D0936371

The
Political Economy
of Agricultural
Pricing Policy

VOLUME 1
LATIN AMERICA

A World Bank
Comparative Study

The
Political Economy
of Agricultural
Pricing Policy

VOLUME 1
LATIN AMERICA

A World Bank
Comparative Study

Edited by
- Anne O. Krueger
- Maurice Schiff
- Alberto Valdés

PUBLISHED FOR THE WORLD BANK
The Johns Hopkins University Press
Baltimore and London

© 1991 The International Bank
for Reconstruction and Development/The World Bank
1818 H Street, N.W., Washington, D.C. 20433, U.S.A.

The Johns Hopkins University Press
Baltimore, Maryland 21211, U.S.A.

All rights reserved
Manufactured in the United States of America
First printing June 1991

The text of this book is printed on paper containing
50 percent virgin pulp, 45 percent recycled preconsumer waste,
and 5 percent recycled and deinked postconsumer waste.

The findings, interpretations, and conclusions expressed in this publication
are those of the authors and do not necessarily represent the views and
policies of the World Bank or its Board of Executive Directors or the countries
they represent. The World Bank does not guarantee the accuracy of the data
included in this publication and accepts no responsibility whatsoever for any
consequences of their use.

The material in this publication is copyrighted. Requests for permission to
reproduce portions of it should be sent to Director, Publications Department, at
the address shown in the copyright notice above. The World Bank encourages
dissemination of its work and will normally give permission promptly and,
when the reproduction is for noncommercial purposes, without asking a fee.
Permissions to photocopy portions for classroom use is not required, though
notification of such use having been made will be appreciated.

The complete backlist of publications from the World Bank is shown in the
annual *Index of Publications,* which contains an alphabetical title list and indexes
of subjects, authors, and countries and regions. The latest edition is available
free of charge from Publication Sales Unit, Department F, The World Bank, 1818
H Street, N.W., Washington, D.C. 20433, U.S.A., or from Publications, The
World Bank, 66 avenue d'Iéna, 75116 Paris, France.

Library of Congress Cataloging-in-Publication Data
(Revised for vol. 1)

The political economy of agricultural pricing policy.

   Includes bibliographical references.
   Contents: v. 1. Latin America—v. 2. Asia.
   1. Agricultural prices—Government policy—Developing countries—
Case studies.   2. Agricultural prices—Government policy—Asia—
Case studies.   3. Agricultural prices—Government policy—Latin America—
Case studies.   I. Krueger, Anne O.   II. Schiff, Maurice W.
III. Valdés, Alberto, 1935-   .
HD1417.P65   1991   338.1'8'091724   90-27232
ISBN 0-8018-4030-9

Contents

Preface   vii

Terms and Abbreviations   xi

1 Measuring the Effects of Intervention in Agricultural
   Prices   1

   Anne O. Krueger, Maurice Schiff, and Alberto Valdés

   The Scope of the Project   3
   Measuring the Impact of Agricultural Pricing Policies   5
   The Quantitative Effects of Intervention in Agricultural
       Prices   8
   The Political Economy of Agricultural Pricing Policies   8
   The International Economic Environment   9
   Regional Findings   10

2 Argentina   15

   Adolfo C. Sturzenegger

   The Economy of Argentina   15
   The Basic Pattern of Price Intervention   19
   The Political Economy of Pricing Policies in the Pampas   31
   Objectives of the Economic Team and the Conflict with the
       Agricultural Sector   40
   Pricing Policies in the Pampas as Equilibrium Results between
       Competing Interests   44
   A Brief Historical Review of Argentina's Trade Policy   46
   Summary and Conclusions   48

3 Brazil   52

   Antonio Salazar P. Brandão and José L. Carvalho

   Overview   53
   The Agricultural Sector   56

The Effects of Agricultural Pricing Policy   64
Other Impacts of Agricultural Pricing Policies   68
The Political Economy of Price Policies   86
Summary and Conclusions   96

4 Chile   100

Alberto Valdés, Hernán Hurtado, and Eugenia Muchnik

Chile and Its Agriculture   101
Measures of Intervention in Agricultural Prices   110
The Impact of Removing Price Intervention, 1960–84   116
The Political Economy of Price Intervention   134
Summary and Implications   140

5 Colombia   144

Jorge García García

An Overview of the Colombian Economy and the Agricultural
   Sector   145
Government Intervention in Agricultural Prices   147
The Effects of Price Intervention on Relative Prices   149
The Political Economy of Agricultural Pricing Policies   182
Conclusions   196

6 Dominican Republic   203

Duty D. Greene and Terry L. Roe

An Overview of the Dominican Economy   204
Agricultural Price Policies   215
The Political Determinants of Agricultural Pricing Policies   236
Conclusion   250
Appendix A. Estimation of a Shadow Equilibrium Exchange
   Rate   252
Appendix B. Additional Empirical Evidence of Government
   Behavior   256

Appendix   261

Anne O. Krueger, Maurice Schiff, and Alberto Valdés

The Impact of Policies on Incentives   261
The Effect of Policies on Economic Variables   266
Government Investment and Expenditure Index   271
Price Variability   272

Preface

This is the first of five volumes summarizing the results of the World Bank research project, A Comparative Study of the Political Economy of Agricultural Pricing Policies. The project consisted of eighteen country studies that employed a common analytical framework and entailed close collaboration between the investigators and the project's three codirectors. This volume deals with the five countries studied in Latin America: Argentina, Brazil, Chile, Colombia, and the Dominican Republic. The remaining thirteen countries are also organized by region in two other volumes, which examine Asia (Volume 2) and Africa and the Mediterranean (Volume 3). Volumes 4 and 5 present a synthesis and comparative analysis of the findings from each country study.

The purpose of the project was threefold: to provide systematic estimates of the degree of price discrimination against agriculture within individual countries and to explain how it changed over time; to determine how this intervention affected such key variables as foreign exchange earnings, agricultural output, and income distribution; and to gain further insight into the political economy of agricultural pricing policy through a study of the motivations of policymakers, the economic and political factors determining the degree of agricultural intervention, and the attempts to reform unsuccessful policies.

Until recently, analysts were primarily concerned with the direct effect that agricultural pricing policies might have on agricultural product and input prices. According to international trade theory and general equilibrium analysis, however, a policy that protects one particular sector of the economy (in this case, industry) is essentially imposing a tax on other sectors of the economy (in this case, agriculture). The tax is likely to raise the real exchange rate, which will then lower the real return to exportables and unprotected import-competing sectors, which account for most of agriculture. Indeed, a country's general economic policies may have far greater indirect effect on agricultural incentives than its agriculture-specific or direct pricing policies do.

That is why this project proceeded on the premise that it is impossible to judge the impact of a developing country's policies without an understanding of the relative importance of direct and indirect intervention. This approach also provides an effective means of evaluating the political economy of agricultural pricing policies across a number of countries, as explained in the final volumes of this series. The systematic examination of the impact of these policies on output, consumption, government budgets, foreign trade, intersectoral transfers, and income distribution in itself contributes a great deal to our understanding of the workings of these policies in developing countries.

Economic growth is such a complex process that it is extremely difficult to interpret accurately. Because it consists of many phenomena changing simultaneously, the effects of particular policies are hard to isolate, especially if the policies have been in place for a long time. To deal with this problem, we asked the researchers to test three hypotheses in each country study: (a) agricultural pricing policies elicit economic responses that affect the evolution of those policies (in the market, for example) and political responses (among pressure groups, bureaucratic organizations, and voter blocs) that affect the evolution of those policies; (b) the results of the policies may differ significantly from—and in some cases be opposite to—what was intended when they were adopted; and (c) the costs of price intervention are usually underestimated and tend to rise over time.

Several criteria were used to select the countries for the project. A foremost concern was to represent a reasonable range of country experience. Therefore, some countries in the group are exporters of food, others are exporters of agricultural (but nonfood) commodities, and still others are importers of food. An effort was also made to achieve some balance between low-income and middle-income countries, as well as among geographic regions. The task would have been impossible to carry out without able researchers willing to participate in the project and to prepare the country reports (published as individual volumes in the World Bank Comparative Studies series).

The countries included in the project, the participants, and their affiliations were as follows:

Argentina	Adolfo Sturzenegger and Wylian Otrera (assisted by Beatriz Mosquera), Fundacion Mediterranea, Buenos Aires
Brazil	José Luiz Carvalho, Universidade Santa Ursula, Rio de Janeiro; Antonio Salazar P. Brandão, Fundaçao Getulio Vargas, Rio de Janeiro
Chile	Hernán Hurtado and Eugenia Muchnik, Catholic University, Santiago; Alberto Valdés, International Food Policy Research Institute (IFPRI), Washington, D.C.
Colombia	Jorge García García, World Bank, Washington,

	D.C.; Gabriel Montes Llamas, Instituto Colombiano Agropecuario (ICA), Bogotá
Côte d'Ivoire	Achi Atsain, Ministère de l'Industrie; Allechi M'Bet, Centre for Economic and Social Research (CIRES), Université Nationale de Côte d'Ivoire, Abidjan
Dominican Republic	Duty Greene, Sigma One Corporation, Quito; Terry Roe, University of Minnesota, St. Paul
Egypt	Jean-Jacques Dethier, World Bank, Washington, D.C.
Ghana	Dirck Stryker, Associates for International Resources and Development (AIRD), Somerville, Massachusetts
Republic of Korea	Pal-Yong Moon, Kon Kuk University, Seoul; Bong-Soon Kang, Seoul National University, Suwon
Malaysia	Glenn Jenkins and Andrew Lai, Harvard Institute for International Development, Cambridge, Massachusetts
Morocco	B. Lynn Salinger, AIRD, Somerville, Massachusetts; Hasan Tuluy, World Bank, Washington, D.C.
Pakistan	Naved Hamid, Asian Development Bank, Manila; Ijaz Nabi, World Bank, Washington, D.C.; Anjum Nasim, Lahore University of Management Sciences, Lahore
Philippines	Ponciano S. Intal, Jr., University of the Philippines, Los Baños; John H. Power, University of Hawaii
Portugal	Francisco Avillez, Instituto Superior de Agronomia, Lisbon; Timothy J. Finan, University of Arizona, Tucson; Timothy Josling, Food Research Institute, Stanford University, Stanford, California
Sri Lanka	Surjit Bhalla, The Policy Group, New Delhi
Thailand	Ammar Siamwalla and Suthad Setboonsarng, Thailand Development Research Institute, Bangkok
Turkey	Hasan Olgun and Haluk Kasnakoglu (with the cooperation of Arslan Gurkan), Middle East Technical University, Ankara
Zambia	Doris Jansen, Development Technologies Inc., Larkspur, California

An advisory board knowledgeable on the issues and experienced in analyzing agricultural pricing policies was assembled to oversee the project. Board members were asked to comment on all aspects of the project and to review various country reports. Board members, their affiliations, and the countries for which they took primary responsibility were as follows:

Romeo Bautista, IFPRI	Korea, Malaysia, Philippines
Hans Binswanger, World Bank	Pakistan, Sri Lanka
Vinod Dubey, World Bank	Côte d'Ivoire, Morocco
Peter Hopcraft, World Bank	Ghana, Zambia
D. Gale Johnson, University of Chicago	Portugal, Turkey
Yair Mundlak, Hebrew University, University of Chicago, and IFPRI	Argentina, Chile, Thailand
Edward Schuh, University of Minnesota	Brazil, Egypt
Marcelo Selowsky, World Bank	Colombia, Dominican Republic

Many other persons helped to bring the project to a successful conclusion, and we thank them here. Project administrator Celina Bermudez and her predecessor Rosario Seoane handled an endless flow of personnel and communications matters; Anne Muhtasib, the project secretary, processed voluminous correspondence and the numerous edited manuscripts; and word processors Myriam Bailey and Estela Zamora provided helpful support. Our research assistants—Lilyan Fulginiti, Emmanuel Skoufias, Pierre Nadji, and Claudio Montenegro—reviewed the results in the many country reports and summary chapters and helped us conduct the statistical analysis for the synthesis volumes. The editor for the project was Phillip Sawicki, assisted by Paul Wolman, Vicky Macintyre, and Mary Ellen Buchanan.

Terms and Abbreviations

Below is a list of terms and abbreviations found in some or all of the chapters in this volume. The more technical terms are explained in detail in the appendix.

ABCAR	Associação Brasileira de Crédito e Assistência Rural
ACAR	Associação de Crédito e Assistência Rural
AGF	Acquisitions of the Federal Government
ANDI	National Association of Industrialists
CACEX	Carteira do Comércio Exterior
CEA	Dominican State-Owned Sugar Enterprise
CFP	Companhia de Financiamento da Produção
CIP	Conselho Interministerial de Preços
COFAP	Comissão Federal de Abastecimento e Preços
CONTAG	Confederação Nacional dos Trabalhadores Agrícolas
CORDE	Dominican Corporation of State-Owned Enterprises
CORFO	Chilean Development Corporation
CP	Coefficient of protection
CPA	Consumer price index for corn, rice, soybeans, and wheat
CPI	Consumer price index
CPI$'$	Consumer price index in the absence of direct price policies
CPI*	Consumer price index in the absence of total price policies
CREAI	The agricultural credit office of the Banco do Brasil
DANE	Departamento Administrativo Nacional de Estadistica
DGPC	Dominican Directorate General of Price Control
E_0	Nominal official exchange rate
E^*	Equilibrium nominal exchange rate
e	Real exchange rate
e^*	Equilibrium real exchange rate
ECLA	Economic Commission for Latin America
EDC	Economic Development Council
EGF	Loans of the Federal Government

EMBRAPA	Empresa Brasileira de Pesquisas Agropecuarias
ERP	Effective rate of protection
ERP_T	Total effective rate of protection
FNC	Fondo Nacional del Café
GDP	Gross domestic product
GEB	Government expenditure bias
GIB	Government investment bias
GMP	Guaranteed minimum price
GNP	Gross national product
IAD	Dominican Agrarian Reform Institute
ICA	International Coffee Agreement
ICO	International Coffee Organization
IDEMA	Instituto de Mercadeo Agropecuario
IFPRI	International Food Policy Research Institute
IMF	International Monetary Fund
INDAP	Instituto Nacional de Desarrollo Agropecurario
INESPRE	Dominican National Institute of Price Stabilization
IRGA	Instituto Rio Grandense do Arroz
LIBOR	London interbank offered rate
MPP	Minimum price policy
NCF	National Coffee Fund
NPR	Nominal protection rate
NPR_D	Nominal protection rate due to direct price policies
NPR_I	Nominal protection rate due to indirect price policies
NPR_{ST}	Short-term nominal protection rate
NPR_{LT}	Long-term nominal protection rate
NPR_T	Total nominal protection rate (includes NPR_D and NPR_I)
P_i, P_A	Domestic agricultural producer prices
P_A', P_i'	Producer prices in the absence of direct price policies (which equal the border price evaluated at the official exchange rate, after adjustment for transport and other margins)
PICOT	Price index for cotton at the consumer level
P_{NA}	Price index of the nonagricultural sector
P_{NA}^*	Price index of the nonagricultural sector in the absence of interventions (under free trade and at the equilibrium exchange rate)
P_{NAT}	Price index of the tradable component of the nonagricultural sector
P_{NAH}	Price index of the nontradable component of the nonagricultural sector
PPP	Purchasing power parity
PRCC	Effective consumer price
PRCF	Effective producer price
P_X	Domestic price of the exportable sector

P_M	Domestic price of the importable sector
PF_X	International price index of the exportable sector
PF_M	International price index of the importable sector
SAC	Sociedad de Agricultores de Colombia
SEA	Dominican Secretariat of Agriculture
SUNAB	Superintendência Nacional de Abastecimento
SNCR	National System of Rural Credit
t_M	Average equivalent tariff (measuring the effect of tariffs and quotas on imports)
TOT	Foreign terms of trade
t_{NA}	Effect of trade policies on the price of nonagricultural tradables
t_x	Average equivalent export taxes
UDR	União Democrática Ruralista
VA	Value added expressed in domestic market prices
VA*	Value added expressed in border prices converted at the equilibrium exchange rate
WPI	Wholesale price index
ΔQ_0	Nonsustainable part of the current account deficit
ΔQ_1	Current account deficit that would result from the removal of interventions on imports t_M and on exports t_x at exchange rate E_0
ϵ_s	Elasticity of supply of foreign exchange with respect to the real exchange rate e
η_D	Elasticity of demand for foreign exchange with respect to the real exchange rate e (defined as positive)

1 Measuring the Effects of Intervention in Agricultural Prices

Anne O. Krueger
Maurice Schiff
Alberto Valdés

Most developing countries have adopted policies that affect agricultural prices, either directly or indirectly through industrial protection and macroeconomic policies. These policies have affected production incentives by making agriculture more or less attractive than other sectors of the economy.

Direct, sector-specific measures have often been the equivalent of direct taxation in that they have kept the prices received by agricultural producers below the levels that would have prevailed in their absence. Among the more important interventions of this type have been the procurement of agricultural outputs by government marketing boards (often the only legal buyers), the establishment of quotas on exports of food crops and other agricultural commodities, and the direct taxation of such exports.

Although some direct interventions have kept producer prices lower than they would have been otherwise, others have benefited agricultural producers. Domestic producers of import-competing food products, for example, have often been protected by quantitative restrictions or tariffs on imported commodities. In addition, the government has often subsidized the costs of farm credit and important agricultural inputs, such as fertilizer. Protection for food producers has been a publicly stated objective of many developing countries, which have sought to raise their level of self-sufficiency in response to the perceived unreliability of world markets (see Valdés 1981, chapter 1). Direct intervention has also been used frequently to stabilize domestic producer prices relative to prices on world markets.

In some developing countries, the government has also intervened in agricultural markets by subsidizing the costs of food for urban consumers. Retail food prices have sometimes been fixed by government edict, or ceilings have been imposed on producer prices. Another approach has been to establish dual pricing systems that keep producer prices high and consumer prices low, with the government making up the difference out of its own budgetary resources.

Subsidizing consumer food prices, however, has frequently proved to be unsustainable because of budgetary and balance-of-payments pressures, which have then forced the government to tax agricultural producers directly. In principle, the fiscal costs of cheap food policies can be reduced by targeting the subsidies to specific groups, such as consumers with income below a certain level. But the effectiveness of such programs has often been limited because the institutional structures needed to implement them have been so complex, and the target groups have been so large.

Agricultural producers have also been strongly influenced by the indirect effects of economywide policies. The principal indirect effects have been (a) exchange rate misalignment because of macroeconomic policies, which reduces the real purchasing power of income received from sales of export- and import-competing commodities; (b) protection for domestic industry, which forces farmers to pay more for agricultural inputs than they would have had to pay for the same goods imported at world prices and also reduces the purchasing power of farm households as consumers of manufactured goods; and (c) appreciation of the real exchange rate because of industrial protection policies, which results in additional taxation of farm producers.

Our comparative analysis of the direct and indirect effects of intervention showed that the effects were similar in most of the eighteen selected countries. Intervention usually reduced agriculture's share of gross national product and led to slower growth in agricultural production and agricultural exports. At the same time, the administrative complexity of intervention increased, and so did illegal activities such as smuggling, as producers and traders sought to evade the costs imposed by price intervention.

Another particularly significant finding was that direct and indirect intervention in combination yielded net taxation of agricultural producers. Even in those countries where direct intervention alone tended to benefit producers, that positive effect was outweighed by the negative effects of indirect intervention.

We found, too, that changing circumstances often forced policymakers to change the policies under which intervention occurred. Apart from their difficulties in foreseeing broad changes in the world prices of agricultural commodities, policymakers often failed to gauge accurately the effects of price intervention on such things as agricultural output, the government budget, and the balance of payments. Moreover, the makers of agricultural pricing policies often failed to anticipate the reactions of specific groups to price intervention. For all these reasons, the policymakers often found it necessary to amend existing policies or to devise new ones.

The rationales for taxing agriculture directly or indirectly include (a) that taxes on agricultural trade are relatively easy to collect in countries where the tax base is thin or the institutional capacity to collect other types of taxes is limited; (b) that not much agricultural output will be forgone by holding down food prices in urban areas, because agriculture is not especially responsive to incentives; and (c) that the terms of trade for primary products seem to be declining over time. Although the dim prospects for exports of primary products prompted early arguments for import-substituting industrialization, a more recent argument has been that markets for agricultural goods are limited not only by the level of final demand but also by the protectionist policies adopted by the industrial countries.

These arguments have now been reappraised by Schultz (1964), Mundlak (1985), Mundlak, Cavallo, and Domenech (forthcoming), and Coeymans and Mundlak (forthcoming). Evidence has accumulated that strongly suggests that agriculture is a dynamic sector that responds positively to price incentives and that "policies which tax agriculture reduce the investment in agriculture, increase outmigration, and reduce the implementation of new techniques" (Mundlak 1985). Much of the earlier pessimism about the trade prospects in agriculture overlooked cost-reducing technological innovations and export growth of nontraditional agricultural commodities, which would give the economies of the developing countries more flexibility to cope with changing conditions in the international economic environment.

The Scope of the Project

Since the early 1970s a great deal of research has been done on development strategies and trade regimes in developing countries. (See, for example, Little, Scitovsky, and Scott 1970; Balassa 1971; Bhagwati 1978; Krueger 1978; 1983; and Krueger, Lary, and Akrasanee 1981.) A recurring finding of such studies is that countries that sought to build their industrial sector through an inward-oriented strategy of import substitution have often been less successful than countries that adopted outward-oriented strategies.

In any case, none of the comparative studies referred to above deals explicitly with the agricultural sector. As a result, the impact of trade and balance-of-payments regimes (and other types of indirect intervention) on agricultural incentives has not been systematically examined.

There are, of course, well-known comparative studies of agricultural pricing policies such as the Stanford Food Research Institute's examination of rice policies in Asia (1975) and the World Bank's case studies of administered agricultural prices, taxes, and subsidies (1976). These, however, deal essentially with sectoral output and input price policies. And a set of studies on the interaction between industrial protection and agricultural incentives has been conducted by the International Food Policy Research Institute (IFPRI) (Bautista and Valdés, forthcoming).

Studies of individual countries to estimate the short-term effects of sector-specific policies on agricultural output, food consumption, and trade flows are common, and one can also find occasional attempts to determine the political factors underlying the selection of agricultural pricing policies in individual countries. These studies, however, do not use the same methodology, nor do they cover the same time period, and the accompanying changes in such important measures as terms of trade, exchange rates, real interest rates, technology, and government investment in the agricultural infrastructure vary both across countries and time. These studies, therefore, do not lend themselves to useful cross-country comparisons of the effects of either direct or indirect intervention. The IFPRI studies mentioned above deal with the impact of industrial protection policies, but they do not analyze the indirect effects of other macroeconomic policies, the quantitative effects of the policies, or the political economy.

The World Bank's agricultural pricing policy project was designed to fill the gap in the literature by assessing the effects of both direct and indirect intervention in agricultural prices over a long period in eighteen representative developing countries. The project used a common conceptual framework and methodology and analyzed the political economy of these interventions. The first step in the process was to measure the impact of direct and indirect intervention on relative prices within agriculture and then to compare the impact on agricultural prices with the impact on prices in the rest of the economy—that is, in the nonagricultural sector. The next step was to estimate the effects of direct and indirect intervention in agricultural prices on (a) agricultural production, (b) consumption of agricultural products, (c) foreign exchange earnings, (d) the government budget, (e) income transfers between agriculture and the nonagricultural sector, and (f) the distribution of income among the various income groups. These estimates, in conjunction with a history of agricultural price interventions in each country, were the basis for an analysis of the evolution of the country's political economy of agricultural pricing policies.

The provision of public goods (irrigation, rural roads, research and extension, rural electrification) is, of course, important to the progress of the agricultural sector. Although analysis of the provision of public goods to agriculture was not a fundamental part of the project, the project authors were asked to measure the transfer of public expenditures and investment to and from agriculture and the net effects of those transfers on agricultural income.

The project also examined the so-called compensation hypothesis—the argument that taxation of agriculture is not necessarily harmful to the sector because the revenues tend to be reinvested in the sector. That hypothesis was tested by two alternative methods and is fully described in volume 4 in this series. Analyzed by the first method, the hypothesis was rejected for most of the countries studied. In most cases, either no relation was found between the provision of public services to the agricultural sector (that is, investment) and price intervention, or else a positive relation was found. In other words, taxation of the agricultural sector in most cases was either accompanied by a reduction in investment in the sector or else had no impact on investment. Analyzed by a second method, the hypothesis was not rejected, but public investment was found to compensate for only a very small fraction of the income lost because of price intervention.

This project, however, did not address such issues as the optimal investment of public goods in the agricultural sector, the optimal taxation of agriculture, or the role of agriculture in overall development strategy. Important as these questions are, they cannot be examined in an analysis that concentrates, like this one, on a single sector of the economy. A broader analytical framework is necessary.[1]

Measuring the Impact of Agricultural Pricing Policies

The various agricultural commodities of the developing countries are often subject to different pricing policies. Food commodities are usually treated differently from nonfood commodities, and the same is true for exportable and import-competing products. The authors of our studies were therefore asked to identify those farm products that they considered reasonably representative of commodity categories in their countries. Table 1-1 shows the twenty-six products selected. The products most frequently studied were rice, wheat, corn, sugar, and cotton.

To estimate the impact of price intervention, it was necessary to have a benchmark price, and we chose border prices. Border prices can be measured easily and provide a uniform comparator for all of the studies. Moreover, border prices represent the opportunity cost of tradables (allowing, of course, for the costs of processing, storing, marketing, and transport) for countries that are price takers in the world market. Of course, one objection to using world prices as benchmark prices is that they are subject to a great deal of short-run instability. We do not argue, however, that optimal allocation of resources requires domestic prices to fluctuate in step with world prices, especially in developing countries that have limited abilities to hedge against changes in world prices.[2] Instead, we simply claim that

Table 1-1. Agricultural Product Classification, by Region and Country

	Latin America					Asia			
Product	*Argen-tina*	*Brazil*	*Chile*	*Colombia*	*Dominican Republic*	*Rep. of Korea*	*Malaysia*	*Pakistan*	*Philippines*
Apples	—	—	X	—	—	—	—	—	—
Barley	—	—	—	—	—	M	—	—	—
Beef	X*	—	M*	—	—	M*	—	—	—
Cocoa	—	—	—	—	—	—	—	—	—
Coffee	—	—	—	X	X	—	—	—	—
Copra	—	—	—	—	—	—	—	—	X
Corn	X	X	—	—	—	—	—	—	M
Cotton	—	X	—	X	—	—	—	X	—
Grapes	—	—	X	—	—	—	—	—	—
Hazelnuts	—	—	—	—	—	—	—	—	—
Milk	—	—	M*	—	—	—	—	—	—
Palm oil	—	—	—	—	—	—	X	—	—
Pork	—	—	—	—	—	M*	—	—	—
Potatoes	—	—	—	—	—	—	—	—	—
Rice	—	M*	—	X*	M*	M*	M*	X*	M*
Rubber	—	—	—	—	—	—	X	—	—
Sheep[a]	—	—	—	—	—	—	—	—	—
Sorghum	X	—	—	—	—	—	—	—	—
Soybeans	X	X	—	—	—	M	—	—	—
Sugar	—	—	—	—	X*	—	—	M*	X*
Sunflowers	X*	—	—	—	—	—	—	—	—
Tea	—	—	—	—	—	—	—	—	—
Tobacco	—	· -	—	—	—	—	—	—	—
Tomatoes	—	—	—	—	—	—	—	—	—
Wheat	X*	M*	M*	M*	—	—	—	M*	—
Wine	—	—	—	—	—	—	—	—	—

—Not applicable.

Note: M = importable; X = exportable; H = nontradable. Asterisks indicate staple commodities; otherwise, commodities are considered to be nonstaples.

a. Consists of mutton and lamb.

a reasonable way to analyze price intervention is to compare relative domestic prices with long-term trends in border prices. In our studies, the authors show the average deviations of domestic prices from border prices over five-year periods and over the entire period covered by the studies. When it existed, the price-setting power of a developing country in a world market (for example, cocoa in Ghana) was taken into account.[3]

With border prices as their reference points, our authors then identified various types of intervention in both producer prices and input prices and quantified their effects on producer receipts. For tradable

Sri Lanka	Thailand	Côte d'Ivoire	Egypt	Ghana	Morocco	Portugal	Turkey	Zambia	Product
									Africa and the Mediterranean
—	—	—	—	—	—	—	—	—	Apples
—	—	—	—	—	X*	—	M	—	Barley
—	—	—	—	—	—	M*	—	—	Beef
—	—	X	—	X	—	—	—	—	Cocoa
—	—	X	—	—	—	—	—	—	Coffee
X	—	—	—	—	—	—	—	—	Copra
—	X	—	M	M	—	M	—	M*	Corn
—	—	—	X	—	—	—	X	X	Cotton
—	—	—	—	—	—	—	—	—	Grapes
—	—	—	—	—	—	—	X	—	Hazelnuts
—	—	—	—	—	—	M*	—	—	Milk
—	—	—	—	—	—	—	—	—	Palm oil
—	—	—	—	—	—	—	—	—	Pork
—	—	—	—	—	—	H*	—	—	Potatoes
M*	X*	M*	X*	M*	—	M*	—	—	Rice
X	X	—	—	—	—	—	—	—	Rubber
—	—	—	—	—	—	X*	X*	—	Sheep[a]
—	—	—	—	—	—	—	—	—	Sorghum
—	—	—	—	—	—	—	—	—	Soybeans
—	X*	—	M*	—	M*	—	X	—	Sugar
—	—	—	—	—	—	—	—	—	Sunflowers
X	—	—	—	—	—	—	—	—	Tea
—	—	—	—	—	—	—	X	X	Tobacco
—	—	—	—	—	—	X	—	—	Tomatoes
—	—	—	M*	—	M*	M*	M*	—	Wheat
—	—	—	—	—	—	X	—	—	Wine

commodities, which included most of those considered, these estimates were conceptually straightforward. They are presented as the effects of direct intervention and are the authors' estimates of the percentage by which the producer price (value added) of each crop exceeded or fell short of the adjusted border price (value added) at the official exchange rate.

The next step was to estimate the impact of indirect intervention on relative agricultural prices. Here, the analytic underpinnings were more complex. In effect, the authors first had to estimate what the exchange rate would have been if the country in question had abandoned tariffs and quantitative restrictions while incurring a sustainable current account deficit—that is, a deficit small enough to be financed through foreign aid and long-term capital inflows. These assumptions allowed the authors to estimate the equilibrium exchange rate that would then have prevailed. (See the appendix to this volume for a discussion of the methods used to estimate the equilibrium exchange rate.) Some authors found it necessary to adapt the project methodology to their own specific situations.

To measure the impact of indirect intervention, an estimate was needed of how much the prices of goods purchased by agricultural producers would have declined if there had been no intervention. Thus, an index of nonagricultural prices was adjusted for the difference in that index if farmers had faced border prices at the equilibrium exchange rate for the tradable goods they purchased. (See the appendix for the methodology used.)

The Quantitative Effects of Intervention in Agricultural Prices

There are good reasons to believe that production of individual crops responds in the short run to changes in relative prices between crops, as well as to changes in relative differences between input and output prices. The estimates of supply elasticities available for many agricultural commodities in several developing countries confirm this belief. Based on such estimates of price elasticity, the authors were asked to estimate the short-run effects of price intervention. They were also asked to estimate the long-run effects—that is, the effects that occurred after producers had fully adapted to a new price environment. In addition to determining the effects of price intervention on agricultural output, the authors assessed the impact of intervention on consumption, foreign exchange, government expenditures, intersectoral income transfers, and income distribution.[4]

The Political Economy of Agricultural Pricing Policies

This project was designed not only to measure the effects of agricultural pricing policies on farm prices and production and other important variables, but also to explain how government intervention in agricultural prices was affected by market forces and political factors.

A number of hypotheses can be proposed as possible explanations of the policies that were adopted in the eighteen countries. It is possible, for example, that much of the discriminatory effect of intervention on agricultural prices, and especially indirect intervention, was a byproduct of the theory that claimed that the best way to achieve industrialization was to adopt the inward-oriented strategy of import substitution. As such, price discrimination against agriculture may have been unintentional. As mentioned earlier, one of the project's findings was the surprising magnitude of the discrimination against agriculture and the related income transfers from agriculture because of industrial protection policies and the exchange rate overvaluation associated with import-substitution regimes.

Another argument is that price intervention that discriminates against agricultural producers was a natural consequence of the political dominance of urban populations. In many countries, policymakers are under pressure to design policies that will benefit urban populations. (For analyses of related policies, see Bates 1981, 1983.)

Discrimination against agricultural prices may also have other causes. Such discrimination might, for example, be an unintended byproduct of transfers of income to the urban poor when budgetary resources are inadequate. Or a government might intervene in domestic agricultural prices because of a desire to protect producers from instability in world prices. This well-intended intervention might have become discriminatory against agriculture as circumstances changed. Another plausible hypothesis is that intervention, which originally discriminated against agriculture, might develop a life of its own as market reactions and political pressures alike prompt further intervention.

To test these hypotheses, the authors were asked to provide an analytical history of pricing policies. One aspect of the task was to evaluate the degree to which announced policies achieved their stated objectives; another was to identify those who gained and those who lost because of price intervention. A surprising degree of inconsistency was found in many countries between stated and actual outcomes. As the two synthesis volumes for this project show, the comprehensive evaluation of the political economy of agricultural pricing policy is a difficult task.

The authors of the country studies were also asked to examine reforms of agricultural pricing policies that occurred during the period studied. This meant, among other things, identifying groups that supported or opposed the existing system, as well as sketching the positions taken by national political parties. In many of the countries, issues of reform played a critical role in the analysis.

The International Economic Environment

The international economic environment played a large role in shaping agricultural pricing policies in the eighteen countries. The period covered in most of the studies runs from the early 1960s to the mid-1980s—a period marked by significant volatility in the prices of major agricultural goods.

Until 1970, the period was one of rapid growth in the international economy under reasonably stable conditions. That was followed by a commodity price boom in the first half of the 1970s, which affected both agricultural and nonagricultural commodities. Although the prices of both agricultural and nonagricultural commodities were differentially affected, the prices of many of the agricultural products studied in this project reached historical peaks at some point in the first half of the decade, often followed by sharp drops. The oil price shock of 1973 played a significant role, of course, in many commodity markets during this time.

The second half of the 1970s was a period of rising worldwide inflation, and commodity prices were affected again. In 1977–78, for example, coffee prices soared but then fell sharply.

In hindsight, the latter half of the 1970s can be described as a permissive period in the world economy. Although inflation rates rose steeply, international interest rates stayed in the range of 6 to 8 percent. As a result, the real value of the developing countries' debts did not increase, despite substantial increases in their borrowing, and debt-servicing obligations did not rise as swiftly as export earnings or real incomes.

With the second oil price shock in 1979 and the ensuing worldwide recession of the early 1980s, the world economy was transformed. Among other things, most commodity prices plunged downward, eventually reaching lows that had not been seen since the 1930s. These lows occurred at the same time that many developing countries began to experience great difficulty in servicing their international debts because of much higher interest rates and a fall in capital inflows that occurred almost overnight. In short, the permissive environment of the 1970s became the harsh environment of the 1980s. Policies that seemed sensible in the earlier decade incurred large penalties in the 1980s. These comparative studies allow the reader to assess the relative importance of domestic and external factors in shaping agricultural pricing policies. Just as important, they demonstrate how a representative sample of the developing countries responded when confronted by the same external stimuli and the same difficulties.

Regional Findings

Three volumes in this series are case studies grouped by region. The first one deals with Latin America, the second with Asia, and the third with Africa and the Mediterranean. Each of these examines the experience of selected countries in the region in regard to the impact of price policies on agricultural incentives, as reflected in direct, indirect, and total nominal protection rates.

A broad view of the similarities and differences in the causes, implementation, and effects of agricultural pricing policy across countries and regions is the subject of volumes 4 and 5, which present syntheses of the case studies from the perspective of economics and political economy.

Our sample consists of eighteen countries, with the following regional distribution. Latin America: Argentina, Brazil, Chile, Colombia, and the Dominican Republic; Asia: the Republic of Korea, Malaysia, Pakistan, the Philippines, Sri Lanka, and Thailand; Mediterranean: Egypt, Morocco, Portugal, and Turkey; and Sub-Saharan Africa: Côte d'Ivoire, Ghana, and Zambia.

Average measures of price intervention for the products selected in the studies are presented in Table 1-2. A number of similarities across regions are immediately apparent. First, over the period examined, direct intervention on importables was positive on average in each of the four regions, and direct intervention on exportables was negative in all regions. Second, direct intervention on all selected products was negative in all regions, indicating that the direct tax on exportables dominated protection on importables. Third, the rate of indirect taxation (due to industrial protection policy and overvaluation of the real exchange rate) was large in all regions (usually exceeding 20 percent), and it dominated the rate of direct taxation in all regions. And fourth, total taxation exceeded 25 percent in all regions.

The impact of price interventions on agricultural incentives also differs among regions. First, indirect taxation over the period studied was largest in Sub-Saharan Africa, amounting to 28.6 percent (it was

Table 1-2. Direct, Indirect, and Total Nominal Protection Rates, by Region, 1960–84

(percent)

Region	Indirect protection	Direct protection	Total	Direct protection of importables	Direct protection of exportables
Asia[a]	−22.9[b]	−2.5	−25.2	22.4	−14.6
Latin America[c]	−21.3	−6.4	−27.8	13.2	−6.4
Mediterranean[d]	−18.9	−6.4	−25.2	3.2	−11.8
Sub-Saharan Africa[e]	−28.6	−23.0	−51.6	17.6	−20.5

Note: The period covered is generally from 1960 to 1984, but it varies somewhat in a number of countries.

a. Republic of Korea, Malaysia, Pakistan, Philippines, Sri Lanka, and Thailand.

b. In South Asia (Pakistan, Sri Lanka), the indirect nominal protection rate was −32.1 percent, while in East Asia (Korea, Malaysia, Philippines, Thailand) it was −18.1 percent.

c. Argentina, Brazil, Chile, Colombia, and Dominican Republic.

d. Egypt, Morocco, Portugal, and Turkey.

e. Côte d'Ivoire, Ghana, and Zambia.

more than 30 percent in Ghana). This was followed by Asia and Latin America (between 21 and 23 percent), with the Mediterranean region the lowest (about 19 percent).

In Latin America, the indirect taxation rate in each country was quite close to the regional average of 21.3 percent. In Asia, there was a significant difference between South Asia (Pakistan and Sri Lanka) and East Asia (Korea, Malaysia, the Philippines, and Thailand). The indirect taxation rate by region was largest in South Asia (32.1 percent) and lowest in East Asia (18.1 percent). In the Mediterranean region, the indirect taxation rate was close to the regional average for Egypt and Morocco, although Turkey's rate was the highest in our sample and Portugal's was the lowest.

Like indirect taxation, direct taxation was also largest in Sub-Saharan Africa (where agriculture in our sample is dominated by export crops), amounting to 23 percent. That region was followed by Latin America and the Mediterranean, with 6.4 percent each, and Asia with 2.5 percent. The average direct taxation rate in Asia was low because of high direct protection in Korea (39 percent). Without Korea, the average rate of direct taxation in Asia was close to 11 percent (with a rate of 25 percent in Thailand). In Latin America, the highest direct taxation rates were found in Argentina and the Dominican Republic (about 18 percent), while in the Mediterranean region the highest direct taxation rate was in Egypt (about 25 percent). Finally, the total taxation rate was larger than 25 percent in all regions, but was about twice as large in Sub-Saharan Africa as in the other regions.

The remaining chapters in this volume provide self-contained summary accounts of agricultural pricing policies in Argentina, Brazil, Chile, Colombia, and the Dominican Republic. Volume 2 of this series covers the six Asian countries, and volume 3 covers six countries in Sub-Saharan Africa and the Mediterranean. In all cases, the chapters are based on longer and much more detailed country reports published in the World Bank Comparative Studies series, The Political Economy of Agricultural Pricing Policy.[5]

Notes

1. Good reference materials on taxation and public finance in developing countries and the relation between public finance and economic development are the World Bank's 1988 *World Development Report*, and Toye (1979).

2. Valdés and Siamwalla (1988) claim that it may be optimal to shift some of the risk to the government, because it may be better able to pool risks from a variety of activities than individual farmers can.

3. In general, world prices for agricultural commodities are highly distorted as a result of price interventions by the European Communities, Japan,

the United States and others. But for the national policymaker in most small and medium-size economies, and for most commodities, the world's opportunity cost of producing these products is irrelevant. We submit that the world price does reflect the economic opportunities a country faces and thus should be used as a reference. Of course, there may be circumstances when a divergence between domestic and world prices is called for, such as a need to protect low-income consumers against short-term world price instability and monopoly power on world markets or a need to protect producers against temporary foreign export subsidies strong enough to cripple the import-competing sector.

4. Computable general equilibrium models are available for several of the eighteen countries included in the project. These were considered by the country authors, who decided not to use them because they found that the particular models for their countries were not satisfactory for the purposes of these studies.

A more complete analysis would also have included measuring the effects of agricultural price intervention on rural-urban migration, wages, and investment flows. Although it was recognized that these long-run effects were important, the authors were not requested to measure them, on the grounds that doing so would have substantially lengthened the time needed to complete the studies. Several authors, however, sought to assess the impact of agricultural price intervention on rural wages over time (see the appendix). Moreover, in the case of Chile, the impact of policy on intersectoral migration and investment flows was estimated. See Mundlak, Cavallo, and Domenech (forthcoming) and Coeymans and Mundlak (forthcoming) for analyses that incorporate such measurements.

5. Data and conclusions from the study of Côte d'Ivoire are used in volumes 4 and 5. That study is being published in Côte d'Ivoire and not in the World Bank Comparative Studies series or in volume 3 of this series.

References

Balassa, Bela. 1971. *The Structure of Protection in Developing Countries*. Baltimore, Md.: The Johns Hopkins University Press.

Bates, Robert H. 1983. *Essays on the Political Economy of Rural Africa*. Berkeley: University of California Press.

―――. 1981. *Markets and States in Tropical Africa*. Berkeley: University of California Press.

Bautista, R., and Alberto Valdés, eds. Forthcoming. *Trade and Macroeconomic Policies in Developing Countries: Impact on Agriculture*. Washington, D.C.: International Food Policy Research Institute.

Bhagwati, Jagdish N. 1978. *Foreign Trade Regimes and Economic Development: Anatomy and Consequences of Exchange Control Regimes*. Lexington, Mass.: Ballinger Press for the National Bureau of Economic Research.

Coeymans, Juan-Eduardo, and Yair Mundlak. Forthcoming. "Agricultural and Sectoral Growth: Chile, 1962–1982." In R. Bautista and Alberto Valdés, eds., *Trade and Macroeconomic Policies in Developing Countries: Impact on Agriculture*. Washington, D.C.: International Food Policy Research Institute.

Krueger, Anne O. 1983. *Trade and Employment in Developing Countries:* Vol. 3, *Synthesis.* Chicago: University of Chicago Press.

———. 1978. *Foreign Trade Regimes and Economic Development: Liberalization Attempts and Consequences.* Lexington Mass.: Ballinger Press for the National Bureau of Economic Research.

Krueger, Anne O., Hal B. Lary, and Narongchai Akrasanee. 1981. *Trade and Employment in Developing Countries,* Vol. 1. Chicago: University of Chicago Press.

Little, I. M. D., T. Scitovsky, and M. Scott. 1970. *Industry and Trade in Some Developing Countries.* London: Oxford University Press.

Mundlak, Yair. 1985. ''The Aggregate Agricultural Supply.'' Working Paper 8511. Center for Agricultural Economic Research, Rehovot, Israel.

Mundlak, Yair, D. Cavallo, and R. Domenech. Forthcoming. ''Agriculture and Growth: The Experience of Argentina, 1913–84.'' In R. Bautista and Alberto Valdés, eds. *Trade and Macroeconomic Policies in Developing Countries: Impact on Agriculture.* Washington, D.C.: International Food Policy Research Institute.

Schultz, T. W. 1964. *Transforming Traditional Agriculture.* New Haven: Yale University Press.

Timmer, C. P., and W. Falcon. 1975. ''The Political Economy of Rice Production and Trade in Asia.'' In L.G. Reynolds, ed. *Agriculture in Development Theory.* New Haven: Yale University Press.

Toye, J. F. J., ed. 1979. *Taxation and Economic Development.* London: Frank Cass.

Valdés, Alberto, ed. 1981. *Food Security for Developing Countries.* Boulder, Colo.: Westview Press.

Valdés, Alberto, and A. Siamwalla. 1988. Chapter 7 in J. W. Mellor and R. Ahmed, eds. *Agricultural Price Policy for Developing Countries.* Baltimore, Md.: Johns Hopkins University Press.

World Bank. 1988. *World Development Report 1988.* New York: Oxford University Press.

2 Argentina

Adolfo C. Sturzenegger

Since the end of World War II, government intervention in agricultural prices has led to much price discrimination against Argentina's main agricultural products. The reasons for this intervention, and its effects, are the subject of this chapter.

The paper begins with an overview of Argentina's economy and agricultural sector, followed by an explanation of the methods used to measure agricultural price intervention during the period 1960–85. Because intervention was implemented primarily through trade and exchange rate policies, the discussion focuses on the rates of nominal and effective protection for the six main products of the Argentine pampas: wheat, corn, sorghum, soybeans, sunflower seeds, and beef. The next section presents the results of simulation analyses designed to measure the effects of price intervention. Price discrimination is then related to the political economy of Argentina.

The Economy of Argentina

Argentina, the second largest country in South America, covers 2,797,000 square kilometers. Its population in 1980 was 28 million; the annual rate of population growth in recent years has been about 1.8 percent. By 1980, approximately 83 percent of the population lived in urban areas—that is, cities with 2,000 or more inhabitants.

Argentina's most fertile and productive land is located within a radius of 500 kilometers of the capital, Buenos Aires. This area, known as the pampas, accounts for more than 50 percent of the country's agricultural output and almost all of its three main products—cereals, oilseeds, and cattle.

In view of the size of its population and its per capita GDP (about US$2,300), Argentina can be considered a medium-size economy. Annual GDP is about US$70 billion.

A little more than a century ago, Argentina was at a very low level of development. Then, in the late nineteenth century, several important events occurred. Domestically, the country achieved political stability. Externally, significant reductions in overseas transport costs for agricultural products and large increases in world demand for these products greatly improved Argentina's export possibilities. Consequently, the lands of the pampas began to command high rents, which set in motion a type of "Vent for surplus" development scheme (Di Tella and Zymelmann 1967) that attracted large inflows of European immigrants and external capital. That foreign capital was invested mainly in economic infrastructure (railways, ports, electricity, and so forth), and, in the years that followed, Argentina found itself on a path of high and sustained growth, marked by rapid expansion of the amount of cultivated land and rapid growth of exports and GDP (Diaz Alejandro 1975; Cavallo and Mundlak 1982).

The Depression of the 1930s altered the conditions for growth. Agriculture's external terms of trade worsened, which, along with the declining availability of land owing to population growth, caused a reduction in agriculture's internal advantage. As export growth slowed, the domestic components of aggregate demand began to play a more important role in the economy (Ferrer 1980). The economy was also affected by a number of general policy changes. There was a moderate increase in tariffs (Diaz Alejandro 1975), and foreign exchange restrictions were imposed in response to balance of payments problems (Macario 1964). These changes improved conditions for the growth of industrial production.

Relative industrial prices increased sharply during World War II, but immediately after the war the international prices of traditional agricultural commodities began to rise. Argentina's taxes on agricultural exports, however, neutralized any beneficial effect that the new terms of trade might have had on domestic agricultural prices. In addition, high tariffs and restrictions on imports were imposed to protect domestic producers from foreign competition. The net result was that agriculture stagnated while the import substitution industry grew rapidly. The scene was set for the "stop-go" performance that has characterized Argentina's economy for much of the past four decades (Berlinski and Schydlowsky 1977).

Overall, the postwar experience consisted of a period of moderate growth followed by stagnation. Between 1950 and 1974, per capita GDP increased at an average annual rate of about 2.3 percent, while total GDP rose about 4 percent annually. Between 1975 and 1985, however, total GDP remained stationary, and GDP per capita decreased substantially. The change from moderate growth to stagnation appears to have been related principally to a decline in productivity rather than to the quantity of resources available. These trends are reflected in table 2-1, which shows the annual rates of growth of total GDP, available reproducible physical capital, and the average product/capital ratio for the period 1960–84.

Table 2-1. Average Annual Growth Rates of GDP, Capital, and Average Capital Productivity, 1960–84

(percent)

Period	GDP (1)	Capital (2)	Average capital productivity (3)
1960–64	4.6	3.3	1.3
1965–69	3.0	4.1	−1.1
1970–74	3.8	4.5	−0.7
1975–79	1.8	4.1	−2.3
1980–84	−1.6	2.2	−3.8
1960–84	2.3	3.6	−1.3

Note: (3) = (1) − (2).
Source: Sturzenegger and Mosquera (1990), Elias (1982).

Annual rates of inflation as measured by implicit GDP prices are given in the last column of table 2-2. Inflation seemed to be manageable until 1970, but in the early 1970s it accelerated and then took off after 1974, when the public budget started to get out of hand. Recently, inflation has become a self-perpetuating process in which rising prices lead to larger budget deficits and smaller real cash balances. This in turn causes prices to jump still higher. In addition, general price indexing has created a high level of inertial inflation.

Table 2-2 provides data on government revenues, expenditures, and budget balances for the period 1961–85. Government is defined in a broad sense to include government at the national and provincial levels, various public enterprises, and the social welfare system. The quasi-fiscal result is the balance of Central Bank accounts, which consists mainly of subsidies to the financial system. Three important points emerge from the data in table 2-2—the ratio of public expenditures to GDP was high; that ratio increased in the second half of the

Table 2-2. Government Accounts and Inflation Rate, 1961–85

(percentage of GDP)

Period	Government revenues (1)	Government expenditures (2)	Net revenues (3)	Quasi-fiscal deficit (4)	Consolidated net revenues (5)	Annual[a] inflation rate (6)
1961–65	34.1	39.2	−5.2	0.9	−4.3	23.9
1966–70	37.2	39.0	−1.8	−0.1	−1.8	16.4
1971–75	34.2	41.8	−7.6	1.9	−5.7	78.0
1976–80	41.3	46.2	−4.9	−1.2	−6.1	200.7
1981–85	43.9	51.3	−6.3	−11.3	−17.6	391.7

a. The annual inflation rate is a simple five-year average (not cumulative).
Note: (3) = (1) − (2).
           (5) = (3) + (4).
Source: Sturzenegger and Mosquera (1990).

period; and deficits have been chronic (only between 1967 and 1970 did the budget balance appear to be reasonable).

The Agricultural Sector

Although agriculture has been overshadowed by industry since the end of World War II, it nonetheless contributes substantially to Argentina's GDP. The share of agriculture in GDP during 1960–85 can be seen in the first column of table 3. The share shows a downward trend, but with an increase in the 1970–74 period.

The share of agricultural imports in total imports was very low, whereas the share of agricultural exports in total exports was large and showed no significant trend (see table 2-3). The last column of table 2-3 shows a positive trend in the share of agricultural exports in total agricultural output. This can be attributed to two factors—some new, highly exportable products (for example, soybeans) appeared later in the period of analysis and production of grain (mostly exported) increased significantly in the second half of the period.

The farmers of the pampas specialize in producing soybeans, corn, wheat, and beef, which account for the bulk of Argentina's export earnings. Soybeans alone—exported as beans, as edible oil, and as crushed soybean pellets—make up one-fourth of total exports. The region is also the main source of food for the Argentine population, supplying more than 85 percent of the grains and oilseeds consumed domestically and about 90 percent of the livestock. Agricultural production in other parts of the country serves mainly the domestic market. Those areas produce more than 80 percent of the country's industrial crops and more than half of its vegetables and fruits.

The fertile soil and favorable climate of the pampas have enabled farmers to rotate crops and livestock and practice double-cropping.

Table 2-3. The Agricultural Sector, 1961–85

		Agricultural Imports		Agricultural exports[a]		
Period	Share of agriculture in GDP (percent)	Value (US$ millions)	Share in total imports (percent)	Value (US$ millions)	Share in total exports (percent)	Share in total agricultural output (percent)
1961–65	14.9	50.4	4.2	787.8	60.1	34.5
1966–70	12.2	72.0	5.4	948.6	60.6	37.9
1971–75	13.5	138.0	5.4	1546.6	56.6	28.4
1976–80	10.3	254.2	4.5	3428.2	53.9	42.5
1981–65	11.2	195.8	3.6	4670.6	56.8	44.9

a. Include sections I, II, and III of NADE.

b. 1985 is not included.

Source: Sturzenegger and Mosquera (1990).

The high quality of the soil also permits them to shift quickly between wheat and feed crops and oilseeds, depending on the expected profitability of each.

Growth and Stagnation in the Pampas

A striking feature of agriculture in the pampas has been wide swings between growth and stagnation. Until the early 1940s, production followed a steady upward path that took Argentina into world markets, where it became one of the biggest suppliers of food and feed grains. This was followed by more than two decades of uninterrupted stagnation after World War II.

Argentina's average annual yield of cereals and oilseeds in the period 1909–39 was 13.2 million tons, but that figure rose to only 16 million tons in 1945–76 (Miro 1982). The situation was even worse in the case of wheat production, which reached the same level in 1960–64 that it did in 1925–29. Corn production in the later period was 33 percent less than it was in the earlier period (Diaz Alejandro 1975). The stagnation is particularly evident in agriculture's export performance. Annual average exports of cereals and oilseeds reached only 7.3 million tons in 1945–76, contrasted with an average 9.5 million tons a year in 1909–39 (Miro 1982).

Moreover, Argentina's share of world exports of wheat dropped from 19.3 percent in 1934–38 to only 2.8 percent in 1971–75. Whereas world exports of wheat increased more than 300 percent, Argentine exports of wheat decreased 42 percent. In the case of feedgrains (corn, sorghum, barley, and so on), Argentine exports dropped from 48.1 percent of world exports in 1934–38 to only 9.5 percent in 1971–75. The example most often cited is corn. In the period 1934–38, corn from Argentina accounted for two-thirds of all world exports, while the United States provided only 8 percent. By 1976–80, however, the situation was reversed. Argentine corn exports had dropped to less than 8 percent of world exports, but U.S. exports had risen to 74 percent (Miro 1982). Beef exports experienced an even greater decline, falling from 56.0 percent of world exports just before World War II (Diaz Alejandro 1975) to almost no exports at present. Beef is now considered primarily a domestic product.

The Basic Pattern of Price Intervention

Trade policy during the 1960–85 period was designed to discriminate against most exportables in relation to importables. This policy was implemented through high tariffs, quantitative restrictions on imports that compete with the industrial sector, and export taxes on the main agricultural and agroindustrial exports.

These policies pushed up the relative prices of importable products and caused a real appreciation of the currency, which resulted in discrimination against traditional exportables (agricultural and agro-industrial goods). Nontraditional exportables were able to escape some of the effects of import substitution protection through export subsidies.

Of Argentina's traditional exportables, those from the pampas were hit hardest by trade policy. Agroindustrial exportables were, in effect, protected in that they benefited from subsidization of their agricultural inputs. Furthermore, the taxes on agroindustrial exports were significantly lower than those on agricultural exports. To compensate in part for the reduced relative prices of agricultural outputs, the government subsidized some of the inputs used in agricultural production. Specifically, it made credit available at subsidized rates of interest, offered tax exemptions for the purchase of farm machinery, and provided financial support for technological research. These policies were expected to raise the level of sectoral incentives and thereby increase agricultural production without raising agricultural prices.

Methods Used to Measure Price Intervention

Argentina's pricing policies were analyzed for the period 1960–85. The products of interest were wheat, corn, sorghum, soybeans, sunflower seeds, and beef. The average shares of each in total agricultural value added during the period were—wheat, 7.9 percent; corn, 7.2 percent; sorghum, 2.6 percent; soybeans, 5.6 percent; sunflower seeds, 2.9 percent; and beef, 28.9 percent.

All of these products are tradable and, as noted, were discriminated against primarily through restrictions on external trade and an overvalued exchange rate. Therefore, price intervention was measured by determining the rates of direct nominal protection (NPR_D), indirect nominal protection (NPR_I), total nominal protection (NPR_T), and total effective protection (ERP_T).

DIRECT NOMINAL PROTECTION (NPR_D).   Protection rates were estimated at the producer level. In the case of crops, the producer prices used were those prevailing in the main harvest month—January for wheat and May for summer crops. In the case of beef, average annual prices were used.

The prevailing relative prices (that is, P_i/P_{NA}) of the selected products were volatile during the study period, and those for most products hit their lowest levels from 1979 to 1981. Overall, prevailing relative prices appeared to experience a small downward trend. If this trend had been accompanied by an equivalent positive increase in agricultural productivity, and if this productivity change had been appropriated by the agricultural sector, land rents would have remained constant in relative terms. However, land rents did not remain constant. These relationships are explored in greater detail in the political economy section.

Relative prices that were free from direct intervention (that is, P_i'/P_{NA}) were more volatile than prevailing relative prices. The weak downward trends in those prices reflect a basically similar trend in the real exchange rate.

The rates of direct nominal protection can be seen in table 2-4. Direct nominal protection was negative for almost every year and every product. In general, direct nominal negative protection was high in absolute value when relative prices without direct intervention were high, and vice versa. As a result, prevailing prices varied somewhat less than prices that were free of direct intervention. For example, when the prevailing real rate of exchange or the international prices of the six products were high, the level of disprotection (that is, taxation) was also high. Thus, variations in direct nominal protection tended to compensate for variations in the real exchange rate or in international prices. These relationships are also explored in detail in the political economy analysis.

INDIRECT NOMINAL PROTECTION (NPR_I). Total nominal protection NPR_T is the sum of direct (NPR_D) and indirect (NPR_I) nominal protection. In contrast to direct intervention, which directly affects relative domestic prices of agricultural commodities, indirect intervention affects these prices through policies that affect the exchange rate and nonagricultural prices.

To calculate NPR_I, we estimated the free-trade equilibrium exchange rate (e^*) and the implicit (or equivalent) tariff on the import-

Table 2-4. Effects of Direct Price Intervention on Relative Producer Prices (NPR), 1961–85

(percent)

Period	Wheat	Corn	Sorghum	Soybeans	Sunflower seeds	Beef
1961–65	−15.8	−4.3	−12.6	n.a.	n.a.	−31.8
1966–70	−12.3	−12.1	−19.3	n.a.	n.a.	−24.4
1971–75	−45.8	−28.8	−29.5	n.a.	n.a.	−23.9
1976–80	−19.0	−18.9	−14.4	−12.5[a]	−25.6[a]	−2.7
1981–85	−20.2	−21.5	−25.4	−22.3	−24.5	−22.5

a. 1976 is not included.
Source: Sturzenegger and Mosquera (1990).

able sector (t_M). An extended version of Diaz Alejandro's (1981) approach was used to compute t_M. He defines CP as

$$(2\text{-}1) \qquad CP = \frac{P_X/P_M}{P^F_X/P^F_M},$$

where

$\quad CP \qquad$ = "antitrade bias" in external trade policy[1]
$\quad P_X, P_M \quad$ = the domestic price index of exportable and importable sectors, respectively, and
$\quad P^F_X, P^F_M$ = the international price index of exportable and importable sectors, respectively.

As seen in equation (2-1), CP gives the relation between internal and external terms of trade. An unbiased value equals 1. A CP of less than 1 signifies discrimination against exportables in relation to importables. When CP is greater than 1, it means that the trade policy causes tradability to increase and thus has a protrade bias. In Argentina, the CP was less than 1. Therefore, trade policy reduced tradability, and there was an antitrade bias.

Since X and M are tradable sectors, it can be said that

$$(2\text{-}2) \qquad P_X = P^F_X E (1 - t_x)$$

$$(2\text{-}3) \qquad P_M = P^F_M E (1 + t_M)$$

where

$\quad E \quad$ = nominal exchange rate,
$\quad t_x \quad$ = per unit implicit direct taxation in the exportable sector, and
$\quad t_M \quad$ = per unit implicit tariff in the importable sector.

Equations (1), (2), and (3) can now be used to obtain another expression for CP:

$$(2\text{-}4) \qquad CP = \frac{1 - t_x}{1 + t_M}.$$

CP can be calculated from equation (2-1) using the four price indexes, P_X, P_M, P^F_M, and P^F_M. However, the calculation of CP from equation (2-1) depends on the base year chosen for those price indexes. Consequently, we need one independent observation of CP to determine the whole CP series. This is done, using equation (2-4) for a year in which the values of t_x and t_M were available. The year 1969 was chosen because an estimation of t_M exists for that year. Industry, excluding agroindustry, was considered the importable sector. A well-known study of implicit protection in Argentina (Berlinski and Schydlowsky 1977) provided the value of t_M for 1969.

Table 2-5. Explicit Export Tax, Implicit Tariff, and Antitrade Bias, 1961–85

Period	$(1 - t_x)$[a]	$(1 + t_x)$[b]	CP[c]
1961–65	0.88	1.60	0.56
1966–70	0.87	1.61	0.55
1971–75	0.82	1.51	0.55
1976–80	0.92	1.64	0.56
1981–85	0.87	1.95	0.45

a. The explicit export tax, t_x, is the ratio of fiscal revenues from total exports over the total value of agricultural and agroindustrial exports.

b. The implicit import tariff, t_M, is obtained from data on CP and t_x.

c. $CP = (P_X/P_M)/(P_X^F/P_M^F) = (1 - t_x)/(1 + t_M)$, where IP_x and P_M are domestic export and import prices, respectively; and F indicates their foreign equivalent.

Note: The figures are annual averages.

Source: Sturzenegger and Mosquera (1990).

Agriculture and agroindustrial production were considered to be the components of the exportable sector. For this sector, t_x was estimated using explicit export taxes. Next, using the computed value of CP for 1969 as a base for the external and domestic price index series of both tradable sectors, we estimated the CPs for the entire period by means of equation (2-1). Finally, we estimated t_M for the entire period by using the following equation:

$$(2\text{-}5) \qquad t_M = \frac{1 - t_x}{CP} - 1,$$

where t_x indicates explicit export taxes estimated for the whole period as described above. The values of $(1-t_x)$, CP, and $(1+t_M)$ for the period are given in table 2-5.

Table 2-5 indicates that the exportable sector (agriculture and agroindustry) was heavily taxed relative to the importable sector (industry unrelated to agriculture). The value of CP implies an overall taxation on exportables of about 44 to 47 percent from 1961 to 1980, and an increase to 55 percent in the period 1981–84 (and reaching 60 percent in 1985). Such taxation had two components: (1) industrial protection as measured by the implicit tariff t_M, which fluctuated from between about 50 percent (in 1971–75) to 95 percent (in 1981–85), with very large annual variation; and (2) tax t_x on exportables that fluctuated from between about 8 percent (in 1976–81) to 18 percent (in 1971–79), with the largest tax of 23 percent occurring in 1973.

Thus, the main factor in the low value of CP seems to have been the industrial protection policy. However, it must be recalled that t_x measures the tax on both agriculture and agroindustry. When only agricultural products are considered, the export tax is much larger, as is evident from the NPR_D calculations shown in table 2-4. For instance,

Table 2-6. Observed and Sustainable Equilibrium Free Trade Exchange Rates, 1961–85

| Period | Observed nominal exchange rate (per thousand US$) (1) | Real Exchange Rate (per thousand 1969 US$) | | Divergence between (2) and (3) (percent) (4) |
		Observed (2)	Sustainable equilibrium with free trade (3)	
1961–65	0.13	0.43	0.50	−14
1966–70	0.3ꞏ	0.36	0.46	−20
1971–75	1.13	0.39	0.39	1
1976–80	90.95	0.34	0.39	−13
1981–85	136408.22	0.31	0.41	−24

Note: (4) = ((2)−(3)) /(3).
Source: Sturzenegger and Mosquera (1990).

in the period 1971–75, the tax on all exportables was 18 percent, while the direct taxes on beef, corn, sorghum, and wheat were 24, 29, 30, and 46 percent, respectively.

Equation (2-4) shows that there was no need to calculate the free-trade equilibrium exchange rate (e^*) to obtain *CP*, the tax on exportables relative to importables. However, the nonagricultural sector also includes nontradables. To estimate the total degree of intervention on agriculture relative to nonagriculture, we had to estimate e^*. This was done using the "elasticity approach" as revised by Dornbusch (1975). It consists of a model with three sectors: exportable, importable, and home. The three sectors are mutual substitutes.

Before the free-trade equilibrium exchange rate could be obtained, the values of the observed exchange rate had to be adjusted to (1) eliminate the effects of temporary disequilibrium factors; (2) correct for the difference between the observed and the sustainable trade balances; and (3) eliminate the effects of the observed trade policy. These adjustments were made using the Dornbusch model, which is similar to that used in the other studies in this volume. It is because of these corrections that we define e^* (see table 2-6) as the "sustainable equilibrium free-trade" real rate of exchange. It is worth noting that direct and indirect taxation tended to be negatively correlated. For instance, when the rate of exchange was low and indirect taxation was large, direct export taxes on agriculture were reduced. After a significant devaluation and a fall in indirect taxes, however, export taxes were usually increased.

TOTAL NOMINAL PROTECTION. Table 2-7 presents computations of the level of total nominal protection (NPR_T). The general pattern was one of strong negative nominal protection for the whole period for all of

Table 2-7. Effect of Total Price Intervention on Relative Producer Prices (NPR$_T$), 1961–85

(*percent*)

Period	Wheat	Corn	Sorghum	Soybeans	Sunflower seeds	Beef
1961–65	−35.0	−26.3	−33.5	n.a.	n.a.	−46.7
1966–70	−35.7	−36.5	−41.7	n.a.	n.a.	−44.3
1971–75	−51.7	−35.7	−36.5	n.a.	n.a.	−31.8
1976–80	−39.4	−42.3	−39.6	−39.1[a]	−47.6[a]	−25.5
1981–85	−47.7	−48.4	−51.4	−48.0	−49.7	−47.1

a. 1976 is not included.

Source: Sturzenegger and Mosquera (1990).

the selected products. Volatility was much less pronounced than it was in the case of nominal direct protection alone because of the negative correlation between direct and indirect protection.

Grains tended to be increasingly taxed over time, while the tax on beef eventually fell. These trends are analyzed in detail in the discussion on political economy. The relative prices of pampean agricultural products appear to have been discriminated against (that is, taxed) by about 40 to 50 percent on average during the period 1960–85. In other words, on average, undistorted relative prices would have been about 70 to 100 percent higher than those that actually prevailed during the period.

TOTAL EFFECTIVE PROTECTION. Incentives for producers may change not only because of variations in producer prices but also because of variations in input prices. It is useful, therefore, to estimate effective protection rates and to compare relative value added with and without intervention. It was impossible to compute relative value added for beef production. For grains, we used three inputs: seeds, fuel, and a composite input consisting of fertilizers, herbicides, and insecticides. The importance of these inputs has been increasing. As a percentage of producer prices, they rose from 10 percent in 1960 to more than 20 percent in 1985.

We estimated only the total effective protection rate (*ERP$_T$*). A comparison of tables 2-7 and 2-8 shows that these effects were very similar to those obtained for total nominal protection.

The Cumulative Effect on Output from Removing Intervention

Our calculations of total intervention were used with price elasticities to obtain an estimate of the effects of price intervention on output (see Sturzenegger and Martinez Mosquera 1990). Price elasticities in agri-

**Table 2-8. Effect of Total Intervention on Relative Value Added
(ERP_T), 1961–85**

(*percent*)

Period	Wheat	Corn	Sorghum	Soybeans	Sunflower seeds
1961–65	−36.0	−27.6	n.a.	n.a.	n.a.
1966–70	−37.6	−39.0	n.a.	n.a.	n.a.
1971–75	−51.0	−33.8	−34.8	n.a.	n.a.
1976–80	−38.7	−42.5	−40.0	−41.4[a]	−51.2[a]
1981–85	−48.3	−49.3	−51.9	−48.6	−49.7

a. 1976 is not included.
Source: Sturzenegger and Mosquera (1990).

culture have received a great deal of attention from economists, both
in Argentina and abroad. Most of the previous studies of the situation
in Argentina agree that prices have been a significant variable in
determining agricultural output in the pampas (see, for example,
Reca 1967; Gluck 1979; Ferrer 1980; Cavallo 1985; Fulginiti 1986).

Most econometric studies of agricultural supply in the region have
found that price responses at the product level are very strong. When
relative prices change within the agricultural sector, there are significant changes in the structure of agricultural output (see, for example,
Reca 1974). These results suggest that sectoral behavior is also
strongly price-responsive. Further evidence of this can be found in
the shift in the proportions of labor and machinery utilized when
relative prices between those inputs changed in the 1950s. Price response has also been strong in the past fifteen years—a time during
which almost the entire sector has been exposed to more profitable
technologies (such as hybrid seeds for corn, sorghum, and sunflower,
and new varieties of wheat) and a new product—soybeans—was
introduced.

At the same time, some studies have found that total production is
not particularly affected by variation in agricultural prices relative to
prices in the rest of the economy, especially when these are short-run
variations. This finding appears to be inconsistent with the one described above. A consistent explanation for both results can be found
in the "fixed assets" argument put forth by Johnson (see Hathaway
1963). These are discussed in detail in Sturzenegger and Martinez
Mosquera (1990).

To summarize, agricultural production in the pampas was highly
sensitive to price changes. Therefore, cross-responses to relative
prices within the agricultural sector were strong. The "fixed inputs"
argument helps to explain the somewhat weaker price responses for
overall output over the short term, but this does not imply that price
responses in the short run are of no consequence, because certain

Table 2-9. Cumulative Change in Output Due to the Removal of Total Invervention, 1961–85

(*percent*)

Period	Wheat	Corn	Sorghum	Soybeans	Sunflower seeds	Beef
1961–65	42	13	73	n.a.	n.a.	77
1966–70	30	24	76	n.a.	n.a.	76
1971–75	68	22	48	n.a.	n.a.	38
1976–80	83	66	−4	13[a]	54[a]	21
1981–85	60	75	104	56	122	70

a. 1976 is not included.
Source: Sturzenegger and Mosquera (1990).

inputs are variable for the sector even over the short term, or are only weakly "fixed." Such inputs include fertilizer, agrochemicals, energy inputs, marginal land (with near-zero rent), tractor hours, and hired labor. In equilibrium situations where prices are reasonably stable, price increases can be expected to elicit normal aggregate responses, even in the short run.

Our calculations on total ERPs were used to estimate the output effects for grains. In the case of beef, for which only proportional changes in prices were estimated, we used NPRs instead of ERPs.

Most of the principal elasticity values were obtained from previous studies, particularly those of Gluck (1979) and Cavallo and Mundlak (1982). The elasticity matrix was completed with the aid of a "calibrated" approximation that took into account agronomical relationships of substitution and complementarity between the six products as well as homogeneity and symmetry conditions. For the calculations of cumulative output effects, we used estimated Nerlove-type coefficients of adjustment. Gluck's review provided helpful data on that.

Table 2-9 shows cumulative changes in the output of each product at five-year intervals that would have resulted from the removal of price intervention. The pattern that emerges is clear. The removal of intervention would have caused production of all the products to increase significantly: 57 percent for wheat, 40 percent for corn, 59 percent for sorghum, 38 percent for soybeans, 98 percent for sunflower seeds, and 57 percent for beef on average over the period. This pattern also indicates that intervention discriminated mainly between agriculture and nonagriculture. Discrimination among the various agricultural products was much weaker.

Table 2-10 presents the levels of production that would have been reached without intervention. The highest total for all crops would have been 69 million tons in 1982. Beef production would have reached a high of 5 million tons in 1969.[2]

**Table 2-10. Volume of Output in the Absence
of Total Intervention, 1961–85**

(millions of tons)

Period	Wheat	Corn	Sorghum	Soybeans	Sunflower seeds	Total crops	Beef
1961–65	9.8	5.6	2.0	0.0	0.6	18.0	4.0
1966–70	8.4	9.4	3.9	0.0	1.0	22.7	4.5
1971–75	10.4	10.5	6.6	0.3	0.8	28.6	3.0
1976–80	15.4	12.8	5.8	2.7	2.1	38.9	3.6
1981–85	17.9	18.3	15.3	7.8	4.6	63.9	4.4

Source: Sturzenegger and Mosquera (1990).

The Effects on Consumption of Removing Total Price Intervention

In computing the effects of price intervention on consumption, we used the own-price elasticity of De Janvry and Nunez (1971) for beef, which is similar to the values reported in other studies. We also assigned a low value to the own-price elasticity of wheat (De Janvry and Nunez estimated it to be -0.015), and to the own-price and cross-price elasticities of corn and sorghum because of competition between these two products as inputs in meat production. All other elasticity values were set to zero. Table 2-11 shows the effects on consumption of removing total intervention. The effect on consumption of wheat and sorghum would have been relatively small. It would have been negligible for corn except in 1975–79, when consumption would have been reduced by 8 percent. The reduction in the consumption of wheat and sorghum would have reached 10 percent or more in the 1980–85 period. The reduction in beef consumption would have been much larger: over 30 percent in 1960–69 and 1980–84, and 14 percent in 1970–79, when total taxation of beef was lowest.

**Table 2-11. Consumption Effects Due to the Removal
of Total Intervention, 1961–85**

(percent)

Period	Wheat	Corn	Sorghum	Beef
1961–65	−6	2	−8	−32
1966–70	−6	−0	−8	−29
1971–75	−13	−3	−3	−18
1976–80	−7	−5	−2	−15
1981–85	−9	−2	−10	−35

Source: Sturzenegger and Mosquera (1990).

The Effects on Foreign Exchange Earnings of Removing Total Price Intervention

The increase in foreign exchange earnings owing to the removal of total intervention for each product has three aspects. It is the result of an increase in the value of output, of a decrease in the value of consumption, and of an increase in the value of imported inputs used in the added production. The results are shown in table 2-12, by product and for the six products as a whole.

There is an important caveat, however. The results in table 2-12 probably overestimate the increase in foreign exchange earnings, chiefly because we did not include the increase in nonagricultural imports that would have resulted from removing tariffs and import quotas. Given our estimate of t_M in table 2-5, we suspect that the overestimate may be large, although industrial exports would have been higher because of devaluation of the local currency (table 2-6).

The figures in table 2-12 indicate that the increase in foreign exchange earnings would have been greatest for beef (because its consumption would have fallen much more than consumption of crops, as is shown in table 2-11), and then for wheat, corn, and sorghum. The effect for soybeans and sunflower seeds would have become significant in the 1980s. The effect for beef would have been as large or larger than for the five crops in every period except 1976–80.

The total annual increase in foreign exchange earnings for the six products would have been over US$1 billion in every year, would have averaged US$2.7 billion a year from 1961 to 1985, would have increased over time, and would have reached over US$6 billion in 1981–85. It would have amounted to over 100 percent of the value of total agricultural exports in every period except 1976–80.

Table 2-12. Change in Foreign Exchange Earnings Due to the Removal of Total Intervention, 1961–85

(millions of US$)

Period	Wheat	Corn	Sorghum	Soybeans	Sunflower seeds	Beef	Total products
1961–65	167	24	33	n.a.	n.a.	1,099	1,323
1966–70	112	84	66	n.a.	n.a.	1,326	1,588
1971–75	622	150	146	n.a.	n.a.	1,151	2,070
1976–80	877	537	−1	97[a]	271[b]	1,277	3,058
1981–85	867	843	723	541	515	3,453	6,940

a. 1976 is not included.

b. 1976 and 1977 are not included.

Source: Sturzenegger and Mosquera (1990).

Table 2-13. Loss in Fiscal Revenues Due to the Removal of Total Intervention, 1961–85

(percent of total national tax revenues)

Period	Loss in export taxes	Loss in import tariffs	Total loss in revenues
1961–65	12	23	34
1966–70	9	17	26
1971–75	13	13	25
1976–80	7	15	22
1981–85	10	11	22

Source: Sturzenegger and Mosquera (1990).

The Effect on the Budget of Removing Price Intervention

Table 2-13 presents the loss of revenues that would have resulted if there had been no intervention. This loss would have been the result of removing export taxes and import tariffs. The results are presented as a percentage of total tax revenues.[3]

Two conclusions can be drawn from table 2-13. First, revenues from export taxes (mainly taxes on agricultural exports) became an increasingly important way to finance public expenditures. They rose from 6.6 percent of national fiscal resources in 1960–62 to 13.0 percent in 1983–85. Second, revenues from import taxes became a less important source of government financing, dropping from 31.7 percent in 1960–62 to only 7.1 percent in 1983–85. This reduction, however, does not necessarily mean a reduction in protection. It only indicates a reduction in explicit protection; implicit protection, in the form of quantitative restrictions, remained very high (see table 2-5).

The Effect on Resource Transfers

Transfers of resources between pampean agriculture and the rest of the economy have been influenced by both price-related and nonprice-related intervention. We computed only the transfers related to price intervention that had dominant effects. Transfers because of government investment were very modest. Although it is obvious that transfers from and to agriculture are related to the general tax system (land taxes, production taxes, income taxes, and so forth), we know of no study that has found a significant pro or anti-agricultural bias in the tax system. Credit policy is another instrument used to transfer resources between agriculture and the rest of the economy. Although this has generally produced transfers in favor of agriculture, they were of minor importance compared with transfers resulting from price intervention.

Table 2-14. Total Real Transfers into Agriculture Due to the Removal of Total Intervention, 1961–85

(percentage of agricultual GDP)

Period	All[a] crops	Beef	Total
1961–65	8.5	32.7	41.2
1966–70	11.5	30.7	42.2
1971–75	15.4	12.3	27.7
1976–80	18.8	12.2	31.0
1981–85	31.1	30.1	61.2

a. All crops include wheat, corn, sorghum, soybeans, and sunflower seeds.
Source: Sturzenegger and Mosquera (1990).

We estimated real transfers as the impact of price intervention on real pampean income, because those interventions affect both nominal income (through change in the producer surplus) and consumer prices of agricultural and nonagricultural products.

The total real transfers out of agriculture shown in table 2-14 are extremely high (40 percent on average). The highest transfers—56 and 91 percent—occurred in 1980 and 1981, respectively, in association with the highest degree of overvaluation of the local currency. Actually, these percentages underestimate the degree of discrimination against the pampean agricultural sector because they reflect only the transfers associated with the six commodities discussed in this paper.

The Political Economy of Pricing Policies in the Pampas

To understand the operations of the main forces that have influenced pricing policy in the pampas, we must first obtain some quantitative indicators of intervention, which can be seen as a sociopolitical mechanism. The quantitative indicators of interest here are the rates of direct and total nominal protection (tables 2-4 and 2-7). We use nominal protection instead of effective protection because direct effective protection was not measured and the rates of total effective protection were close to those for total nominal protection, as can be seen by comparing tables 2-7 and 2-8.

The analysis here covers only four of the products (wheat, corn, sorghum, and beef) because data on the other two (soybeans and sunflower seeds) were incomplete (see table 2-15). Measurements that are available for these two products were fairly similar to those for the other grains (see tables 2-4 and 2-7).

We concentrate on explaining the level of direct nominal protection because this the relevant variable for testing any hypothesis concerning the political economy. The regression results presented below will clarify the role that direct intervention (export taxation) played in stabilizing relative prices and incomes.

Three Facts to be Explained

Three facts need to be explained concerning the quantitative indicators of intervention and, in particular, the direct nominal protection rate NPR_D:

- Short-run or annual variations in NPR_D (export taxes) during the period of analysis. The coefficients of variation were wheat, 0.31; corn, 0.25; sorghum, 0.20; and beef, 0.20.
- Long-run variations or trends in the same NPR_D rates. For example, significant negative trends exist in NPR_D for grains, whereas there is no trend for beef (see table 2-16). Annual percentage rates were wheat, -1.4; corn, -1.8; and sorghum, -1.2. These rates indicate that grains were increasingly taxed during the period of analysis.
- On average, the negative NPR_D in relation to products of the pampas was high at the beginning of our period of analysis and remained high throughout the period (see table 2-4). That starting point and this general pattern cannot be explained without reference to the decades immediately preceding our period of analysis.

We will examine whether the various hypotheses that have been raised explain these three facts, and we will then suggest a hypothesis that does.

The Stabilizing Export Tax

We begin with the nominal direct protection (NPR_D) estimated in table 2-4. For any product i, the relationship between the relative producer price, border price, and protection rate NPR_D is:

$$(2\text{-}6) \qquad 1 + NPR_D = \frac{P_i/P_{NA}}{P_i'/P_{NA}}$$

where $P_i(P_i')$ is the actual (border) price of agricultural product i, and P_{NA} is the nonagricultural price index.

Rearranging terms, and noting that $P_i' = P_{Fi}E$ (law of one price, where P_{FI} is the international price of product i), we have

$$(2\text{-}7) \qquad \frac{P_i}{P_{NA}} = \frac{P_{Fi} E}{P_{NA}} (1 + NPR_D).$$

and with some further rearrangement, we obtain

(2-8) $$\frac{P_i}{P_{NA}} = \frac{P_{Fi}}{P_F} \cdot \frac{E \cdot P_F}{P_H} \cdot \frac{P_H}{P_{NA}} (1 + NPR_D)$$

where P_F is the world price of Argentine tradables and P_H is the price of home goods.

It is important to note that P_i'/P_{NA} (relative prices without direct intervention) varied more than did P_i/P_{NA} (observed relative prices). The coefficients of variation in these two cases were: wheat, 0.39 and 0.20; corn, 0.27 and 0.24; sorghum, 0.27 and 0.23; and beef, 0.27 and 0.23.

These values suggest that export taxes may have helped to stabilize the observed internal relative prices of products from the pampas. If they played such a role, a negative correlation should exist between P_i'/P_{NA} and NPR_D.

In table 2-15 we tested the possibility of a stabilizing role. We used equation (2-8), which separates P_i/P_{NA} into three components: the world price of the product in relation to world prices of Argentine tradables (P_{Fi}/P_F); the observed real rate of exchange ($e = E_{PF}/P_H$); and the relative domestic price of home goods and nonagricultural goods (P_H/P_{NA}), which depends on trade policies affecting tariffs, export taxes, and subsidies on tradables outside the pampas, and on e. We also used a trend variable to capture long-term variations in export taxation; for beef, a dummy variable was included to take care of periodic overreactions in the observed prices of beef caused by what has been called the "cattle cycle."

The results are satisfactory. Note the stability of the coefficients of the relative world prices of the products (except for sorghum) and of the observed real exchange rate among products. Both variables are also highly significant. The elasticity of export taxation in both cases is about −0.70.

Also note that the explanatory variable e in the regressions in table 2-15 is the observed and not the equilibrium real rate of exchange. In the short run, e is very volatile (Sturzenegger and Mosquera 1988). This volatility is primarily because of short-run changes in monetary and macroeconomic conditions, and changes in exchange rate policy. Therefore, e can be considered independent of export taxation in the short run and can be tested as one of the explanatory variables of export taxation.

Table 2-16 presents additional regressions, again using relative prices without direct intervention as the main explanatory variable, but now in its compact form, P_i'/P_{NA}. In the top part of table 2-16, the explained variable is again the coefficient of direct protection for any of the four products. In the bottom part of the explained variables are

Table 2-15. Export Tax Regression

$(1+NPR_D)^a$	C	$(P_{Fi}/P_F)^a$	e^a	$(P_H/P_{NA})^a$	Trend	DUMCAR	AR(1)	R^2	D.W.
Wheat	−0.49	−0.70	−0.66	−1.08	−0.014	—	0.31	0.62	1.93
	(−0.86)	(−2.66)	(−2.10)	(−0.58)	(−1.34)	—	(1.22)		
Corn	−0.79	−0.67	−0.83	−2.19	−0.018	—	—	0.66	2.06
	(−2.48)	(2.13)	(−4.66)	(−3.18)	(−3.23)	—	—		
Sorghum	−0.64	−1.12	−0.68	−0.98	−0.015	—	—	0.68	2.00
	(−2.43)	(−4.53)	(−4.26)	(−1.08)	(−3.05)	—	—		
Beef	0.30	−0.64	−0.84	−3.05	0.002	0.19	0.83	0.85	1.71
	(0.75)	(−5.82)	(−4.10)	(−2.70)	(0.14)	(6.84)	(5.05)		

— Not available.

Note: The variables are defined as: C, constant; P_{Fi}/P_F world price of product i in relation to world prices of Argentine tradables; e, the observed real exchange rate; P_H/P_{NA}, the relationship between home goods and nonagricultural goods; DUMCAR, a dummy variable for beef; AR(1), the lagged dependent variable.

Source: Sturzenegger and Mosquera (1990).

Table 2-16. Determinants of Direct Intervention and Producer Prices

$(1+NPR_D)^a$	C	$(P'_i/P_{NA})^a$	Trend	DUMCAR	AR(1)	R^2	D.W.
Wheat	−0.07	−0.67	−0.014	—	—	0.79	1.84
	(−1.15)	(9.02)	(−3.97)				
Corn	−0.05	−0.52	−0.018	—	—	0.59	1.79
	(−0.87)	(−5.15)	(−4.16)				
Sorghum	−0.30	−0.49	−0.012	—	—	0.57	1.98
	(−4.75)	(−5.32)	(−2.98)				
Beef	0.36	−0.39	0.003	0.21	0.46	0.82	1.80
	(2.01)	(−4.76)	(0.72)	(7.24)	(2.06)		
Producer prices relative to P_{NA}							
Wheat	−0.07	0.33	−0.014	—	—	0.70	1.84
	(−1.15)	(4.41)	(−3.97)				
Corn	−0.05	0.48	−0.018	—	—	0.75	1.79
	(−0.87)	(4.72)	(−4.16)				
Sorghum	−0.30	0.51	−0.012	—	—	0.74	1.98
	(−4.75)	(5.52)	(−2.98)				
Beef	0.36	0.61	0.003	0.21	0.46	0.90	1.80
	(2.01)	(7.60)	(0.72)	(7.24)	(2.06)		

—Not available.
Note: P'_i/P_{NA} is defined as relative prices without direct intervention; see table 2-15 for the other variables.
a. Variables in log form.
Source: Sturzenegger and Mosquera (1990).

internal relative prices. There is an algebraic relationship between the coefficients of P_i'/P_{NA} in any pair of regressions (see Sturzenegger and Mosquera 1990).

From the results of tables 2-15 and 2-16, we know that P_i'/P_{NA} is the main explanatory variable of short-run variations in export taxes. Nominal direct protection reacts negatively to changes in P_i'/P_{NA}. When P_i'/P_{NA} improves, protection decreases (that is, export taxes rise), and vice versa. Export taxation, therefore, stabilizes the internal relative prices of the products in question. Its function is to maintain preexisting relative internal prices. Changes in these prices are not completely neutralized in the short run. Part of any change in P_i'/P_{NA} in the short run is still transmitted to the actual internal relative prices P_i/P_{NA}, as is shown in the bottom part of table 2-16. This point will become more significant when we examine Argentina's political economy.

Long-Run Variations

Long-run variations provide additional evidence of the stabilizing role played by export taxes and also help to clarify the specific nature of this role. To explain the trends in the NPR_D for each product and the long-run behavior of export taxation in general, we examined the long-run behavior of internal relative prices and of changes in the productivity of variable factors (see tables 2-17 and 2-18).

We found significant negative trends in the relative prices of grains: wheat, -2 percent; corn, -2.7 percent; and sorghum, -2.1 percent (see table 2-17). A negative (although not statistically significant) trend (-1.2 percent) is also evident in the case of beef. This pattern in relative prices is owing to negative trends in direct nominal protection

Table 2-17. Trends in Relative Producer Prices

Relative producer prices[a]	C	Trend	AR(1)	R^2	D.W.
Wheat	0.02	−0.020	0.24	0.45	1.75
	(0.20)	(−3.19)	(1.13)		
Corn	−0.016	−0.027	0.32	0.55	1.84
	(−0.13)	(−3.45)	(1.60)		
Sorghum	−0.40	−0.021	0.27	0.42	1.86
	(−3.23)	(−2.75)	(1.33)		
Beef	1.63	−0.012	0.42	0.25	1.57
	(9.70)	(−1.12)			

a. Variable in log form.
Source: Sturzenegger and Mosquera (1990).

Table 2-18. Trends in Exogenous Productivity

Output (in log)	C	$(P_t/P_{NA})_{t-1}$	S_{uP}	Trend	AR(1)	R^2	D.W.
Wheat	−7.80 (−5.25)	0.36 (1.84)	1.13 (6.40)	0.020 (3.29)	0.00 (0.02)	0.83	1.43
Corn	−6.86 (−4.07)	0.17 (1.20)	1.05 (5.03)	0.035 (6.43)	—	0.80	2.00
Sorghum	−6.87 (8.52)	−0.03 (0.21)	1.06 (8.71)	0.023 (2.23)	—	0.96	1.66
Beef	−4.28 (−1.20)	$(P_B/P_{NA})_{t-1}$ 0.42 (−2.97) $(P_B/P_{NA})_{t-2}$ 0.06 (0.55)	0.53 (1.58)	0.00 (0.02)	0.04 (0.13)	0.62	2.01

Note: $(P_t/P_{NA})_{t-1}$ is defined as relative producer prices at time $t-1$; $(P_B/P_{NA})_{t-1}$, $(P_B/P_{NA})_{t-2}$ are the relative producer prices of beef at time $t-1$, and $t-2$, respectively; S_{uP} is the harvested surface per product P.

Source: Sturzenegger and Mosquera (1990).

(increasing taxation) and the fact that relative prices without direct intervention (P_i'/P_{NA}) also showed negative trends, although they were rather weak.

At first glance, these results seem to suggest that export taxes did not play a stabilizing role in the long run. Although border prices without intervention showed negative trends, direct nominal protection rates also showed negative trends. However, the stabilizing hypothesis gains additional support from regression results indicating large increases in the productivity of variable inputs (see table 2-18). The levels of production for each product are regressed on three variables: relative prices lagged by one period, harvested area, and a trend variable. These regressions were used to estimate the long-run rate of variation in the productivity of inputs independent of price changes. It can be seen that there were important increases in exogenous productivity in grain production: wheat, 2 percent; corn, 3.5 percent; and sorghum, 2.3 percent. These increases were somewhat stronger than the negative trend in prices. For beef, no increase in productivity was detected. There was a negative trend in relative prices, but it was not statistically significant.

These results indicate that intervention had something of a stabilizing effect in that the more productive products were taxed the most. For corn, high increases in productivity were followed by a significant increase in the annual rate of taxation of 1.8 percent (see table 2-16); for beef, there was no increase in productivity or in taxation.

The results suggest that export taxes tended to stabilize agricultural income to a greater extent than agricultural prices in the long run. It seems that relative agricultural income has declined, however, owing to the fact that the net change between increases in exogenous productivity and decreases in relative prices (nil in wheat, 0.8 percent in corn, 0.2 percent in sorghum, and probably negative in beef) were apparently lower than increases in productivity in Argentina as a whole.

Although the previous results are very satisfactory, we also tested other explanatory variables. These included the annual rate of inflation measured by the CPI, the level of fiscal deficits measured as shares of GDP, the annual credit subsidy to products of the pampas as measured by Penna and Palazuelos (1987), and a dummy variable that was used to test the propopulist nature of the Illia and Peron governments. None of the results was statistically significant (see Sturzenegger and Mosquera 1988).

The Forces Behind Export Taxes

Until now, our analysis has demonstrated that export taxes helped to stabilize internal prices and incomes in the pampas between 1960 and

1985. The forces that generated this type of price intervention were the government, the agrarian lobby, and the industrial lobby.

THE GOVERNMENT. Here, the word "government" refers primarily to the executive branch. External trade policy, including export taxes, falls under the aegis of the president and his economic team, which consists of the Economics Minister, and the secretaries of the Treasury, Domestic Trade, Industry, Agriculture, Foreign Trade, and Planning. Every administration during the period of study had to move within a conflicting context in implementing its agricultural policies because of different interests between the economic team and the agricultural sector.

Argentina had two kinds of agriculture secretaries during the study period. One was more technically oriented than the other, somewhat resistant to pressures from the agriculture sector, and more impelled to find ways of reducing the conflict between the economic team and the pampean sector. The other tended to pay much more attention to sectoral interests.

We do not take the standard approach of welfare economics, which assumes that governments are altruistically oriented toward the public interest. On the contrary, we believe that governments are largely composed of different groups and individuals who seek to enhance their own special interests. Attempts to serve the public interest are not excluded, but they are deemed to be relatively minor.

It is also assumed here that private agents in pluralistic societies try to maximize their welfare in several ways, only one of which is the production of useful goods or services. Another activity is lobbying, which has been defined as

> the use of resources to obtain government regulations that enhance the incomes of members of some particular group in the society by raising the prices of goods they sell, or by lowering the prices of goods they purchase. (Wellisz and Findlay 1986).

When the existence of pressure groups and lobbying activities is acknowledged, the assumption of full autonomy of decisionmakers has to be rejected. This is made more certain in our case for three reasons.

Argentine governments were very unstable during the period of analysis. No elected president remained in power for a complete term, and during periods of nonconstitutional government the armed forces constantly threatened to change the leadership. Economic teams were even more unstable than presidents. Unstable administrations are weak and seek short-run results. They fear social unrest and try to prevent conflict by acceding to political pressures.

Then, there was a clear and permanent pattern of government

intervention in agricultural prices during the entire period. If full autonomous governments were assumed, it would be difficult to reconcile this permanent pattern with the fact that different types of governments have been in power since 1960. Economic pressure groups, however, were constantly active in Argentina (see, for example, Diaz Alejandro 1975; Imaz 1964). The persistence of the pattern of intervention seems not to be consistent with the assumption of full autonomy of the various governments in determining policy, but may be consistent with governments limited by pressure group actions.

Finally, it was not difficult for special interests to prevent government policies from being implemented. Agrarian interests, for example, blocked the introduction of land taxes. Industrial interests rejected explicit subsidies and insisted on such implicit types of protection as quantitative restrictions and tariffs.

When governments have their own special interests and limited autonomy, it is customary to view government intervention as compromises between the goals of different pressure groups and the goals of government. This concept can also be used to explain intervention in the prices of pampean commodities.

Objectives of the Economic Team and the Conflict with the Agricultural Sector

We have mentioned that Argentina's economic policymakers continually sought to achieve short-run objectives. Three such objectives were dominant: general price stability, fiscal equilibrium, and correcting shortages of foreign exchange.

It seems clear that changing the level of taxes on agricultural exports was not considered an appropriate short-run instrument for accomplishing the third objective, given that the main variable for short-run corrections of foreign exchange shortages was the rate of exchange, the short-run elasticity of grain production in the pampas was considered to be low, and there were possible perverse short-run effects (negative short-run elasticity) in the case of beef. Former members of the National Meat Board cited several instances in which they failed to convince the Economic Minister to reduce export taxes on beef. The ministers were clearly more interested in stabilization or fiscal equilibrium than in increasing beef exports.

We, therefore, suggest that, for most of the period of analysis, price intervention was guided by two objectives—general price stability and deficit reduction. Export taxes on the products of the pampas appeared to be an excellent way of dealing with those two problems in the short run. Such taxes both reduced prices and increased fiscal revenues. Furthermore, they can be collected swiftly and more easily than other taxes. Moreover, other things being equal, a reduction in the prices of wage goods implies a reduction in public sector salaries.

If Argentina had had a well-developed tax system, it would have been possible to reduce the deficit and to reduce inflationary pressures with fewer allocative costs than those resulting from export taxes (see, for instance, Llach and Fernandez Pol 1985). But the tax collection system is inefficient, and deficits are chronic. Because export taxes served the short-run objectives of economic policymakers, they gave rise to an ongoing conflict between the government, which preferred high export taxes, and agricultural interests, which preferred low export taxes.

However, a stabilizing export tax that varies with world commodity prices, or with real rates of exchange, cannot be fully reconciled with the existence of governments whose primary and permanent objectives are general price stability and fiscal equilibrium. Reductions in export taxes would increase the fiscal deficit and would be inflationary. We indicated above that we tested the empirical relations between export taxes and those two macroeconomic problems, and ended up with poor results. Thus, the existence of those two objectives was not enough to explain the levels of export taxes on agricultural products.

Indeed, it is difficult to find any government objective that explains the stabilizing export tax. Industrialization or improving real urban wages can only explain export tax increases but not export tax reductions. One objective that is compatible with a stabilizing export tax is a desire to stabilize income between the agricultural and urban sectors. But would the government have allowed reductions in export taxes merely to stabilize agricultural incomes when such reductions conflicted with the much more pressing and persistent need to reduce inflation and obtain fiscal equilibrium? The following references to this question are instructive. The Triannual Plan for National Reconstruction and Liberation (1974), for example, states that agricultural prices

> should hold a stable relation with non-agricultural prices, avoiding sudden income transfers between sectors which affect industrial development and the level of welfare of the people.

and also that

> price stability is a key objective of this policy. An attempt will be made to de-link internal prices from variations in world prices (Miro 1982).

The 1985 national agricultural program (PRONAGRO) states:

> In this sense, a stabilization of agricultural prices will be promoted through a flexible policy of export taxes in order to regulate variations that the country, as a price taker, does not control. The flexible use of export taxes means using them as an instrument of incomes

policy for the sector and avoiding their utilization for only fiscal purposes (Secretaria de Agricultura, Ganaderia y Pesca 1985).

It may be impossible to find better definitions of a stabilizing export tax. These definitions suggest that such taxes were applied by fully autonomous policymakers who sought to stabilize pampean relative prices. We disagree with this conclusion because, given the existence of chronic conflict between the government's chief economic advisers and the agricultural sector, the more demanding objectives of those advisers were always fiscal equilibrium and general price stabilization. If they had been fully autonomous, they would have not implemented export tax reductions. If they accepted these reductions, it was because other forces were in action.

The Agrarian Lobby

The activities of interest groups in Argentina take various forms; meetings and social activities with legislators, politicians, and bureaucrats; the financing of studies that support legislation favorable to their interests; monetary contributions to election campaigns; money or other rewards for legislators and regulators; public opinion campaigns; direct participation in government by members of the groups; and threats of different kinds.

The rural sector in Argentina, one of those interest groups, consists of several hundred thousand farmers dispersed throughout the country. The literature on the economic theory of regulation (Olson 1971; Baldwin 1982) suggests that a group of this type finds it difficult to sustain a high level of lobbying activity. Free riding is a severe problem. Another is that the benefit each member of a large group obtains from favorable action is usually very small. Also, it is difficult to coordinate and monitor a very large group. Some members of the group may not weigh the costs and benefits of intervention and may, therefore, not be willing to support it.

Given the costs of organizing an effective rural lobby, we assume asymmetry in the degree of activity of that lobby. When the position of the group is below some parity level, members of the group become more aware of the need to recapture the loss suffered, and the level of lobbying activities becomes very high. In contrast, when the position of the group is better than "parity," its level of lobbying activity tends to diminish.

The possibility of such asymmetries, which is a key assumption in the explanation of the stabilizing role of export taxes, is usually an important consideration in studies pertaining to the economic theory of regulation. Baldwin (1982), referring to the work of Olson, has pointed out that:

Usually a lobbying organization is not formed immediately or, if the organization already exists, resources are not forthcoming in significant amounts from the membership upon the emergence of a new common interest for a group. A crisis or repeated series of crises may be necessary to shock the individuals in the group into establishing the organization or increasing the contributions to it.

In addition, Posner (1974) has noted:

> Coase, however, suggests the interesting possibility that when a business is in decline, managers may find it profitable to shift their attention from improving their business operations to improving the political environment, another potential source of profits. There is a further point: the costs of becoming informed about opportunities for enhanced profits through government regulation may be greater than the costs of perceiving losses that regulation might reduce.

Specifically, we assume that the agrarian lobby becomes very active when facing significant reductions in income or when facing the possibility of being taxed through direct taxes (for example, on land) on the agricultural sector. It becomes much less active when prices and income are high.

The Industrial Lobby

Pricing policy is also affected by a second pressure group, the industrial lobby, which acts to lower relative agricultural prices in two different ways (Brock and Maggee 1978). First, the industrial sector as a whole acts in "a Stolper-Samuelson" direction trying to improve its prices relative to agricultural prices to induce a functional redistribution of income from land to industrial capital (Stolper-Samuelson theorem). Also, through industrial labor, wage goods (mainly wheat and beef) become inputs to industrial production. It should be beneficial, therefore, to reduce the cost of such important inputs for industry. In any case, when the industrial lobby acted, its interests were compatible with those of urban labor.

Second, such lobbying activity was also undertaken in "a Cairnes direction" to obtain sector-specific redistributions of income by raising the returns to those factors that are relatively specific to some industrial sectors. The factors that make it difficult for the rural lobby to organize itself are much less troublesome in the industrial sector. We assumed, therefore, a low level of asymmetry in the degree of activity of the industrial lobby.

The agricultural sector in the pampas is involved in another conflict, this time with industrial interests. One side of the conflict is of the Cairnes type. Because many products of the pampas are small-country exportables, producers do not benefit greatly from the development of processing industries. But these industries benefit greatly from low input prices. The other side of the conflict is of the Stolper-Samuelson type. Industry as a whole benefits from low prices for pampean products because these low prices imply lower wage costs and a higher real rate of exchange. The only industrial sector interested in high agricultural prices, or in high production in the pampas, was the sector that provides production inputs, such as agricultural machines and agrochemicals.

Pricing Policies in the Pampas as Equilibrium Results between Competing Interests

We postulate that pricing policies in the pampas were equilibrium results from competing actions. On one side were those interested in reducing export taxes on products of the pampas (the agrarian lobby); on the other were those interested in increasing those taxes (the economic team and the industrial lobby).

Figure 2-1 shows the political economy process of price intervention in the pampas. The export tax rate is represented on the horizontal axis. The vertical axis shows the marginal "benefits" *MB* and marginal "costs" *MC* of export taxes. The benefits accrued to the government and industrialists, whereas the costs were incurred by producers in the pampas.

The *MC* curve indicates, for agrarian interests, the marginal costs of additional export taxes, given P'_A/P_{NA}, and of exogenous productivity (P_R). The curve shows the costs, as they are perceived by those interests, of not lobbying; so, the *MC* curve can also be viewed as the activity level of the agrarian lobby. Such costs increase with higher export taxes because of asymmetry in the activity levels of that lobby. In other words, when taxation reaches a level that reduces rural incomes below their parity level, the marginal cost of not lobbying for tax reduction rises rapidly.

The *MB* curve indicates the marginal benefits of export taxes, and is a measure of the incentive for additional taxes, given predetermined levels of inflation *(INF)* and fiscal deficits *(DEF)*; it is also a measure of the incentive for lobbying for additional taxes for industrial interests. These benefits decrease very slowly because there is little, if any, asymmetry in the motivations and lobbying activity levels of both actors.

Given the postulated shape of the curves, the equilibrium solutions are located in the steep part of the curve *MC*. Consequently, movement of the *MB* curve to *MB'* because of changes in the *INF* and *DEF* variables does not significantly change the equilibrium levels of ex-

Figure 2-1 The Political Economy "Market" For Export Taxes on Products of the Pampas

Marginal "costs"
and marginal "benefits"
of export taxes

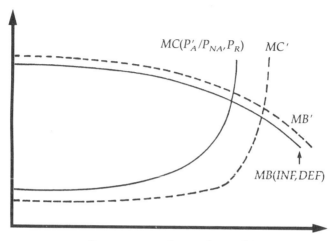

Export tax rate for products of the pampas

port taxes. Export taxes, therefore, are not particularly sensitive to changes in these two variables. This finding is consistent with the poor regression results obtained when those two variables were used.

At the same time, movements of the MC curve will cause significant changes in export taxes, as shown by the dotted MC' curve. The MC curve moves when relative prices without direct intervention and exogenous productivity change. When these two variables increase, the MC curve will move to the right and the equilibrium level of export taxes will increase. For instance, if P_A'/P_{NA} is higher for the same level of export taxes, observed prices (P_A/P_{NA}) and observed income will be higher. This will reduce the "costs" of export taxes and deactivate the agrarian lobby. The MC curve will move to the right, and export taxes will increase.

This is our political economy hypothesis of variation of direct price intervention in the pampas. It is consistent with the short- and long-run variations that were described in the first part of the discussion. One item yet to be explained, however, is the high level of price intervention (both direct and total) in the first year of the period of analysis. Because of the stabilizing effect of intervention and the lack of a major trend in relative prices without intervention, the level did not drop during the period.

We have attempted to explain short- and long-run changes in price discrimination. To explain the high average level of price discrimination, we need to examine the origins of present trade policy.

A Brief Historical Review of Argentina's Trade Policy

During the first three decades of this century, agricultural products were free of direct discrimination and experienced only weak indirect discrimination through a tariff of approximately 20 percent on imports (Diaz Alejandro 1975). Several important events then took place to change the situation. Initially, relative international prices began to favor industrial products. Then, balance of payments problems developed. In response, the government imposed foreign exchange restrictions, which, in turn, protected industry (Macario 1964). Finally, the previous level of tariffs was slightly increased (Diaz Alejandro 1975). This set of factors, together with internal changes in relative factor prices, which also favored industry, encouraged additional industrialization.

It seems that intervention did not play a stabilizing role at that time because, despite a reduction in international relative agricultural prices, intervention changed in favor of industrial production. This does not mean that a rural pressure group mechanism was not at work. The rural lobby, still basically a cattlemen's lobby, was mainly worried about the threat to its external markets if England decided to import the cattle it needed from the Commonwealth countries. The Roca-Runciman treaty put an end to such speculation.

During World War II, there was a strong external impetus for further industrialization. Although industrial exports increased significantly (Diaz Alejandro 1975), the war made it impossible to bring in imports, and importable goods attained a high level of de facto protection. According to Cavallo and Mundlak (1982), relative prices between agriculture and imported products decreased 9.2 percent a year during the war. There were also significant changes in income distribution, but all of these changes were related to external circumstances and not to external trade policy.

The adjustments in relative prices can be seen in table 2-19, which shows the relation between the prices of agricultural exportables and the prices of industrial products. A downward adjustment of 30 percent occurred during the war, owing to a reduction in the relative prices of products of the pampas. These prices did not change for ten years after the war.

As table 2-19 indicates, internal relative prices declined mainly because of a 23 percent reduction in external relative prices. Thus, the

**Table 2-19. Indexes of Internal and External Prices
between Agricultural and Industrial Products, 1935–54**

Period	Internal relative prices (1)	External relative prices (2)	Relation between both relative prices (3)
1935–39	100	100	100
1940–44	70	77	91
1945–49	68	114	62
1950–54	70	88	81

Note: (3) = (1)/(2)
Source: Naciones Unidas (1958).

relative prices of products from the pampas declined mainly because of the war and not because of changes in trade policy.

After the war, the industrial sector found it necessary to use internal economic stimuli (Llach 1984) in response to the normalization of the world economy. This normalization led to an increase in agriculture's external relative prices of over 45 percent in the five years following World War II (see column 2, table 2-19). Also, industrial exports decreased and industrial import flows were gradually reestablished. The industrial sector, which had prospered from the de facto protection provided by the war, now had to support its expansion in the growth of internal demand and in trade policy protection. To stimulate demand, it was necessary to increase real wages. This increase was to be achieved through a transfer of increases in land rents that were expected to take place in the rural sector after high international agricultural prices were transmitted to domestic prices. The transfer from the pampas was implemented mainly through high direct price discrimination against the region's agricultural products. Then, Argentina found it necessary to protect domestically produced importables. To do so, it introduced high tariffs and quantitative restrictions on imports.

This intervention, applied during Juan Peron's administration, discriminated against the pampas and favored the importable sector, and was a remarkable example of a stabilizing intervention. Although this government policy unquestionably favored immediate industrial development, it did so through intervention that prevented any substantial changes in the high industrial relative prices that prevailed during the war. Without it, relative prices would have changed dramatically in favor of the rural sector.

The data of table 2-19 support this view. Note that, although the external relative prices for products of the pampas rose by 48 percent in the period 1945–49, internal relative prices remained stationary. This situation was the result of a stabilizing trade policy that strongly discriminated against the pampas.

The same stabilizing pattern can be verified for the next five-year period—from 1950 to 1954—although in this case it worked in the other direction. As external relative prices declined, price discrimination against the pampas eased, so that internal relative prices remained the same.

Our political economy hypotheses are consistent with the external trade policy of the early postwar years. The industrial lobby was already very strong. It should have been very active, according to the Stolper-Samuelson formula, because of the threats to its short-run survival associated with the weakening of external incentives and with the real rate of exchange effects that would have occurred if agricultural prices had been allowed to rise to the high levels prevailing in world markets. If both factors had not been neutralized, a significant portion of the industrial sector could have disappeared.

It seems that during the war years the agrarian forces either accepted lower relative prices or were unable to successfully oppose them, undoubtedly because they were the result of external and uncontrollable circumstances. After the war, the agrarian lobby accepted the new structure of relative prices. This structure became the basis for the parity levels prevailing after the war.

The government decided to support the industrial lobby after the war because it wished to avoid short-run unemployment and to improve the welfare of urban labor, which formed the popular base of the peronist movement.

Summary and Conclusions

Price discrimination against agricultural production in the pampas was remarkably high in the postwar period and greatly affected its long-run growth. Implicit taxation resulting from total intervention in the prices of the six products of the region was about 45 percent in 1960, and remained more or less at that level until 1985. This rate of taxation implies that relative producer prices were only 55 percent of those that would have prevailed without intervention. When relative value added is used instead of relative prices, the picture is more or less the same.

The economy reached this point in two stages. The first occurred before the war. Import taxes, which encouraged import substitution and thus protected industrialization, subjected the pampas to indirect taxation of about 20 percent. This can be considered a moderate level of protection, because it did not seem to stem the vigorous growth of the agricultural sector in those years.

The second stage started during World War II, when internal agricultural relative prices among tradables dropped 30 percent, to a level that substantially favored industry. This change, however, was not policy-induced; it was a result of the circumstances of war. But immediately after the war, when external relative prices substantially improved for agriculture, the government adopted a proimport substitution policy that severely discriminated against agricultural products. This policy maintained the wartime structure of relative prices. The price discrimination that evolved during these two stages was responsible for the high level of total taxation at the beginning of the period of analysis. The second stage, in particular, produced adverse effects on agricultural production in the pampas. Only within the past two decades has growth resumed, mainly as a result of significant technical improvements. During the period of analysis, the level of income in the pampas remained more or less constant, with internal relative prices falling somewhat and productivity increasing.

Eventually, Argentina's taxation of agriculture will probably change. The agrarian lobby is beginning to understand the implications of its asymmetric behavior. If, in addition, Argentina can strengthen its tax system and reduce inflation and the fiscal deficit, it will no longer feel pressed to use export taxes on agriculture to stabilize the economy.

Notes

This paper is a condensed version of *Trade, Exchange Rate, and Agricultural Pricing Policies in Argentina,* World Bank, 1990.

1. Diaz Alejandro calls CP the "protectionist bias of commercial policy" (coefficient of protection). This does not seem to be an adequate definition because any protection implies disprotection. In Argentina, it is usually called the "antiexport bias" but this definition is not precise because the coefficient simultaneously reflects an "antiimport bias." When CP is less than 1, the "antitrade" denomination is precise; trade will be lower, and the economy more closed.

2. To gain some idea of whether these results were reasonable, we compared them with the results of a detailed study of the potential for increasing agricultural production in the pampas (Oris de Roa 1984). We found somewhat smaller output effects than Oris de Roa did for the period 1977–81 but greater effects (14 percent larger) for the period 1980–85. The latter comparison is perhaps more valid than the former, since potential output was underestimated in Oris de Roa's study because fertilizer use was not included in the calculations. This leads us to believe that the results obtained in our computations are reasonable.

3. This is a simple partial equilibrium estimation, in which the consequent losses of revenues would have to be offset by other taxes or by other means of financing public expenditures.

References

The word "processed" describes works that are reproduced from typescript by mimeograph, xerography, or similar means; such works may not be cataloged or commonly available through libraries, or they may be subject to restricted circulation.

Baldwin, Robert E. 1982. "The Political Economy of Protectionism." In *Import Competition and Response.* Edited by Jagdish Bhagwati. Chicago: University of Chicago Press.

Berlinski, J., and D. M. Schydlowsky. 1977. *Incentives for Industrialization in Argentina.* IBRD.

Brock, William A., and Stephen P. Maggee. 1968. "The Economics of Special Interest Politics: The Case of the Tariff." *American Economic Review* 68, no. 2.

Cavallo, D. F. 1985. "Exchange Rate Overvaluation and Agriculture (The Case of Argentina)." Background paper for *World Development Report 1986.* Washington, D.C.: World Bank.

Cavallo, D. F., and Y. Mundlak. 1982. *Agriculture and Economic Growth in an Open Economy: The Case of Argentina.* IFPRI, Research Report, no. 36. Washington D.C.: International Food Policy Research Institute.

De Janvry, A., and A. Nunez. 1971. "Analisis de demanda para productos agropecuarios en Argentina." *Económica* 17: no. 3.

Diaz Alejandro, C. F., 1975. *Ensayos sobre la historia económica Argentina.* Amorrortu Eds.

———. 1981. *Tipo de cambio y terminos de intercambio en la Republica Argentina 1913-1976.* C.E.M.A., Documentos de Trabajo No. 22, Buenos Aires.

Di Tella, G., and M. Zymelmann. 1967. *Las Etapas del Desarrollo Económico Argentino.* Buenos Aires: Editorial Paidos (PAIDOS).

Dornbusch, R. 1975. "Exchange Rates and Fiscal Policy in a Popular Model of International Trade." *American Economic Review* (December).

Elias, V. 1982. "El crecimiento económico argentino y sus determinantes: 1970-1980." *Ensayos Económicos,* BCRA no. 21.

Ferrer, A. 1980. *La Economia Argentina.* Mexico.

Fulginiti, L. E. 1986. "The Structure of Agricultural Technology: The Case of Argentina." Processed.

Gluck, S. 1979. "Reseña de estimaciones de oferta agricola pampeana." *Ensayos Económicos,* June. Buenos Aires.

Hathaway, D. E. 1963. *Government and Agriculture.* New York.

Imaz, J. L. 1964. *Los que mandan.* Buenos Aires.

Llach, J. J. 1984. "El Plan Pinedo de 1940, su significado historico y los origenes de la económia politica del peronismo." *Desarrollo Económico* 23, no. 92 (February-March).

Llach, J. J., and Fernandez Pol, J. 1985. "Sustitucion de las retenciones a las Exportaciones Agropecuarias por un impuesto a la Tierra Libre de Mejoras y Subsidios Explicitos al Consumo de Alimentos." *Estudio* 8, no. 34.

Macario, S. 1964. "Proteccionismo e industrializacion en America Latina" *Boletin Económico de America Latina* 9, no. 1 (March).

Miro, D. 1982. *Politicas de Precios Efectivas para Inducirel Aumento de la Overta Agricola.* Bolsa de Cereales de Buenos Aires, Buenos Aires. Processed.

Naciones Unidas, Comisión Económica para America Latina. 1958. *El Desarrollo Económico de la Argentina.* Mexico.

Olson, M. 1971. *The Logic of Collective Action.* Cambridge, Mass: Harvard University Press.

Oris de Roa, C. 1984. *El despertar de los granos. Evaluación del potencial de producción y sus limitantes en la Argentina.* Buenos Aires.

Penna, J. A., and Palazuelos, R. 1987. *La desprotección del sector agricola argentino en la ultimas decadas,* Centro de Investigaciones sobre Politicas Agropecuarias (CISPA), Documento de Investigación No. 7.

Posner, R. A. 1974. "Theories of Economic Regulation." *Bell Journal* 5, no. 2 (Autumn).

Reca, L. G. 1967. *The Price and Production Duality within Argentine Agriculture, 1923–65,* Ph. D. diss. University of Chicago (December). Processed.

———. 1974. *El Sector Agropecuario y los Incentivos Económicos en torno a la experiencia Argentina en las ultimas dos decadas.* Banco Ganadero Argentino, Temas de Economía Argentina: El Sector Agropecuario 1964/73. Buenos Aires.

Secretaria de Agricultura, Ganaderia y Pesca. 1985. *PRONAGRO.*

Sturzenegger, A. C., and B. Martinez Mosquera. 1990. *Trade, Exchange Rate, and Agricultural Pricing Policies in Argentina.* A World Bank Comparative Study. Washington, D.C.

Wellisz, S. and R. Findlay. 1986. *Income Appropriation and Rent-Seeking.* Processed.

3 Brazil

Antonio Salazar P. Brandão
José L. Carvalho

Although postwar Brazil has been marked by intensive industrialization that has made the country a significant factor in world commerce, agriculture is still an important part of the Brazilian economy. This chapter discusses the government's extensive intervention in agricultural prices during the period 1966–83, with particular attention to the food crops rice and wheat, and to three exportables—corn, cotton, and soybeans. All told, these five crops occupy 60 percent of Brazil's cropland.

Despite Brazil's position as the world's leading coffee producer for many years, relatively little attention is paid to it in this chapter. One reason is that coffee's importance to the Brazilian economy has greatly diminished over the past thirty years or so. Another is that the coffee sector in Brazil has been the subject of innumerable studies (see, for example, Carvalho Filho 1977; Delfim Netto 1979; Malta 1985). It, therefore, seemed more pertinent to concentrate on the five commodities named above, because it is the future prospects of those five crops that dominate debate over Brazilian agriculture today.

Section one of this chapter presents an overview of Brazil, including physical aspects, political institutions, and socioeconomic characteristics. The economic description touches on the most important aspects of Brazil's recent economic growth.

In section two we describe the agricultural sector. We also present a broad description of governmental intervention in the economic system, covering primarily the actions that have affected the agricultural sector.

Measures of relative protection are calculated in section three. Thus, measures of the effects of direct and indirect government intervention on agricultural prices are computed at the producer and consumer levels.

The principal consequences of these interventions are estimated in section four, in terms of their impact on output, consumption, and foreign exchange. Because the government also intervenes in agriculture by means of its expenditures, we tried to estimate the impact of these interventions on the government budget. Moreover, because some of the transfers to or from agriculture do not appear in the government budget, an estimate of the net transfers is made. To obtain these estimates, certain assumptions had to be made because the commodities under consideration do not include the whole agricultural GDP. The principal income distribution implications are also considered

Finally, in section five, the political economy of pricing policies is discussed, including an overview of the main interest groups involved in each commodity considered and an attempt to relate the results of the policies to the behavior of these groups. Through a simple regression analysis, an attempt is made to detail how policymakers' objectives explain agricultural pricing policy results.

Overview

Brazil, which occupies almost half of the South American continent, is located chiefly between the equator and the Tropic of Capricorn. Its geological characteristics include low mountains and rocky plateaus along the coast, the rain forest regions of the Amazon, and a woodland savannah known as the Campo Cerrado that occupies much of the interior south of the Amazon. Brazil's climate is tropical, with average temperatures ranging from 16 to 28 degrees centigrade. Rainfall exceeds 1,000 millimeters a year except in the northeast, a generally arid region.

About one-third of the country (that is, 248 million hectares) was classed as agricultural in 1970. About 30 million hectares were used for crops, with much of the rest used for livestock herds that amounted to an estimated 217 million animals, including 98 million cattle.

The population of Brazil is spread unevenly over the country's 8.5 million square kilometers. About 80 percent of the population is concentrated in the southeast (45 percent) and northeast (35 percent). In 1985 the total estimated population was 135 million, 57 percent of whom were 24 years old or younger. The rate of population growth is 2.49 percent a year. About 30 percent of the population was urban in 1940, but by 1980 the fraction of the population living in urban areas had increased to 67 percent. With an average population density of slightly less than 16 inhabitants per square kilometer, Brazil cannot be considered a populous country.

Life expectancy at birth is roughly 63 years. Infant mortality is about 100 per thousand children born alive. The illiteracy rate is about 33 percent among children between seven and fourteen years old, and about 26 percent for the population above fifteen years. Of those who enter elementary school, only 37 percent complete their second year. Twelve percent complete eighth grade, 4 percent complete secondary school, and only 2 percent earn college degrees.

The president of Brazil is elected for a six-year term indirectly by delegates from the states and the National Congress. The National Congress is bicameral, consisting of a Senate and a Chamber of Deputies. Senators are elected from the states for an eight-year term, and there are two senators from each state or federal territory. The number of federal deputies per state depends on the number of registered voters in each state. Historically, the president has been the dominant power because of both the strong power the presidency is given by law and the organization of Brazilian politics into numerous clienteles. These two characteristics are responsible for the autarchic institutions created to perform specific tasks for the executive.

In 1964 the legally constituted civilian government of Brazil was displaced by the military, whose successive candidates held the office of president from 1964 until 1985. During the military era, the National Congress was prevented from functioning effectively; various presidents selected by the military governed by presidential decree.

Economic Growth in Brazil

Brazil has had a fast-growing economy for many years, and the rate of economic growth accelerated after World War II. From 1952 to 1973 the average annual rate of industrial growth was about 9 percent, while the average rate of agricultural growth was about 5 percent.

The first petroleum price shock in 1973 did not affect Brazil. Through domestic economic policies, the government succeeded in isolating the country from the energy crisis. Nonetheless, the gross domestic product (GDP) growth from 1974 to 1979 dropped to 7 percent a year. When the world was hit by a second petroleum shock in 1979, followed by a sharp increase in international interest rates, Brazil could not postpone an adjustment to the new relative prices. In 1981 Brazil experienced a negative GDP growth (−1.5 percent). In 1982 the growth rate was slightly less than 1 percent, while in 1983 it once more turned negative (−3.2 percent).

In the 1960s, total annual trade volume corresponded, on average, to 13.3 percent of GDP, while for the 1970s this percentage rose to 16.5. After the first oil shock, however, trade volume dropped to about 6.5 percent of GDP (see tables 3-1 and 3-2).

Brazil imports mainly machinery and high technology equipment, oil, nonferrous metals, coal, and wheat. Almost all of the consumer durables demanded internally are domestically produced. About 35 percent of exports consist of manufactures: automobiles and parts,

Table 3-1. Growth Rates of Gross Domestic Product (GDP) and of Economic Sectors, and Sector Share of GDP, 1960–83

Period	Average Annual Growth Rate (percent)				Sector Share in Nominal GDP Annual Average (percent)		
	GDP	Agriculture	Industry	Service	Agriculture	Industry	Service
1960–64	5.9	4.1	6.7	6.6	21.6	25.5	52.8
1965–69	6.5	3.3	6.7	6.9	13.0	33.8	53.3
1970–74	9.8	5.6	12.2	11.5	12.0	36.0	52.0
1975–79	6.4	4.4	7.2	4.9	13.1	34.3	52.6
1980–88	0.9	3.1	−1.0	0.4	12.4	33.1	54.5

Source: Getúlio Vargas Foundation—Conjuntura Económica.

light machinery, textiles, furniture, shoes, and processed food (including coffee and orange juice). The country's principal agricultural exports are soybeans, sugar, and coffee beans. Total exports in 1983 amounted to almost US$22 billion.

Real income per capita has grown continuously since World War II, except in the periods 1964–66 and 1980–83. Although classified as a middle-income country, Brazil's income distribution is quite concentrated and has become more so during the past twenty-five years. Regionally, income in Brazil is concentrated in the southeast.

With respect to agricultural income, however, the southeast has been losing importance, with its share or such income falling from about 55 percent in 1949 to about 32 percent in 1980. The so-called center-south, however, which includes the southeast, south, and center-west regions, has maintained its share of about 76 percent of overall agriculture income during the last twenty-five years.

Brazil has suffered from inflation since the beginning of the century, and the problem became considerably worse after World War II. The annual rate of inflation reached 90 percent in 1964, when the military took over the government. With the implementation of a stabilization program in 1964–67, inflation started to decline. By the

Table 3-2. Gross Domestic Product (GDP) and Components, 1960–83

Period	Real GDP (US$ Millions, 1970)	Real GDP Per Capita (US$ Millions, 1970)	Share of GDP			
			Total Investment	Total Savings	Exports	Imports
1960–64	27,574	372	19.1	11.1	7.1	7.6
1965–69	34,082	397	22.0	12.7	6.2	5.8
1970–74	54,039	550	27.1	18.4	7.4	9.6
1975–79	80,568	727	26.5	21.4	7.0	9.0
1980–83	95,528	774	21.6	15.7	6.9	7.8

Source: Getúlio Vargas Foundation—Centro de Contas Nacionals.

end of 1973, when inflation was about 15 percent, the first petroleum price shock reversed the decline in inflation. However, the acceleration of inflation in the 1970s cannot be attributed to the oil crisis alone. Both monetary and fiscal policy became considerably more expansive after 1974. With the second oil shock in 1979, inflation accelerated to 110 percent in 1980. This mark was broken in 1983, when inflation reached 200 percent.

The Agricultural Sector

During the postwar period the roles of agriculture were to produce "cheap food," to produce raw materials for the domestic market, and to generate foreign exchange. Schuh (1975) pointed out that relatively abundant supplies of land and labor in Brazil eliminated the inducements to technical change in agriculture that were present in other countries. Instead of allocating resources to increase productivity in the sector, Brazil imposed price controls and quantitative restrictions on exports for the purpose of reducing prices for urban consumers. Moreover, commercial policy favored urban consumers through implicit and explicit taxes on agriculture.

According to a 1980 agricultural census, Brazil's agricultural sector accounted for approximately 55 percent of the value of all production in the primary sector. The most important products in the crop sector that year were soybeans (13.5 percent of total crop value), sugarcane (13 percent), corn (12 percent), coffee (10.5 percent), rice (9.8 percent), edible beans (8.7 percent), manioc (5 percent), cotton, cocoa, and wheat (3 percent each), and oranges (2.5 percent). Together, these accounted for 83.5 percent of the value of crop production. In 1980, when the area harvested was 48.7 million hectares, 23.5 percent of those hectares were devoted to corn, 18 percent to soybeans, 12 percent to rice, 9.5 percent to beans, 7.6 percent to cotton, 6 percent to rice, 5 percent to sugarcane and coffee, 4 percent to manioc and oranges, and 1 percent to cocoa. That adds up to 97.6 percent.

Food production increased steadily during the 1966–83 period; output in 1983 was roughly twice the level of 1966. Both pulses and root crops showed very poor performance during the period, however. Production levels were roughly the same in 1983 as they had been in 1966. Note also an instability in the production of edible beans, which was a consequence of the weak technological base for the crop. Cereals and edible oils fared better, as production doubled between 1966 and 1983.

After 1973, the amount of land devoted to rice, coffee, and manioc stabilized, but the area devoted to cotton declined by 42 percent. Wheat displayed a high degree of instability and a declining trend in area between 1960 and 1983. Two crops (edible beans and corn) experienced some growth in area, while cocoa, sugarcane, oranges, and soybeans showed sizable growth.

Production levels of cotton, coffee, edible beans, and wheat showed no distinct trend. Coffee production remained almost constant after 1964, taking into account the biannual variation characteristic of this crop. Production of edible beans increased during the 1960s but not after 1973. Manioc showed a declining trend after a large expansion in the 1960s.

The rise in agricultural production was sufficient to prevent major scarcities in the domestic market, and the terms of trade between agriculture and industry were almost constant until the end of the 1960s. Short-term variations in the terms of trade were quite common, however, reflecting specific problems in domestic supply.

During the 1970s the rate of growth of output continued at high levels. Nonetheless, the terms of trade again began to favor agriculture. This was true for both food commodities and exportable agricultural commodities (Homem de Melo 1979).

The high average rate of growth characteristic of Brazilian agriculture has been much more the result of expansion in the amount of land devoted to farming than the modernization of the sector. In 1940 there were 2.30 hectares of arable land per worker in the agricultural sector. This rose to 3.95 hectares in 1980 (an increase of more than 70 percent), notwithstanding an 85 percent increase in the number of workers in the sector.

Agriculture's share of GDP has been declining, as has the share of agricultural employment in total employment. Despite extensive labor migration, there is still a large difference between incomes in the farm and nonfarm sectors. According to the 1980 census, average income in agriculture was Cr$6,668 per month (cruzeiros of August 1980), while in the nonagricultural sector average income was Cr$13,912. The ownership of land is quite concentrated, and there has been no major change since 1940.

Economic growth in Brazil during the postwar period has been dominated by industrial growth and by the strategy adopted to develop the industrial sector. Nonetheless, exports of agricultural goods have accounted for a large share of the value of exports. To finance its development strategy, in fact, the country has relied heavily on taxation of agricultural exports (see table 3.3). It is well known that export taxes on coffee financed the infrastructure necessary to build the industrial complex of São Paulo. Because Brazil is the world's largest coffee exporter, the taxation of coffee export earnings was justified as a way of maintaining the world price of coffee. Taxation of the earnings of sugar exporters has also been a source of revenue of the government.

To achieve its domestic agricultural objectives—cheap food and adequate raw materials—the government has relied chiefly on controlling the marketing of agricultural products, on price controls, and on quantitative restrictions on agricultural exports. As the economy has become more complex, additional instruments have been brought into play: intensified price controls (usually price ceilings at the retail level, but occasionally at the wholesale level), expanded credit (especially for marketing activities), the creation of government stocks, and larger imports of food and raw materials to prevent increases in consumer prices. In Brazil, imports must be authorized by Carteira do Comércio Exterior (CACEX) (an agency of Banco do Brasil), which issues a document that allows importers to accept foreign exchange.

In some cases, the government has chosen to control the profit margins of retailers without directly affecting the level of agricultural prices. In other cases, export embargoes have been utilized to maintain domestic supply, or—as is frequently the case with soybeans—to counteract (or take advantage of) the situation in the world market. Another frequently utilized instrument is the allocation of fixed proportions of sales in the domestic and export markets.

One can identify three distinct periods in the recent history of agricultural policies in Brazil. The first period includes principally the decade of the 1950s, which was marked by concern with output losses as well as recommendations for investments in rural infrastructure. The best-known study dating from this period identified a lack of commercialization infrastructure as the major bottleneck in agriculture (see Smith 1969). Large investments in highways and storage capacity were then made and, in view of an abundant supply of high-quality land, the production response was quite good. It appears, however, that those were the only measures favorable to agriculture in that period. Any other agricultural measures were a response to some specific problem, usually a crisis in the supply of food to urban centers (Smith 1969; Homem de Melo 1979).

Discrimination against the agricultural sector through commercial policy persisted during most of the 1960s. In this period, no agricultural policy (in the sense of a consistent set of instruments with goals to be attained) was established. As in the 1950s, there sometimes were problems in supplying food to urban centers, but concerns about the rural infrastructure became secondary. The authorities interpreted the persistence of urban food supply problems as an indication of monopoly in marketing, but this interpretation was replaced in the mid-1960s by the view that lack of incentives to increase agricultural production were the origin of the problem. The immediate reaction, though, was to enlarge the government's role in marketing through governmental enterprises and through regulations that permitted SUNAB (Superintendência Nacional de Abastecimento), a new agency, to control prices, confiscate stocks, and determine profit margins in the agricultural markets.

The perception that limitations to expansion of production can occur evolved only in the second half of the 1960s. It was then that subsidized credit and minimum agricultural prices were first utilized, and that major liberalization measures were taken. These included lowering tariffs and a change in exchange rate policy that amounted to abandoning fixed exchange rates and adopting minidevaluations according to the purchasing power parity (PPP) rule.

A more comprehensive agricultural policy only began to develop in Brazil in the 1970s. The two most important instruments utilized were credit at concessionary rates and a minimum price policy (MPP). It is during this period that a concern with agricultural research and agricultural technology emerges. Empresa Brasileira de Pesquisas Agropecuarias (EMBRAPA), a federal enterprise for agricultural research, was created in 1973.

Agricultural Policy Instruments

The policy instruments that have been used are, basically, minimum prices, credit, marketing and price controls, fertilizer-use incentives, extension, and basic research. Thus, for example, when the government is concerned with food supply, it tends to set higher minimum prices for food crops and to facilitate access to credit by producers of those commodities.

MINIMUM PRICES. A minimum price is price insurance to the farmer. When a minimum price is set, the probability distribution of prices is truncated in such a way that a part of the area under the curve is no longer relevant, because the price cannot go (in principle) below that minimum. With risk-averse farmers, this will lead to a rightward shift in the supply curve which will, in turn, lead to higher levels of production (Carvalho 1978). It should be noted that the policy is not a buffer stock policy; the minimum price is set in such a way that it is at or near equilibrium. Because this involves estimations, frequently, the price is too high (forcing the government to purchase a substantial share of the harvest) or it is too low (thus reducing the effectiveness of the policy). The government agency in charge of policy is the Companhia de Financiamento da Produção (CFP).

The minimum price policy consists of setting minimum prices for the major commodities of corn, cotton, rice, and soybeans. The government stands ready to buy any quantity at that price. It also provides credit (at concessionary rates) to facilitate the formation of stocks.

Timing is a key feature of the policy. The crop year in the center-south starts in the third quarter of the year and ends in the second quarter of the following year. Thus, the bulk of production is harvested from April to June, while planting decisions are made between

July and November. Minimum producer prices are announced by July.

The two instruments utilized under the minimum price policy are Acquisitions of the Federal Government (AGF) and Loans of the Federal Government (EGF). It is through the former that, whenever necessary, the government buys from producers. This happens more frequently in years of unexpectedly poor crops, and when minimum prices are at high levels.

The EGF is a credit program open to any qualified farmer. Access to EGF is limited by usual banking rules and by the amount of financial resources allocated to the program. The financial agent of the policy is the Banco do Brasil.

Credit Policy

A National System of Rural Credit (SNCR) was created in the mid-1960s in response to domestic supply problems. The new system was the successor to CREAI—the agriculture credit office of the Banco do Brasil—which was created in 1937. One of the most important innovations introduced by the SNCR was the inclusion of all banks as suppliers of credit to agriculture. This "participation" was obtained by special regulations that required the banks to allocate a specific proportion of deposits to the rural credit system. Also, a proportion of the reserve requirement could be used for agricultural loans. The proportion of deposits required to be loaned to agriculture has increased in recent years.

As adjustments were made in the economy at large in the aftermath of the 1982 Mexican default, Brazil's agricultural credit policy was also changed. The interest rate subsidy, which had been part of the policy since the beginning, was substantially reduced.

During most of the 1970s, interest rates on agricultural loans were fixed and independent of the rate of inflation. These rates differed depending on purpose and programs, but the average rate was 15 percent. Real interest rates were negative throughout the decade of the 1970s (da Mata 1982). When the inflation rate reached a plateau at the end of that decade, the nominal rates were adjusted, but the real rates remained negative. In the crop year 1983–84 the subsidy was reduced, and the nominal rate was equal to the monetary correction of the period plus 3 percent per year.

Brazil's credit policy for agriculture has been subject to criticism by many economists both within and outside the government. The main concern has been over the incentive given to substitute personal resources for bank loans (Sayad 1977), so that the net increase in production has been much less than desired. Because risk is an important element in agriculture, one could argue that a subsidy would compensate the sector for the excess risk and bring the supply curve closer to the marginal cost curve. This has not been the case in Brazil. The subsidies are larger than necessary to reach that goal, and it is obvious that a misallocation of resources takes place. To have access to the subsidy, an individual must be a landowner. In many circumstances, those attracted to agriculture by this financial gain utilize land differently than those for whom agricultural activity is the main source of income. Usually, large landowners develop extensive livestock activity, which is neither labor- nor management-intensive. The policy has tended to preserve or increase inequality in the distribution of agricultural income.

A significant distortion introduced by credit policy in Brazil concerns storage. Marketing credit is mainly an incentive to retain production after the harvest. In other words, it is a mechanism to induce the private sector to hold stocks and to stabilize prices. The practical consequences of this, however, have been exactly the opposite. Typically, in a year in which a good crop occurs, credit incentives to the private sector to pile up stocks are so large that the market price does not fall as it otherwise should. Domestic demand is then filled by imports.

Marketing and Price Controls

Ensuring food supplies for the urban sector has always been a major concern of the government. During the 1950s and 1960s, this concern was expressed in the form of investments in marketing, transport, and storage infrastructure as well as price controls of agricultural products at the consumer level. The investment in transportation and storage resulted from a consensus that the problems of supplying Brazilian cities with food were the result of losses during the commercialization process—losses estimated then at 20 to 25 percent of all agricultural produce.

Expansion of Brazilian agricultural production has also depended on the creation of a transportation infrastructure. Public investment in this area has lagged, however, because the construction of local roads linking production areas to the main highways is a municipal responsibility. Because of a concentration of fiscal revenues at the national level in 1964, municipalities have had fewer resources to pay for expansion of the transport infrastructure.

State intervention in agricultural marketing initially occurred during the World War II with the creation of the Coordenacao de Mobilizacao Economica which, in 1951, became the Comissão Federal do Abastecemento e Preços (COFAP). In 1954, COFAP was turned into a council and, finally, in 1962, into a superintendency—SUNAB. SUNAB has discretionary powers to intervene in the market through

Table 3-3. Agricultural Imports and Exports, 1960–83

Period	Agricultural Imports[a] Value (US$ Millions)	Share of Total Imports (percent)	Agricultural Exports[b] Value (US$ Millions)	Share of Total Exports (percent)
1960–64	265	18.7	1,150	85.7
1965–69	290	18.4	1,439	78.4
1970–74	571	9.1	3,146	67.3
1975–79	1,363	8.7	6,471	55.7
1980–88	2,039	9.6	7,126	41.7

Source: Getúlio Vargas Foundation; F.A.O.—Production Yearbook.

price and profit margin controls, food stock sales, export embargoes, and food importation. Industrialized agricultural products are also subject to price controls imposed by CIP (Conselho Interministerial de Preços).

A major concern in controlling agricultural product prices has been to restrain inflation. Unfortunately, the long-term effects of such efforts have been negative. Declines in crop profits have tended to cause shifts of resources to other sectors, or to other activities within the same sector, which may help to explain the relative contraction of the food production sector. In addition, price controls tend to diminish the incentives to modernization.

Fertilizer Policy

The use of fertilizers in Brazilian agriculture has been increasing significantly. From 1960 to 1980 it increased approximately fourteenfold. Of this total, 50 percent are phosphoric fertilizers, which are necessary because Brazilian soils are deficient in that nutrient; potassium and nitrogen correspond to 30 and 20 percent, respectively (Levy 1982).

The use of fertilizers is differentiated according to crops. Thus, in the period 1975–77, 75 percent of fertilizer was utilized for only six products: soybeans, sugarcane, wheat, coffee, rice, and corn.

Import substitution has taken place in this industry since the late 1960s. In 1974 the Economic Development Council (EDC) approved a plan whose objective was to make Brazil self-sufficient in fertilizer production by the year 1980 (Braga 1981). Domestic production has increased significantly since then, and today most phosphate fertilizer, is produced internally as is a large proportion of nitrogen fertilizer. Potassium fertilizer, however, is still entirely imported.

Import substitution was accompanied by measures to increase consumption. After 1966 fertilizer use was subsidized by special interest rates on loans for purchase, or directly through price. Nominal interest rates on fertilizer loans have been lower than inflation since 1970.

Imports of fertilizer have been subject to a policy known as *contingenciamento*. To be able to import a quantity of a product, importers have had to buy a certain amount of the same product domestically, at a higher price. These rates of *contingenciamento* have varied over time (see Santana 1984).

Rural Extension and Basic Research

In 1953 Associação de Crédito e Assistência Rural (ACAR) started to provide rural extension service. Gradually, the ACAR experience was absorbed by other states, and in 1956 the Ministry of Agriculture created a national system of credit and rural extension by placing all state extension services under a national association—ABCAR (Associacao Brasileira de Credito e Assistencia Rural).

The rural extension programs have not been subjected to thorough evaluation. Nonetheless, two studies provide us with some indication of their contributions. Alves and Schuh (1984) analyzed the Minas Gerais ACAR, using individual data collected in the crop year of 1963/64. Their findings indicate that ACAR support was effective in providing what they call price efficiency. Thus, under the technical assistance of ACAR, farmers tended to use their resources efficiently. They imply, however, that ACAR was not effective in promoting the use of modern technology.

Dias (1974), using a 1971–72 countrywide sample of 1,686 farmers under the ABCAR programs, concluded that, given the technological knowledge in Brazil, ABCAR had a positive impact on the use of new techniques by farmers who produced at low technological levels.

After the first petroleum price shock in 1973, agricultural research became an important potential source of production increase. Technical knowledge developed elsewhere had to be adapted to the country's specific conditions. In 1974 the federal government created an enterprise for agricultural research under the Ministry of Agriculture—EMBRAPA. Agricultural research is developed by EMBRAPA's national centers, which are spread over the country. The research efforts of the centers are concentrated on a few agricultural products. They have been developing new agricultural techniques as well as seed improvements. A great deal of effort is directed toward disseminating EMBRAPA's research findings.

To conclude this section, we should mention that there are other policies for the agricultural sector that are not considered in our discussion. One of these is income taxation of the sector. Income tax for agriculture is around 1 percent of total revenue from the income tax, while agriculture's share of income from the tax is approximately 10 percent. This is a consequence of a large number of rebates and special treatments given to the sector.

Other policies exist for the agricultural sector that are not discussed here. They include special fiscal incentives for the acquisition of tractors and machinery, credit insurance (see Lopes and Dias 1986), a value added tax (ICM) levied by the states (Bressan Filho 1978), and a complicated land tax system that ultimately collects insignificant revenues.

The Effects of Agricultural Pricing Policy

The approach followed to quantitatively evaluate the effects of price policies consists of computations of various price ratios under distinct policy scenarios. First, one observes the prevailing price ratios between food and nonfood agricultural goods and between agricultural and nonagricultural goods. These price ratios are then recomputed on the assumption that the policy scenario is one from which direct taxation or subsidization of agricultural commodities has been removed.

The next step consists of recomputing the price ratios on the assumption that indirect intervention in prices is also removed. Thus, an equilibrium exchange rate is computed and applied to both agricultural and nonagricultural commodities to obtain the prices in domestic currency. Nonagricultural prices are also corrected for taxes and subsidies.

The final step is consideration of value added. Corrections were made for direct taxation and for the discrepancy between the equilibrium exchange rate and the official exchange rate for fertilizer prices. In addition, an estimate was made of undistorted value added for each product, and the ratios between value added in distorted and undistorted situations are compared.

Effects of Direct Intervention on Producer Prices

The relative prices that would have prevailed in the absence of direct intervention were obtained by taking the FOB average export (or CIF average import) price and then subtracting (or adding) transportation and other transaction costs. For the period 1976–82, most of the data were taken from a study by Brandão and Cavalho (forthcoming). For the other years they were estimated according to the methodology described in appendix D of the same work.

In table 3-4 the relative differences between these price ratios and the prevailing price ratios are shown. Here, as in all relative differences presented, we used the following: (observed ratio—undistorted ratio)-undistorted ratio. When the result is positive, the commodity

Table 3-4. Effect of Direct Price Interventions on Relative Prices at Farmgate, 1966–83

Year	Cotton–Rice	Cotton–Wheat	Soybeans–Rice	Soybeans–Wheat	Corn–Rice	Corn–Wheat
1966	—	−0.404	—	—	—	−0.040
1967	—	−0.435	—	—	—	0.062
1968	—	−0.436	—	—	—	−0.102
1969	−0.261	−0.412	—	—	0.168	−0.070
1970	−0.543	−0.449	−0.499	−0.407	−0.158	−0.006
1971	−0.665	−0.331	−0.661	−0.324	−0.383	0.232
1972	−0.608	−0.330	−0.604	−0.324	−0.176	0.406
1973	−0.226	0.054	−0.388	−0.167	0.296	0.764
1974	−0.058	0.292	−0.167	0.142	0.068	0.464
1975	−0.096	−0.068	−0.249	−0.226	−0.024	0.006
1976	0.220	0.079	−0.293	−0.374	0.428	0.263
1977	0.208	−0.367	−0.172	−0.566	−0.867	−0.023
1978	−0.143	−0.326	−0.410	−0.535	0.130	−0.110
1979	−0.294	−0.273	−0.252	−0.230	−0.203	−0.180
1980	0.109	0.372	−0.281	−0.111	−0.128	0.395
1981	0.154	0.011	0.118	−0.021	0.486	0.301
1982	−0.044	−0.107	−0.486	−0.519	0.006	−0.060
1983	0.182	0.303	−0.029	−0.070	0.087	0.198

— Not available.

Note: Computed as $\dfrac{\text{observed price ratio} - \text{undistorted price ratio}}{\text{undistorted price ratio}}$

Source: Author's calculations.

was protected (that is, subsidized) in relation to the undistorted situation. Of the three export goods considered in the study, cotton and soybeans show a consistent pattern of suffering discrimination vis-à-vis food commodities. Corn, on the other hand, was protected for a number of years.

For cotton, compared with rice and wheat, the average difference during 1969–83 was −0.14 in relation to rice, and −0.10 in relation to wheat. Until 1975, the relative disprotection with respect to rice was higher than with respect to wheat, but after that the pattern is not clear.

For soybeans, the situation was somewhat similar. It was discriminated against, but the pattern of discrimination was more consistent than it was for cotton. The average difference during 1970–83 was −0.31 in relation to rice and −0.26 in relation to wheat. Until 1975, the penalization of rice was higher than that of wheat.

Corn was not discriminated against as much as the other two export crops. The situation was actually quite favorable in a number of years. The average relative discrepancies in the period 1970–83 were 0.11 and 0.17 in relation to rice and wheat, respectively.

Table 3-5.   Effect of Direct Price Interventions on Relative Prices (to Nonagricultural Prices), 1966–83

Year	Cotton	Corn	Soybeans	Rice	Wheat
1966	−0.144	0.378	—	—	0.436
1967	−0.207	0.492	—	—	0.405
1968	−0.221	0.240	—	—	0.381
1969	−0.156	0.335	—	0.143	0.435
1970	−0.083	0.655	−0.014	0.967	0.664
1971	−0.093	0.671	−0.083	1.707	0.356
1972	−0.174	0.735	−0.166	1.106	0.234
1973	−0.080	0.540	−0.273	0.188	−0.127
1974	−0.087	0.035	−0.193	−0.031	−0.293
1975	0.027	0.109	−0.147	0.136	0.102
1976	0.217	0.425	−0.294	−0.002	0.128
1977	0.076	0.663	−0.262	−0.109	0.701
1978	−0.011	0.305	−0.319	0.154	0.467
1979	−0.231	−0.132	−0.185	0.089	0.058
1980	0.026	0.044	−0.335	−0.074	−0.252
1981	0.055	0.358	0.022	−0.086	0.044
1982	0.038	0.092	−0.441	0.086	0.162
1983	0.151	0.059	−0.054	−0.026	−0.116

— Not available.

Note: Computed as $\dfrac{\text{observed price ratios} - \text{undistorted price ratio}}{\text{undistorted price ratio}}$

Source: Author's calculations.

The effects of direct intervention in agricultural prices versus non-agricultural prices are presented in table 3-5. The effect of direct intervention in soybean prices was negative during virtually the entire period, as it was for cotton until 1974. There is, however, a difference in the behavior over time. For soybeans there appears to be no trend in the magnitude of the difference, but for cotton there is a clear trend toward reduction of taxation. The average level of the relative difference was −0.05 for cotton and −0.20 for soybeans.

The situation of the other crops was somewhat similar—that is, usually they were protected by direct intervention. It is clear that corn was the most protected by direct intervention. It is clear that corn was the most protected commodity (average relative difference of 0.33). One must interpret these results with some care in view of the particular nature of this crop. Brazil was a net exporter of corn until 1977 and then became a net importer. Our study considered it an exportable, however, because some studies have indicated a high potential for Brazil in world markets. Some analysts treat this crop as a nontradable because of the behavior just described, and because direct price comparisons show that the domestic price is usually above the FOB price and below the CIF price.

The picture that emerges for rice and wheat is somewhat similar. The average relative differences are 0.28 and 0.21 for rice and wheat, respectively. The levels of protection for rice were very high in the early 1970s and then declined, with more recent years demonstrating disprotection. Roughly the same is true for wheat.

In summary, there appears to have been a clear tendency for the government to tax the export crops and to protect food crops.

Effects of Direct and Indirect Intervention

Indirect interventions are tariffs and subsidies on imports and exports of nonagricultural goods. To estimate the total effects of government intervention, one must estimate an equilibrium exchange rate and correct the prices of nonagricultural goods. Correction of the exchange rate involved the methodology proposed by Roe and Greene (1986), which assumes constant elasticities of supply and demand of foreign exchange. The equilibrium exchange rate is defined as equal to zero, with tariffs and exports taxes eliminated.

Effects of Direct and Indirect Intervention on Producer and Consumer Prices

The differences between observed prices and prices corrected for total intervention are shown in tables 3-6 through 3-9. Such intervention meant that crops were discriminated against most of the time. The average relative differences were −21.8 for cotton, −34.6 for soybeans, 9.9 for corn, 4.2 for rice, and 0.3 for wheat.

For cotton, protection was negative over all the period (with the exceptions of 1976 and 1983), but there was a tendency for taxation to diminish in the most recent period. Soybeans were taxed over the period, and taxation increased over time (with the exceptions of 1981 and 1983). Corn appears as a protected commodity, but the level of protection seems to decrease in the more recent years. Rice was protected in the early years but later was taxed. The situation for wheat was the most striking. Despite all the direct subsidies given to that commodity, it endured high levels of indirect taxation in some years. The average level indicates that the net effect of direct and indirect intervention combined was almost zero.

Intervention at the producer level generated distortion in the prices of rice and wheat at the consumer level. The methodology is described in Brandão and Carvalho (forthcoming), appendix F. Rice was highly taxed during most of the period; when it was subsidized (1976, 1978, and 1980), the subsidy was relatively small. Wheat policy penalized consumers until 1972. Consumers were then subsidized at increasing rates. The level of the subsidy to consumers as well as to

Table 3-6. Effect of Direct and Indirect Output Price Interventions on Relative Prices, 1966–83

Year	Rice-UPNA	Wheat-UPNA	Cotton-UPNA	Soybeans-UPNA	Corn-UPNA
1966	—	0.254	−0.253	—	0.203
1967	—	0.213	−0.315	—	0.288
1968	—	0.151	−0.351	—	0.033
1969	.000	0.256	−0.261	—	0.168
1970	0.644	0.391	−0.234	0.176	0.383
1971	1.152	0.078	−0.279	−0.271	0.328
1972	0.670	−0.022	−0.345	−0.338	0.376
1973	−0.011	−0.274	−0.234	−0.395	0.282
1974	−0.247	−0.451	−0.291	−0.373	−0.196
1975	−0.086	−0.113	−0.174	−0.134	−0.108
1976	−0.161	−0.052	−0.023	−0.407	0.197
1977	−0.242	0.449	−0.084	−0.372	0.416
1978	−0.130	0.105	−0.255	−0.487	−0.017
1979	−0.199	−0.221	−0.434	−0.041	−0.361
1980	−0.295	−0.430	−0.219	−0.493	−0.205
1981	−0.223	−0.112	−0.103	−0.131	0.155
1982	−0.134	−0.073	−0.172	−0.554	−0.128
1983	−0.111	−0.193	0.051	−0.137	−0.033

— Not available.

Note: Computed as $\dfrac{\text{observed price ratio} - \text{undistorted price ratio}}{\text{undistorted price ratio}}$

Source: Author's calculations.

producers was reduced in the early 1980s owing to pressure to reduce the public deficit.

Corn, cotton, and soybean consumers (mostly processing industries) were taxed in about a third of the years studied.

Other Impacts of Agricultural Pricing Policies

We now present estimates of the impact of intervention on agricultural production, consumption, foreign exchange earnings, and the government budget. We also estimate transfers into and out of the sector as well as the income distribution impacts.

Effects on Production

To measure the impact of price intervention on agricultural production, we assumed that supply is a function of expected prices. Direct and cross-supply price elasticities were borrowed from other studies. The distortions for prices used here refer to unit value added; therefore, the estimates for the elasticities used were corrected accordingly.

**Table 3-7. Effect of Direct and Indirect Consumer
Price Intervention on Relative Prices (Agriculture
to Non-Agriculture), 1966–83**

Year	Corn	Cotton	Rice	Wheat	Soybeans
1966	—	−0.238	—	0.297	—
1967	—	0.063	—	0.334	—
1968	—	−0.148	—	0.396	—
1969	—	−0.096	—	0.329	—
1970	0.230	0.558	1.481	0.525	—
1971	−0.157	−0.255	3.292	0.230	—
1972	0.361	−0.374	1.584	0.174	—
1973	0.102	0.980	0.316	−0.090	−0.038
1974	−0.407	−0.323	0.049	−0.359	−0.008
1975	−0.279	−0.270	0.228	−0.300	0.539
1976	−0.173	n.a.	−0.074	−0.385	0.042
1977	0.000	0.000	0.000	0.000	0.000
1978	−0.390	0.049	−0.057	−0.333	−0.140
1979	−0.523	−0.553	1.445	−0.553	−0.127
1980	−0.409	0.051	−0.037	−0.680	−0.149
1981	−0.247	−0.250	0.201	−0.358	−0.094
1982	−0.416	−0.486	0.574	−0.221	−0.038
1983	−0.109	−0.422	0.411	−0.303	0.196

— Not available.

Note: Computed as $\dfrac{\text{observed price ratio—undistorted price ratio}}{\text{undistorted price ratio}}$

Source: Author's calculations.

Table 3-10 shows the difference between observed and "free trade" production of the five commodities based on short-run elasticities.

For cotton, intervention in prices produced output losses during the period 1971–83 (with the exception of a small gain in 1977). The largest loss in output occurred in 1980, with production 6 percent below its nonintervention level. For corn the situation was just the opposite—output was greater over most of the period. The most damaging effects occurred for soybeans. In many years one notices losses on the order of 15 to 20 percent. In 1983, soybean production was 39 percent below the nonintervention level. In the case of rice, there were output gains until 1974 and losses from then on. For wheat, a consistent and often substantial loss in production was observed.

Effects on Consumption

From the distortions in consumer prices (table 3-11), consumption under the nonintervention assumption was estimated and is reported in table 3-12, as obtained from the above price distortions, the corresponding estimated elasticities, and the actual apparent consumption

Table 3-8. Effect of Direct and Indirect Output Price Interventions and of Input Price Interventions on Relative Values Added, 1966–83

(percent)

Year	Cotton Rice	Cotton Wheat	Soybeans Rice	Soybeans Wheat	Corn Rice	Corn Wheat
1966	—	—	—	—	—	—
1967	—	—	—	—	—	—
1968	—	—	—	—	—	—
1969	—	—	—	—	—	—
1970	−0.593	−0.502	−0.561	−0.462	−0.223	−0.60
1971	−0.726	−0.377	−0.722	−0.370	−0.463	0.20
1972	−0.661	−0.381	−0.658	−0.375	−0.220	0.40
1973	−0.243	0.100	−0.417	−0.152	0.339	0.90
1974	−0.022	0.522	−0.191	0.259	0.098	0.70
1975	−0.103	−0.067	−0.292	−0.264	−0.024	0.00
1976	0.254	0.091	−0.330	−0.417	0.490	0.20
1977	0.301	−0.398	−0.168	−0.615	1.081	−0.00
1978	−0.136	−0.346	−0.449	−0.583	0.158	−0.10
1979	−0.301	−0.267	−0.278	−0.243	−0.218	−0.10
1980	0.140	0.520	−0.332	−0.109	0.158	0.50
1981	0.197	0.025	0.137	−0.027	0.576	0.30
1982	−0.026	−0.098	−0.556	−0.589	0.024	−0.00
1983	0.219	0.370	−0.032	0.089	0.116	0.25

— Not available.

Note: Computed as $\dfrac{\text{observed value added ratio} - \text{undistorted value added ratio}}{\text{undistorted value added ratio}}$

Source: Author's calculations.

of the product, estimated from current data on production, exports, and imports (for details, see appendix F of Brandão and Carvalho forthcoming).

It is important to note that here we are working with the percent change in the price of each product and not with the relative price change. The relevant prices for consumers are those relative to the consumer price index. Because the estimated own-price elasticities take inflation as given, these computations disregard any effect that the liberalization of agricultural pricing policy would have had on inflation.

The following points emerge from table 3-12:

- Because corn was taxed in the early years of the 1970–83 period, severe reductions occurred in the level of consumption. After 1974 the situation changed, and higher levels of consumption are observed.

- With the exception of the 1960s and some years in the 1970s, actual consumption of cottonseed oil was above the nonintervention situation, which indicates a tendency to subsidize consumption, especially in the more recent period.

Table 3-9. Effect of Direct and Indirect Output Price Interventions and of Input Price Interventions on Relative Value Added Agricultural/Nonagricultural, 1966–83

(percent)

Year	Cotton	Soybeans	Corn	Rice	Wheat
1966	—	—	—	—	—
1967	—	—	—	—	—
1968	—	—	—	—	—
1969	—	—	—	—	—
1970	−0.250	−0.190	0.434	0.845	0.506
1971	−0.291	−0.283	0.388	1.582	0.138
1972	−0.338	−0.331	0.525	0.955	0.070
1973	−0.143	−0.339	0.516	0.132	−0.221
1974	−0.194	−0.334	−0.095	−0.176	−0.471
1975	−0.155	−0.333	−0.081	−0.058	−0.094
1976	0.057	−0.435	0.257	−0.157	−0.031
1977	−0.042	−0.387	0.533	−0.264	0.592
1978	−0.146	−0.455	0.145	−0.012	0.306
1979	−0.385	−0.365	−0.312	−0.121	−0.162
1980	−0.118	−0.483	−0.103	−0.226	−0.419
1981	−0.091	−0.136	0.198	−0.240	−0.113
1982	−0.193	−0.632	−0.152	−0.172	−0.172
1983	0.036	−0.177	−0.052	−0.150	−0.244

— Not available.

Note: Computed as $\dfrac{\text{observed value added ratio} - \text{undistorted value added ratio}}{\text{undistorted value added ratio}}$

Source: Author's calculations.

- Rice was subsidized most of the time, and actual consumption usually exceeded distortion-free consumption.
- Soybean oil consumption was always above the nonintervention situation (except in 1983), although the difference tended to be a small proportion of total consumption.
- For wheat, the consumption subsidy was important during the 1970s, which had a large impact on the rise in actual consumption levels. In 1974, 1976, 1978, 1979, 1980, 1981, 1982, and 1983 the difference was more than one million metric tons.

The message conveyed by this is quite clear. Brazil pursued a policy of subsidizing wheat consumption, and subsidies were more frequent in the 1970s and 1980s.

Effects on Foreign Exchange Earnings

The impact of intervention in agricultural prices on foreign exchange earnings was also estimated. The procedure adopted was to take the dollar price of the commodities multiplied by the difference between

Table 3-10.   Short-Run Effects on Output of Direct and Indirect
Interventions, 1966–83

(percent)

Year	Cotton	Corn	Soybean	Rice	Wheat
1966	—	—	—	—	—
1967	—	—	—	—	—
1968	—	—	—	—	—
1969	—	—	—	—	—
1970	—	—	—	—	—
1971*	−4.0	5.7	−4.3	21.7	11.7
1972*	−4.6	4.5	−6.2	47.5	−1.7
1973	−5.3	6.7	−20.8	28.7	−4.7
1974	−2.2	6.9	−23.9	3.5	−12.3
1975	−3.0	−1.2	−27.0	−4.7	−18.2
1976	−2.5	−1.1	−23.0	−1.6	−9.3
1977	−0.9	3.4	−27.9	−4.2	−9.4
1978	−0.7	7.6	−16.3	−7.0	9.6
1979	−2.4	2.0	−24.0	−0.3	−0.2
1980	−6.0	4.2	−25.0	−3.3	−11.5
1981	−1.9	−1.3	−34.3	−6.0	−19.9
1982	−1.5	2.9	−11.4	−6.6	−6.1
1983	−3.1	−2.1	−39.0	−4.8	−15.4

— Not available.

Note: Columns in the table are: $\dfrac{\text{observed production} - \text{undistorted production}}{\text{undistorted production}}$

Source: Author's calculations. See Brandão and Carvalho (forthcoming), chapter 5.

the change in consumption (that is, actual minus nonintervention)
and add the results. The estimation of the change in fertilizer consumption was made with input-output coefficients also utilized in
computing value added.

Table 3-13 displays the short-run impacts. Notice that for export
and food crops, the columns indicate the potential gain from liberalization (or, in other words, the loss actually incurred), although the
column for fertilizer indicates the increase in the value of imports
owing to liberalization (this, therefore, enters with a negative sign in
the calculation of the total effect).

The results are straightforward. For export crops, the loss averaged
around 10 percent per year. The impacts resulting from intervention
in food crop and fertilizer prices were smaller. The total effect reflects
essentially the loss in foreign exchange earnings from export crops.

Effects on the Government Budget

The interest here is in computing the effects of agricultural price
policy on the governmental budget. Because of severe data limita-

Table 3-11. Consumer Price Distortions for Selected Agricultural Products, 1966–83

Year	Corn	Soybean Oil	Wheat Flower	Cottonseed oil	Rice
1966	—	—	0.0149	−0.0409	—
1967	—	—	0.0146	0.2944	—
1968	—	—	0.0704	0.0451	—
1969	—	—	0.0044	0.0890	—
1970	0.6553	—	0.1655	0.9234	0.7746
1971	0.1249	—	−0.0551	−0.0872	2.0477
1972	0.7872	—	−0.1030	−0.2352	0.8294
1973	0.4599	−0.0634	−0.3085	1.4133	−0.0664
1974	−0.2602	−0.0949	−0.5420	−0.2260	−0.3035
1975	−0.1135	−0.0999	−0.5056	−0.1742	−0.1934
1976	0.0186	−0.0594	−0.5647	n.a.	−0.3895
1977	0.2089	−0.1144	−0.3066	0.115	−0.3548
1978	−0.1448	−0.1163	−0.4635	0.3518	−0.2938
1979	−0.3372	−0.1106	−0.6436	−0.4286	0.8150
1980	−0.1958	−0.1500	−0.7501	0.3171	−0.2994
1981	−0.0641	−0.1742	−0.5419	−0.1432	−0.2028
1982	−0.2765	−0.1258	−0.4459	−0.4143	0.0414
1983	0.0407	0.0245	−0.5322	−0.3789	−0.1192

— Not available.

Note: Computed as $\dfrac{\text{observed price}-\text{undistorted price}}{\text{undistorted price}}$

Source: Author's calculations. See Brandão and Carvalho (forthcoming), appendix F.

tions, the results presented here must be considered carefully. It should be remembered that these computations account for the entire agricultural sector, not only the five commodities that have been considered. This was necessary because it is impossible to isolate government expenditures on agriculture by crop.

The only revenue items considered were the export tax and the ICM tax, which is a state value-added tax. The expenditures considered were the wheat subsidy, credit subsidy, and fertilizer subsidy. It should be noted that negative export taxes and negative subsidies might occur, and that they therefore represent subsidies and taxes, respectively.

Exports of raw agricultural goods, except for coffee, are almost nonexistent. Soybeans, sugar, and cocoa are exported as processed goods—such as soybean meal or oil; brown, refined, or crystalized sugar; and cocoa meal or butter. (Instant coffee, though, is not considered an agricultural export.) In the case of sugar, only exports of brown and refined sugar were considered. For cocoa and soybean, all exports were considered.

Table 3-14 summarizes our results in terms of current cruzeiros and

Table 3-12. Actual and Distortion-Free Consumption for Five Commodities, 1966–83

(values in 1,000 metric tons)

Year	Cottonseed oil Actual	Cottonseed oil Distortion free	Corn Actual	Corn Distortion free	Rice Actual	Rice Distortion free	Soybean oil Actual	Soybean oil Distortion free	Wheat Actual	Wheat Distortion free
1966	1,629	1,594	10,755	—	5,512	—	247	—	2,995	3,022
1967	1,503	1,793	12,402	—	6,760	—	245	—	3,075	3,102
1968	1,752	1,796	11,580	—	6,494	—	301	—	3,470	3,624
1969	1,671	1,757	12,045	—	6,282	—	384	—	3,720	3,730
1970	1,612	3,277	12,747	31,074	7,458	8,666	574	—	3,802	4,221
1971	1,892	1,806	15,482	17,442	7,507	11,889	1,928	—	3,648	3,531
1972	1,733	1,535	15,411	52,865	7,072	8,313	2,883	—	4,195	3,951
1973	1,991	8,486	14,149	24,141	7,138	7,053	1,309	1,265	4,976	4,199
1974	1,838	1,634	15,164	12,287	6,708	6,360	2,667	2,535	5,258	3,967
1975	1,642	1,499	15,189	13,781	7,788	7,526	2,732	2,590	3,870	2,970
1976	1,253	—	16,380	16,674	9,698	9,062	2,242	2,172	6,642	4,961
1977	1,866	1,988	17,936	21,966	8,585	8,070	3,388	3,187	4,674	3,948
1978	1,526	1,892	14,817	13,108	7,140	6,781	2,248	2,113	7,025	5,497
1979	1,636	1,324	17,822	13,673	8,306	9,734	3,257	3,070	6,577	4,745
1980	1,585	1,920	21,960	18,670	10,013	9,501	5,531	5,109	7,457	5,142
1981	1,703	1,579	22,012	20,811	8,321	8,028	2,656	2,424	6,570	4,958
1982	1,872	1,524	21,299	17,055	9,870	9,944	2,862	2,677	6,051	4,774
1983	1,421	1,176	18,191	18,883	8,056	7,887	2,866	2,905	6,418	4,865

— Not available. Because of the way the distortion free prices at the consumer level were computed, this price for cotton in 1976 was negative. For details see Brandão and Carvalho (forthcoming), appendix F.

Source: Author's calculations.

Table 3-13. Short-Run Direct Effects of Price Interventions on Foreign Exchange Earnings, Gains or Losses with Liberalization, 1966–83

(millions of U.S. dollars)

Year	On export crops US$	On export crops % Total exports	On food crops US$	On food crops % Total exports	On fertilizer imports	Total effect US$	Total effect % Total exports
1966	—	—	—	—	—	—	—
1967	—	—	—	—	—	—	—
1968	—	—	—	—	—	—	—
1969	—	—	—	—	—	—	—
1970	—	—	—	—	—	—	—
1971	—	—	−492.13	—	—	—	—
1972	—	—	−355.91	—	—	—	—
1973	−184.65	−2.58	−182.98	−2.56	−5.19	−362.44	−5.07
1974	1,059.42	11.14	403.66	4.25	53.23	1,409.84	14.83
1975	1,073.08	11.60	457.43	4.52	87.25	1,543.26	15.25
1976	179.46	1.57	573.25	5.01	45.28	707.43	6.18
1977	70.72	5.55	381.66	2.78	58.56	1,083.83	7.91
1978	206.40	1.41	464.30	3.16	19.13	651.57	4.44
1979	2,201.65	12.26	−147.88	−0.82	51.78	2,001.98	11.14
1980	1,880.84	8.08	907.15	3.90	147.94	2,640.06	11.34
1981	2,742.85	10.18	795.46	2.95	210.94	3,327.37	12.35
1982	1,517.24	6.46	489.41	2.09	37.00	1,969.65	8.39
1983	2,473.35	10.20	561.42	2.32	147.39	2,887.38	11.91

— Not available.

Note: For cotton in 1976, distortion in consumer is with PPP. For cotton in 1973, the same distortion as in 1972 was used.

Table 3-14.   Effect of Price Policy on Government Budget, 1960–83

(values in current CR$ 1,000,000)

Year	Total revenues (1)	Total expenditures (2)	Net revenue (3)	Net revenue as % of GDP (4)
1960	14	22.9	−8.9	−0.3
1961	19	41.7	−22.7	−0.5
1962	35	89.9	−54.9	−0.7
1963	52	205.2	−153.2	−1.1
1964	129	475.5	−346.5	−1.3
1965	1,605.2	487.8	1,117.4	2.6
1966	2,555.1	420.7	2,130.4	3.4
1967	3,589.0	515.3	3,073.7	3.7
1968	4,790.6	806.7	3,983.9	3.5
1969	6,607.5	1,113.9	5,493.6	3.6
1970	8,344.2	994.3	7,349.9	3.8
1971	9,907.0	2,338.6	7,568.4	2.9
1972	12,607.6	3,030.9	9,576.7	2.7
1973	15,461.9	7,595.3	7,866.6	1.6
1974	21,293.6	26,607.7	−5,314.1	−0.7
1975	22,732.9	36,391.5	−13,658.6	−1.4
1976	21,139.8	74,743.0	−53,603.2	−3.3
1977	34,218.7	80,750.7	−46,532.0	−1.9
1978	41,704.6	107,547.8	−65,843.2	−1.8
1979	33,008.1	240,222.5	−207,214.4	−3.4
1980	91,394.8	1,119,365.8	−1,027,971.0	−8.1
1981	108,262.6	884,779.4	−776,516.8	−1.6
1982	112,733.2	1,337,556.8	−1,224,823.6	−1.0
1983	1,018,967.2	3,011,760.5	−1,992,793.3	−0.5

Source: Brandão and Carvalho (forthcoming), chapter 5.

as a percentage of GDP. The effects were negative from 1960–64 and from 1974–83, but were positive in the period 1965–73. Until 1965 the amount of government expenditures on agriculture were similar to the amount of credit subsidy. From 1966–72, owing to some negative subsidies to wheat consumers the credit subsidy was higher than total expenditures on agriculture. From 1973–82 the credit subsidy averaged about 45 percent of the total in 1983. Thus, governmental expenditures associated with price policies were basically subsidies to credit.

Governmental net expenditures on agriculture averaged, in the period 1960–64, about 0.78 percent of GDP and presented an increasing trend from 0.3 percent of GDP in 1960 to 1.3 percent in 1964. In the period 1965–73, the government extracted net revenue from the farm sector that, on average, corresponded to about 3.1 percent of GDP. From 1974 to 1983, net expenditures on agriculture produced an average reduction of 2.4 percent of GDP, with a relatively high 8.1 percent in 1980.

Transfers to and from Agriculture

To compute transfers into and out of the agricultural sector, we considered price intervention in terms of its total effects (that is, direct and indirect effects), not simply in terms of government revenues and expenditures. Thus, the calculations include transfers on account of policies for exportables and importables, fertilizer policies, the subsidy granted through concessionary interest rates for rural credit, the income tax, and government investment in agriculture.

Table 3-15 presents the estimated value of transfer disaggregated to show direct and total effects. The figures are presented as a percentage of agricultural GDP to facilitate comparisons with other countries. We also show these transfers with the interest rate subsidy included and excluded.

Except in 1974, agriculture (with credit included) received positive transfers because of direct intervention that averaged 8 percent.

Table 3-15. Direct and Total Transfers for the Five Commodities, Due to Output and Input Price Interventions out of (−) and into (+) Agriculture, 1966–83

(percentage of agricultural GDP)

	Transfers as proportion of agriculture GDP			
	Credit included		Credit excluded	
Year	Direct	Total	Direct	Total
1966	4.53	4.75	2.05	2.28
1967	5.35	4.78	2.99	2.42
1968	2.91	1.75	−0.25	−1.40
1969	6.79	5.64	3.65	2.50
1970	18.34	16.60	14.40	12.67
1971	19.55	16.10	14.99	11.54
1972	14.51	11.08	10.43	7.00
1973	2.72	−0.56	−0.81	−4.08
1974	−2.96	−13.97	−8.77	−19.79
1975	5.38	−2.97	−4.70	−13.06
1976	9.01	4.31	−3.43	−8.13
1977	8.19	5.80	−2.67	−5.06
1978	7.48	4.70	−2.09	−4.87
1979	7.67	1.93	−4.79	−10.53
1980	22.79	18.98	−7.50	−11.31
1981	9.56	6.77	−0.45	−3.24
1982	3.54	−1.35	−6.75	−11.64
1983	0.81	−1.83	−3.83	−6.47

Source: Author's calculations.

When credit is excluded, there was a reduction in the pre-1972 positive percentages, and they become negative from 1973 on. Moreover, the difference between the two series (with and without credit) becomes greater after 1973. Clearly, during the second part of the 1970s and in the early 1980s the government compensated for its discrimination against agriculture by means of credit subsidies.

When total transfers (that is, those caused by both direct and indirect intervention) are considered, the results are qualitatively similar. However, the positive percentages are smaller, the negatives are larger (in absolute value), and some that were positive become negative. The average value was around 4.6 percent with credit included and −3.4 with credit excluded. Because credit is concentrated among larger farmers (Wright and Rego 1982) in the most developed regions and in some ''noble'' commodities (soybeans, for example), it appears that what took place in Brazil was a system of perverse compensation. The agricultural sector as a whole was taxed, while a small proportion was not only able to avoid the tax but also to receive a very sizable subsidy.

In table 3-16 we evaluate transfers for the agricultural sector as a whole, using the transfers previously calculated by the respective shares of the five commodities in the agricultural sector. This is not entirely appropriate, because there is no a priori reason for the average level of protection or disprotection to be equal to that for the five commodities. The qualitative behavior is essentially the same as observed for the five commodities, however, because credit was a major proportion of transfers. Even when credit is excluded, the qualitative behavior does not change much in relation to what has been noticed previously. It is important to emphasize, however, that the transfers sometimes reached very high proportions of agricultural GDP. For example, in 1980 they exceeded 40 percent (including credit).

As mentioned earlier, there was an increase in income concentration in agriculture during the 1970s. The data presented here indicate that the credit subsidy was largely responsible for that.

Index of Government Bias

To assess the attitude of the government toward agriculture, we computed a government expenditure bias (GEB), defined as the ratio of government expenditures for agriculture as a share of total government expenditures, divided by the share of undistorted agricultural GDP to total GDP. Undistorted agricultural GDP was estimated as the value of agricultural GDP plus net transfers out of agriculture owing to price intervention minus the credit subsidy (see Brandão and Carvalho forthcoming, chapter 6).

The value of GEB is not, in itself, an indication of government bias. There is no a priori presumption that this index should be one. Its

Table 3-16. Direct and Overall Net Transfers to Agriculture due to Price and Nonprice Policies, 1966–83
(percentage of agriculture GDP)

	Credit included		Credit excluded	
Year	*Direct*	*Total*	*Direct*	*Total*
1966	12.57	13.19	5.69	6.31
1967	14.38	12.84	8.03	6.50
1968	16.42	13.45	8.32	5.34
1969	29.78	26.93	21.97	19.11
1970	53.19	49.12	43.97	39.90
1971	54.37	46.37	43.81	35.82
1972	42.14	34.29	32.79	24.95
1973	14.46	6.68	6.09	−1.68
1974	−0.87	−35.15	−18.97	−53.26
1975	28.86	11.00	7.31	−10.55
1976	35.19	25.91	10.64	1.36
1977	27.57	23.05	7.07	2.55
1978	25.52	20.66	8.79	3.93
1979	21.91	11.86	0.10	−9.95
1980	48.68	41.92	−5.09	−11.86
1981	26.44	20.89	6.52	0.98
1982	14.62	5.56	−4.45	−13.51
1983	7.72	1.35	−3.50	−9.87

Source: Author's calculations.

evolution, however, may provide some clues about government behavior toward the sector.

Table 3-17 shows two periods of different average levels of GEB. The index moves to a higher plateau after 1974. This, as column 2 indicates, was the result of a sharp increase in government expenditures on agriculture as a proportion of total expenditures. This result should be interpreted with care, however, because it may only reflect an increase in expenditures on the bureaucracy. Nonetheless, the GEB index was computed excluding current expenditures from government expenditures in agriculture. This alternative GEB is reported in table 3-18. We did not expect to remove the main problems with the ' GEB measure, but only to adjust its level to the possible bias generated by expenditures on the bureaucracy.

Income Distribution Impacts

Here, we attempt to estimate the impact of intervention in agricultural prices on income distribution. Data limitations allowed us to consider only two groups of urban consumers—families with wage income of one to five times the minimum wage and families with income of one to thirty times the minimum wage. We also estimated the impact of intervention on "poor" and "rich" farmers.

Table 3-17. Index of Government Expenditure Bias (GEB) with Respect to Agriculture, 1966–83

(percent)

Year	Share of undistorted agricultural GDP on GDP-factor cost[a]	Share of government agricultural expenditures in total expenditures	GEB
1966	—	—	—
1967	—	—	—
1968	13.7	24.02	1.80
1969	11.38	27.14	2.39
1970	7.46	24.35	3.26
1971	7.76	23.10	2.98
1972	9.13	24.52	2.69
1973	13.06	23.02	1.76
1974	18.44	23.52	1.28
1975	12.80	45.83	3.58
1976	12.68	53.02	4.18
1977	14.14	52.36	3.70
1978	12.87	52.21	4.06
1979	13.37	46.88	3.51
1980	9.16	48.86	5.33
1981	11.67	38.13	3.27
1982	11.93	38.08	3.19
1983	13.99	40.90	2.92

— Not available.

a. Undistorted agricultural GDP was calculated as agricultural GDP plus net transfer out due to price policy less subsidy due to credit policy.

Source: Author's calculations.

IMPACT ON URBAN CONSUMERS. This impact was determined by comparing the urban consumer cost of living that would have existed if intervention had not occurred with the cost of living given the adopted pricing policy. The indirect effect was mainly defined by exchange rate distortion provoked by exchange rate policy.

To compute the effects, we had to construct CPIs for the urban consumer income groups. The idea was to construct indices that included the prices of the five products, other agricultural goods, and nonagricultural goods. Because cotton is an agricultural good but not a food product, the CPI was defined as follows:

$$CPI = w_1 \, PICOT + w_2 \, CPA + w_3 \, CPA\text{-}OTH + w_4 \, P_{NA}$$

where

CPI	=	the consumer price index
PICOT	=	price index for cotton at consumer level
CPA	=	consumer price index for four agricultural goods defined as follows:

Table 3-18. Alternative Index of Government Expenditure Bias (GEB) with Respect to Agriculture, 1966–83

(percent)

Year	Share of undistorted agricultural GDP on GDP-factor cost[a]	Share of government agricultural expenditure in total expenditure	GEB
1966	—	—	—
1967	—	—	—
1968	13.37	7.29	0.55
1969	11.38	9.06	0.80
1970	7.46	6.09	0.82
1971	7.76	6.07	0.78
1972	9.13	8.77	0.96
1973	13.06	10.38	0.80
1974	18.44	9.45	0.51
1975	12.80	16.97	1.33
1976	12.68	17.28	1.36
1977	14.14	19.15	1.35
1978	12.87	17.26	1.34
1979	13.37	17.54	1.31
1980	9.16	21.56	2.35
1981	11.67	20.23	1.73
1982	11.93	15.96	1.34
1983	13.99	16.34	1.17

a. Undistorted agricultural GDP was calculated as agricultural GDP plus net transfers out due to price policy less subsidy due to credit policy.

Note: This table has been constructed with government expenditures in agriculture excluding running expenditures.

Source: Author's calculations.

$$CPA = \sum_{i=1}^{4} \beta_i P_i, \qquad \text{where}$$

$i=1$ corn; $i=2$ rice; $i=3$ soybean; and $i=4$ wheat. The weights, β_i's, vary according to the consumer income group and were normalized to total one. The original weights were obtained from the national CPI. These weights were obtained from a household survey conducted in nine metropolitan regions as well as Brasilia during 1974–75. Because distortion-free prices would not be computed for the entire period (1966–83), they were computed with the existing information.

The consumer price index for other agricultural goods (CPA-QTH), was obtained as follows:

$$CPA\text{-}OTH = \frac{CPIF - a\,CPA}{(i - a)} \qquad \text{where}$$

$CPIF$ = consumer price index for food in Rio de Janeiro as computed by the Vargas Foundation;
a = relative importance of agricultural goods in $CPIF$ in 1973
w_1 = sum of weights of cotton products as defined in the household survey (w_1 = 0.005565)

w_2 = sum of weights of agricultural goods considered in this study, which assumed the following values: 1966–69, 0.043793; 1970–72, 0.090524; 1973–83, 0.0105341.

w_3 = weight of other agricultural products not included in $w2$. For the corresponding periods, w_3 assumed the following values: 0.388845; 0.3421140 and 0.3273339

w_4 = weight of nonagricultural goods on consumer price index as computed by the Vargas Foundation for 1973; w_4 = 0.561797.

In computing CPI^*k (that is, the urban consumer price index free from total intervention, we used the earlier expression with the relevant definition for each index: $PICOT^*$, CPA^*, $CPA\text{-}OTH$, and UP_{NA} normalized for 1977=100). In defining $CPI'k$, the urban consumer price index free from direct intervention, we proceeded in the same fashion, using $PICOT'$ and CPA' but maintaining $CPA\text{-}OTH$ and P_{NA} unchanged.

Distortion-free prices to consumers were estimated in a way that did not permit a breakdown into the effects form direct and total intervention. Because the indirect effect was mainly a result of exchange rate policy, we took the total distortion-free prices and reintroduced the exchange rate distortion by multiplying these prices by e/e^*, where e is the current exchange rate and e^* the equilibrium exchange rate.

In nine of the seventeen years (1967–83) considered, direct intervention penalized the low-income consumers (table 3-19). If we consider the effects of total intervention, low-income consumers were penalized in seven years. Average losses for low-income consumers were higher than for high-income consumers—about 70 percent higher if we consider direct intervention and 30 percent higher if total intervention is considered. The yearly average income losses owing to direct intervention were about 0.47 percent of the previous year's income for low-income consumers and about 0.27 for higher income consumers. For total intervention, these averages were 1.23 percent and 0.97 percent, respectively.

Effects on Producer Prices

Because agricultural products are the sources of farmers' income, we should distinguish the prices received by poor and rich farmers. Unfortunately, this information was not available. Alternatively, we thought of using regional proxies for poor and rich farmers. Thus, the price received by farmers in the northeast, or in a particular state of

Table 3-19. Income Distribution Effects of Agricultural Pricing Policies, 1966–83

Year	Direct Effect		Total Effect	
	Poor	Rich	Poor	Rich
1966	—	—	—	—
1967	0.022	0.011	0.045	0.037
1968	−0.003	−0.001	−0.007	−0.007
1969	0.002	0.005	0.020	0.018
1970	−0.012	−0.012	−0.034	−0.029
1971	−0.008	−0.002	0.000	0.005
1972	0.014	0.008	0.016	0.011
1973	0.045	0.023	0.046	0.026
1974	0.012	0.014	0.084	0.076
1975	−0.014	−0.009	−0.013	−0.005
1976	0.029	0.009	0.010	0.000
1977	−0.005	−0.001	−0.037	−0.039
1978	−0.002	−0.005	−0.043	−0.049
1979	−0.029	−0.003	−0.010	0.001
1980	0.056	0.022	0.051	0.033
1981	−0.021	−0.011	0.030	0.051
1982	−0.024	−0.013	−0.015	−0.007
1983	0.018	0.011	0.040	0.043

— Not available.

Note: Comparisons are made with respect to previous year. Percentual change is obtained by multiplying present figures by 100. Poor = consumers with income from 1 to 5 minimum wages. Rich = consumers with income from 1 to 30 minimum wages.

Source: Author's calculations.

the region, would represent the price received by poor farmers. Because the south region, in particular the state of São Paulo, has a more developed agriculture compared with the northeast, the price received by farmers in this region would represent the price received by rich farmers.

Unfortunately, this approach could not be used. Farmers in the northeast sometimes receive a higher price than farmers in the south, but that does not mean that they are doing relatively better. The difference might have been owing to production cost differentials or transportation costs. To identify who is doing better requires information on regional production costs, transportation costs, and consumer prices that are not available. The difference between "poor" and "rich" farmers could emerge, therefore, only from differences in consumption behavior.

The income distribution impact of the agricultural pricing policies are calculated as follows:

$$\frac{Yk - \tilde{Y}k}{\tilde{Y}k} \times 100$$

where Yk is actual real income of rural consumer-producers of category k and $\bar{Y}k$ is the undistorted (corrected for direct or total intervention in each case) real income of rural consumer-producers of category k. Real income was obtained as the product of observed production and percent value added, deflated by the rural CPI. Undistorted real income takes undistorted value added, deflated by an undistorted CPI.

To compute the rural CPI, we proceeded in a fashion similar to the urban CPI. The difference was related to the weights. In the case of rural consumers, the weights were taken from a rural family survey conducted by the Vargas Foundation during 1961–62 for the states of Rio Grande do Sul, Santa Catarina, São Paulo, Minas Gerais, Espirito Santo, Pernambuco, and Ceara.

Table 3-20 displays the accumulated values of gains and losses during 1970–83. In the case of direct intervention, the losses were larger for "poorer" farmers and the gains were smaller. Total intervention effects on income distribution between "poor" and "rich" farmers were negligible, indicating that indirect pricing policy roughly compensated for direct pricing policy in terms of income distribution.

Another important dimension of the income distribution consequences of government intervention was the impact on rural wages and, therefore, on rural-urban migration. To infer the effects of pricing policies on the rural labor market in the long run is difficult, especially because there are very few data on rural-urban migration in Brazil. Hence, analysis was limited to the effects on rural wages in the short run. To do that, a very simple short-run labor market model was adopted. It was assumed that, in the short run, the rural labor supply is vertical—that is, that the opportunity cost of labor in rural areas was low compared with current wages, and that the labor force cannot migrate to the urban sector. The rural demand for labor is assumed to be given by the marginal productivity of labor in agriculture. This assumption has been criticized in the economic development literature, and average productivity has been indicated as the relevant demand for labor given in family transfers in agriculture. Because we are interested in paid rural wages and not family labor force, we took the marginal approach. Although the existence of this family labor market has some effect on the formal market, these effects are disregarded here.

The rural wage equation is shown in table 3-21. The results indicate that the prices received by farmers had very little effect on wage rates, and that both the rental on land and agricultural GDP were the most important variables in the wage regression. This information is compatible with the fact that the use of new land has been the most important source of agricultural growth in Brazil.

To estimate the impact of price policy on wages, we first estimated

Table 3-20. Income Distribution Effects of Agricultural Pricing Policy Intervention, 1970–83

Commodity and type of farmer	Direct pricing policy effect on income	Total pricing policy effect on income
Corn		
Poor	+100.00	+100.00
Rich	+146.29	+99.89
Cotton		
Poor	−100.00	−100.00
Rich	−58.49	−100.01
Rice		
Poor	+100.00	+100.00
Rich	+146.29	+99.86
Soybean		
Poor	−100.00	−100.00
Rich	−99.45	−100.06
Wheat		
Poor	+100.00	−100.00
Rich	+146.23	−100.18
Total		
Poor	+100.00	−100.00
Rich	+146.41	−100.05

Note: Original variations accumulated from 1970 to 1983 and converted into indices. Gains (+) or losses (−) are compared for kind of farmers for each crop and for direct or total pricing policy effects.

Source: Brandão and Carvalho (forthcoming) tables 7.9–7.12.

distortion-free rural wages by taking the estimated equation and replacing the observed variables by their distortion-free estimates. This was done for prices received by farmers and agricultural GDP. The other variables, as well as the ordinary least squares (OLS) regression residual, were maintained at their current levels.

It is apparent that the rural wage was relatively higher owing to the adopted policies than it would have been had intervention ended.

Table 3-21. Rural Wage Equation Dependent Variable: Real Wage in Agriculture

Independent Variables	Coefficient	t-Statistics
Constant	1.54	1.57
Price received	0.11	1.42
Tractor rental price (PT)	0.00	0.00
Land rental price (PL)	0.18	2.67
Agriculture GDP (AGDP)	0.19	2.98
$R^2 = 0.96$	DW = 2.27	

Source: Author's calculations.

Only during a short period in the mid-1970s would liberalization of the market have been favorable to workers in agriculture.

The Political Economy of Price Policies

The development strategy adopted by Brazil after World War II favored the industrial sector. It was argued that gains from trade were biased in favor of industrialized countries (the center), thus inhibiting industrial development in less developed countries (the periphery). Developed by Gunnar Myrdal, this argument gained momentum in Latin America owing to the work of ECLA (Economic Commission for Latin America), and in particular the writings of Raul Prebisch. There was, it was argued, an inexorable tendency for the terms of trade to deteriorate on the periphery because: (1) the periphery exported natural resource-based goods (agricultural goods, minerals, and wood) and imported industrial goods from the center; (2) industrial goods contain more value added than natural resource-based goods and, therefore, are more expensive; (3) demand for natural resource-based goods, owing to increases in consumer income, would increase more slowly than demand for industrial goods; and (4) technical progress would not be fast enough to reduce industrial prices so as to compensate for lower prices for primary goods.

These arguments sounded very logical to Latin American policy makers. From 1914 through 1945, Latin American economies had suffered from external shocks, such as wars and depressions. In the Brazilian case, these shocks gave birth to industrial activity to produce domestic substitutes for imports that could not be obtained. The external shocks proved that LDCs could avoid losses from trade by favoring inward-directed growth through an industrialization-based import-substitution strategy.

The infant industry argument complemented the inward-directed growth strategy. The idea was that a new industrial venture needs to be protected from foreign competition because of high installation costs and the necessity of a learning-by-doing period, after which production costs would decline to their mature level. Although Brazil had experimented with protection for certain activities, it was only with the implementation of this industrial development strategy that protection was consistently used as a policy instrument.

But protection is not sufficient for industrial takeoff. Investments are needed, not only to increase producing capacity but also to build the urban infrastructure required by new industry. Thus, the strategy adopted by the government was to attract foreign capital to invest in producing capacity and provide the urban infrastructure for industrial development. Brazilian laws on foreign capital have been quite liberal, although foreign capital cannot be invested in the so-called strategic sectors. Exchange rate policy favored imports of capital goods; the trade deficit was financed by commercial arrears and borrowing abroad.

Although quite popular among government officials, Arthur Lewis's theory of an infinitely elastic supply of urban labor based on rural migration did not impress pragmatic businessmen. Immediately after the war, an industrial labor force training program was established by the private industrial sector. The industrial enterprises contributed 1 percent of their total wages to this program, and the government, in turn, created technical high schools in urban areas to train youngsters in industrial skills. The job opportunities that were opened up by industry in urban areas, the social assistance provided free of charge by the government, and cheap housing and food all attracted the most qualified rural workers, thereby penalizing the rural sector by preventing income from increasing—or even depressing it through price controls—and by reducing labor force quality.

The rationale for maintaining a low urban cost of living was that low urban wages would assure the profitability of industrial activity. In the 1950s, the predominant argument used by officials was that low urban wages would attract foreign capital, especially when coupled by fiscal benefits and subsidies.

Agriculture was to play an important role by providing the foreign exchange necessary to pay for capital imports. In Brazil, however, the agricultural sector was dominated by large, inefficient farms (latifundios), whose production did not respond to price incentives. The supply of agricultural products, therefore, was static in the short run.

Under these circumstances, as argued by the structuralists, industrialization produces urbanization, and as the urban population increases, so does the demand for food. Increases in food prices then pressure urban wages and, therefore, industrial prices, upward. Because farmers do not respond to price incentives by increasing production levels, they automatically gain rent increases. Thus, as the industrial sector expands and urbanization occurs, inflation accelerates. Therefore, agricultural price controls were the long-run solution to the food supply problem.

ECLA reasoning had a marked influence on Brazilian policymakers. Intervention was aimed at controlling inflation, while other policies were adopted to promote industrialization. Foreign exchange rate policy strongly penalized the agricultural sector while favoring industry. Industrial policies, including export incentives for manufactures, also had negative effects on the agricultural sector, particularly when the protected industry used agricultural products as inputs.

One could argue, however, that agriculture benefited from subsidies for tractors, fertilizers, and credit. This is true, but upon closer examination it is apparent that a large part of these subsidies represented a spillover effect from industrial protection. Subsidies for tractor production were allowed during the beginnings of this industry. Importing tractors, meanwhile, was prohibited, which increased the demand for domestic tractors. A similar situation occurred with fertilizers. For a short period, fertilizer production was subsidized because domestic prices to farmers were equal to international prices plus transportation costs. As domestic production increased owing to the petroleum price shock of 1974, part of the subsidy came to be appropriated by farmers.

The Making of Policy

Some agricultural groups in Brazil have been more organized than others in pressing for benefits. Spatial concentration of production has been the most important element in determining the success of agricultural pressure groups.

Export crops in particular provided the appropriate conditions for creating producer associations in Brazil. Producers of some crops, especially coffee, sugarcane, cocoa, and cotton, have been strongly affected by economic policies. As they perceived the way in which these policies affected their businesses, they organized themselves into associations to lobby for their interests.

The concentration of power in the hands of the executive branch is responsible for two important characteristics of lobbying in Brazil. The first is the secondary role played by the legislative in regulating economic activities. In general, economic policies are not voted on or discussed in the Congress. Economic regulations are decided by councils of ministers, which are executive autarchies that have, for all practical purposes, the power of modifying, interpreting, or even bypassing the law.

Although the power of the bureaucracy in Brazil has shifted lobbying efforts from the legislative to the executive, one should not minimize the relative importance of the legislative in directing economic policies. After 1974, as democratic procedures were restored, the importance of the legislature increased, becoming crucial from 1984 onward. It is clear that the legislative is now an important channel of pressure. Members of Congress have acted in many instances as lobbyists for specific groups or specific interests. In earlier years, when agriculture was responsible for a large share of GNP, representation of the sector was strong (see, for example, Mueller 1983). A good example of the agricultural sector's influence is the low income tax on agricultural earnings.

Pricing and credit policies are mostly determined by the Banco do Brasil, which has the power to issue money. On the one hand, this system is quite flexible, because no limit is imposed a priori on total financial resources to be used in implementing policies. On the other hand, it is quite risky because the government does not commit any resources to the agricultural sector in advance. The system thus creates a continuous tension between the ministries of agriculture and finance over miminum prices, agricultural credit parameters, and so forth. Over the last decade and a half, the minister of agriculture as a rule has been the loser in the process, because the inflationary aspects of policy have been considered to be of the greatest importance. The minimum prices set by the ministry of finance have been much lower than ministry of agriculture studies have recommended.

Nonetheless, the Banco do Brasil has consistently conceded more financial resources to the agricultural sector through its policies on credit than originally approved by the Ministry of Finance. Most probably, this has been a deliberate decision by Banco do Brasil to retain its position as the primary bank for the agricultural sector. Maintaining the Banco do Brasil as the principal bank for the agricultural sector has been supported by a large fraction of urban society as well as the rural sector.

Another aspect of the process of policy formulation in Brazil that deserves explicit consideration has to do with pressure groups. Each crop studied here is important to a number of groups interested in influencing governmental policy that will affect their markets. We can identify, for each one of them, besides consumers, the following important groups:

- Corn. Producers are not well organized, owing to the dispersion of production (Pastore, J. et al. 1976); the feed production industry which has as clients the pork, livestock, and poultry producers; and the crushing industry, which produces oil and starch.
- Cotton. Center-south and northeast producers; exporters; the textile industry; the cotton processing industry.
- Rice. Producers of irrigated rice, especially in the state of Rio Grande do Sul, and producers of nonirrigated rice, widespread around the country; the processing industry.
- Soybean. Bean producers; exporters; the crushing industry; the feed production industry; feed consumers.
- Wheat. Domestic producers; millers; the wheat based food and feed industries.

Rio Grande do Sul wheat producers have been a quite strong and active political group. The wheat self-sufficiency objective has been defended by all gauchos (natives of Rio Grande do Sul), politicians from all parties, intellectuals, agronomists, and even housewives. Millers, spread over the country, do not represent an opposing lobby, because their gains from wheat policy are independent of the price received by domestic producers. They are protected from competition by governmental licensing and production quotas.

Rice producers benefit from direct pricing policies, and the irrigated rice growers in Rio Grande do Sul also benefited from subsidized credit. From 1971 through 1983, rice growers obtained from the Banco do Brasil about 16 percent of all agricultural credit for operational costs. For marketing rice, the Banco do Brasil lent about 19 percent of total agricultural marketing credit during the same period.

The erratic policy adopted for soybeans might be a result of the export lobby. When the international price increases, the government usually takes action to guarantee supplies to the domestic market. But as restrictions are imposed on exports, the crushing industry and exporters start to pressure government officials to liberalize exports, arguing that export reduction will increase average costs owing to excess crushing capacity.

Exports of cotton have been declining because of high domestic prices as compared with international prices, and strong pressure from the textile industry to reduce exports of cotton so as to increase its own supplies. Pressured by cotton producers, the government increased the real minimum price of cotton, and raw cotton had to be subsidized to be exported. Under these circumstances, the textile industry, which benefited by export subsidies to manufactures, pressured the government to prohibit raw cotton exports while allowing the industry to export cotton textiles. Because cotton is not subject to the cheap food objective, the foreign exchange objective directs policy toward this commodity. The northeast perennial crop, as opposed to the center-south annual crop, is represented by a very strong political group. The northeast is a poor region, and any economic activity in the region must be preserved at any cost. Thus, the cotton policy is becoming more erratic as the textile industry, mainly located in the center-south, argues for benefits that conflict with the demands of northeast cotton growers.

Corn producers benefited from direct pricing policies during the entire period (1966–83), except in 1979. Corn is grown throughout the country during most of the year, and Brazil was a net corn exporter in the past. In part this was owing to the relatively small role played by this grain as a food. With the development of the pork and poultry industries as well as the feed industries, domestic demand for corn then increased substantially. The reduction in relative consumer prices of chicken and pork led to an increasing demand for these products. As final demand increased, so did the demand for feed-mix and, therefore, for corn.

In this situation, the pork and poultry industries became quite dependent on domestic production, and regional crop failures had to be compensated by imports, which are controlled by the government and subject to delays. To prevent fluctuation in the supply of feed-mix, and acting in their own interests, the feed industries provided farmers in their regions with technical assistance and credit in addition to that provided by the Agricultural Credit System. Concern about the continuous availability of corn made the feed industry a pressure group with the same interests as corn producers. This has also been the case for the feed-mix industry, because their products were very rarely subject to price controls.

After the mid-1970s, with the redemocratization of the country, Brazilian politicians became interested in consumer protection. Several neighborhood associations have been created in the major cities of Brazil, sponsored by individual politicians rather than by political parties. Their effectiveness as pressure groups, though, has been very modest.

Theoretically, farmers' organizations and cooperatives in Brazil should be important pressure groups, but very little farm organization has been observed in the country, although the cooperatives have been quite active in lobbying, especially in Rio Grande do Sul, where the wheat-soybean cooperative is located. Also located in Rio Grande do Sul is Instituto Rio Grandense do Arroz (IRGA), a research institution created in the late 1930s by the rice producers. IRGA has been quite active in providing technical support to the Rio Grande do Sul rice lobby, although it has now been practically transformed into a state autarchy.

The "Sociedade Rural Brasileira" traditional farmers' organization, has not been a very active lobbying group. Recently (1985–86), a new association was created—the União Democrática Ruralista (UDR), which came into existence as a reaction to government land reform projects. It started as a localized movement of livestock producers, but by 1986 it had become a national association of all farmers. Its success derives not only from the common interest of all farmers in Brazil in the agrarian reform law, but also from new rural leadership and organizing capacity.

Agrarian reform laws during the early 1960s generated several local movements either in favor of reform or against it. None of these movements evolved on a national level. UDR's success is directly linked to its vigorous organization, administration, and financing. Organized in the same way as the political parties, UDR will most probably become a party explicitly representing the interests of the rural sector.

Labor movements in the rural sector have been restricted to local or regional areas and have existed only briefly. If the high costs of organizing formal farmers' associations have impeded their development, even greater difficulties exist for organizing and maintaining rural labor associations. In addition, the formal market in rural areas is important only to certain regions and to rural activities associated with large crop or animal production farms. Nonetheless, after the expansion of sugarcane plantations, share croppers became quite active in organizing rural labor movements. Together with workers on the orange plantations, which have been growing very fast in the last ten years or so owing to growth in orange juice exports, and other temporary workers in the rural areas of the center-south, they organized a rural workers' federation known as Confederação Nacional dos Trabalhadores Agrícolas (CONTAG). It seems that CONTAG is shaped by the philosophical concepts of the national urban labor movements that emerged after 1979 with the political redemocratization of the country, and its interests are similar to those of the urban workers.

Policy Intentions and Policy Results

In table 3-22, we attempt to identify policy objectives in Brazilian agriculture and their relative importance over time. The weights in the table were obtained from grades, given by the authors, from one to ten, for each objective according to our perception of its importance—the more important the objective, the higher the grade. In reporting our final grades, we considered similar grades assigned by a group of specialists who participated in a seminar at Santa Ursula University in Rio de Janeiro in January 1987. Reported grades are normalized to add up to one and should reflect the intended policy objectives.

If we take the period after 1966, a period for which we can compute the effects of agricultural pricing policies, we see that, except for supporting domestic industry and processing industries, the policy results did not coincide with policy objectives. Consumer welfare was introduced after the first petroleum price shock, but its relative importance, although small, has been increasing. Measures such as price controls and subsidies were adopted to favor consumers. On several occasions price controls provoked a shortage of the controlled product, which resulted in black markets that actually produced income redistribution. In some cases, the income redistribution favored poor consumers who stood in line to buy the product at the controlled price to resell it at a higher price to other consumers. In other cases, a long chain of beneficiaries developed that generally excluded consumers. Supermarkets have a gentleman's agreement with the government wherein the latter sell products to the former at a price compatible with the fixed consumer price. On some occasions, this drives down the price received by farmers. On other occasions, producers as well as intermediaries have benefited from illegal pro-

Table 3-22. Relative Importance of the Objectives of Agricultural Pricing Policies

Objectives	Prior to 1930	1930-39	1940-45	1945-54	1954-65	1965-70	1970-79	1980s
Consumer welfare	—	—	—	—	—	—	0.083	0.132
Farmer income	0.333	0.278	0.333	0.242	0.194	—	—	—
Government revenue	0.333	0.278	—	0.152	0.226	—	—	—
Foreign exchange	0.333	0.278	0.333	0.152	0.258	0.208	0.278	0.263
Self-sufficiency	—	—	—	—	—	—	—	—
Price stability	—	—	—	0.152	—	0.345	0.194	0.263
Regional Equity	—	—	—	—	—	—	—	—
Nutrition	—	—	—	—	—	—	—	—
Support of domestic industry	—	0.167	0.333	0.303	0.323	0.345	0.278	0.184
Support of processions industry	—	—	—	—	—	0.103	0.167	0.158

— Not available.
Source: Author's calculations.

cedures. For example, because it had a large stock of beans, the government intended, by selling from stock, to maintain the price of the product. Thus, beans were sold by the government to intermediaries, who did not try to sell to retailers because consumers reject stale beans. The wholesalers instead sold government beans to bean producers who, in turn, sold the beans back to the government as if they has just been produced. The price of beans was, therefore, maintained for quite some time. Direct price subsidies to consumers have been supported by politicians as the best way to protect consumers, and, in fact, some consumers have benefited from the wheat subsidy. Nonetheless, the target population (low-income families) benefits less than others. Thus, with respect to consumers, policy results differ from policy intentions.

All export incentives favored manufactures after 1968; the only export taxes referred to agricultural or mining products. Thus, it also seems clear that, although the government adopted a goal of generating foreign exchange through agricultural exports, other objectives (such as protecting domestic industry and controlling inflation) outweighed the foreign exchange objective. This explains export embargoes, taxes, and import contingencies for products in demand in the industrial sector, such as sugar, cotton, and soybeans.

An Attempt to Identify Systematic Policy Behavior

To assess the consistency of the government in formulating agricultural pricing policies, we estimated some regression equations inspired by Lattimore (1974) and Lattimore and Schuh (1976). These regression equations attempt to explain the reasons for intervention by the government. We consider that agricultural policy intervention can be explained by policymaker objectives as reflected in foreign exchange availability, the level of world prices, and the rate of unemployment.

The comments below are based on the best results among the estimations we made. It is important to note that the world price was not significant as an explanatory variable. Moreover, we also defined a variable that reflects foreign exchange requirements in a given year—value of imports plus interest paid minus export revenue. This variable did not contribute to a better understanding of government intervention through the regressions. We then utilized foreign exchange availability (IMC), which was defined as export revenue plus reserves minus interest costs. We also included a dummy variable to reflect the years for which agricultural growth was below average, but this variable generated no better understanding of government behavior.

The dependent variable was specified in a number of alternative ways for each crop. *NPT* is the distortion in relative price as computed before and is given by:

$$((P_A/P_{NA})/(UP_A/UP_{NA}))$$

where P_A is the price of the agriculture commodity, P_{NA} is the price index of nonagricultural goods, and UP_A and UP_{NA} are respectively the above prices corrected for total intervention. *NPB* is the same as *NPT*, except that prices are only corrected for direct intervention (P_{NA} is corrected only for tariffs and subsidies). NP_A is the total distortion in absolute prices of agricultural goods; it is given by $o(P_A/UP_A) - 1.C.$ *NPD* is the same as NP_A, except that prices are only corrected for direct interventions. All of the previous measures refer to producer prices.

For consumer prices we have *NCA*, which is the consumer equivalent of NP_A, and *NCT*, which is the equivalent of *NPT*. Based on the results obtained, some general remarks can be made. First, one notices that inflation tends to show up as the most important variable. This variable is certainly more important for the food items, such as rice and wheat. Second, the availability of foreign exchange does not seem to be relevant for the commodities considered, with the exception of wheat. This is in line with what one should expect, since the other two important commodities in terms of trade—soybeans and cotton—were considered much more important as inputs to domestic industry than as generators of foreign exchange. As mentioned above, wheat is the most important agricultural import in Brazil; the negative impact of the availability of foreign exchange indicates that in times of abundance of foreign reserves, the government reduces protection to wheat producers. Third, cyclical effects seem to influence the government. When the economy is operating with high levels of employment, the level of protection to farm producers is reduced. One can hypothesize that this reflects concern with migration flows to the urban centers. When employment is high, it is easier to absorb those abandoning the rural sector. Thus, the government reduces protection even if it means an increase in the rural—urban migration flow. Fourth, for the two important export crops (soybeans and cotton), neither inflation nor foreign exchange availability seems to have had much effect. One possible explanation in the case of soybeans is that the government does not look at this crop as an important source of revenue; its main concern is with meal and oil, which have more importance in the generation of foreign exchange than exports of beans per se. Fifth, the low values of the R^2 indicate either that there are some explanatory variables that are missing, or that there is a high degree of randomness in government behavior. This last hypothesis cannot be easily discarded.

One may look at these results from another perspective. Clearly, for rice and wheat there is concern for consumers' wellbeing in spite of producer pressure groups. The constants in the regressions tend to be significant, especially in the case of producers. This can be interpreted as the effect of the behavior of pressure groups. Thus, for rice the constant is positive for producers, indicating that they would tend to receive protection of the order of 50 percent (or more) in the absence of inflation or cyclical effects. For consumers of rice, the constant indicates that in the absence of inflation and cyclical factors, there would be a sizable tax; consumers' pressure groups do not seem to be very effective. In the case of wheat, the constant indicates that producers would receive a rate of protection of 16 percent (or more) if the explanatory variables of inflation and GAP (an estimate of the difference between actual and trend GDP) were set at zero. Consumers, however, would receive a subsidy of approximately 12 percent. For soybeans, the cycle in important, but the constants in the regressions for producers tend to be important, also. That is, if inflation were zero and the economy were growing exactly at its long-run rate, soybean producers would be taxed approximately 20 percent. For cotton, the situation is similar—the constant for producers is very significant and indicates a tax on producers of at least 15 percent. Finally, for corn the constant is the most significant coefficient in the regressions—producers would be entitled to a protection of at least 25 percent and consumers would be taxed by more than 35 percent.

Pressure groups seem to be most effective in the cases of soybeans and cotton. This is no surprise, given that these two crops are inputs in the production of important commodities. In the case of corn, the industry has not been as effective. One possible explanation for this may be that there are multiple uses for corn in industry, and that the various users may not have common interests. It may also be that, in its present stage, the corn-processing industry does not need a subsidy to continue its growth, while the soybean complex, developed more recently, is still in need of high protection. Although this is an interesting possibility, the results for cotton contradict that hypothesis, because the textile industry was established during the very first industrial development period in Brazil.

Summary and Conclusions

An attempt has been made to give an interpretation of the process of policy formation in Brazil with respect to the five commodities considered. Beginning with a descriptive presentation of the various policy epochs, empirical estimates of regression equations were presented to capture the behavior of the government in the period 1966–83.

It seems that inflation (or consumers' well-being) has been an important concern of the government in its agricultural price interventions, especially with respect to food crops. Pressure groups seem to have significantly affected soybeans and cotton, and there seems to be a very high degree of randomness in the behavior of the government. Interestingly enough, in the case of wheat, the variables explain more than 80 percent of the variability in level of intervention. In fact, the R^2 in the regression analyses confirms the hypothesis raised before. Thus, the more that interest groups with conflicting interests pressure the government, the more erratic is the conduct of the agricultural policy, and, therefore, the less important are the variables used to explain policy results.

References

Alves, E.R. and G.E. Schuh. 1984. "The Economic Evaluation of the Impact of the Extension Programs: A Suggested Methodology and an Application to ACAR in Minas Gerais." In *Brazilian Agriculture and Agricultural Research* Levon Yezaniantz, ed. Brasília DF: EMBRAPA.

Avila, Luiz Gonçalves. 1985. *Desenvolvimento Industrial e Rendimento da Terra: Um Estudo de Caso*. Escola de Pós-Graduação em Economia-EPGE, Série Teses no. 11. Rio de Janeiro: Fundação Getúlio Vargas.

Azevedo, Aroldo de, ed. 1972. *Brasil, A Terra e o Homem*. São Paulo: Editora Nacional.

Barbosa, Fernando Holanda. 1983. *A Inflação Brasileira no Pós-Guerra: Monetarismo Versus Estruturalismo*. Rio de Janeiro: IPEA–PNPE.

Braga, H.C., G.M.C. Santiago, H. Kume, J.A. Rosa, and M. Carvalho, Jr. 1981. "*Cus tos de Insumos Básicos e Competitividade das Exportações*." Rio de Janeiro: Fundação Centro de Estudos do Comércio Exterior.

Brandão, Antonio Salazar P. and José L. Carvalho. Forthcoming. *Trade, Exchange Rate, and Agricultural Pricing Policies in Brazil*. A World Bank Comparative Study. Washington, D.C.

Bressan Filho, Ângelo. 1978. *Alguns Aspectos da Política Tributária para o Setor Agrícola no Brasil*. Brasília, DF: Comissão de Financiamento da Produção.

Burns, E. Bradford. 1970. *A History of Brazil*. New York: Columbia University Press.

Carvalho, José L. 1978. "A Fixação de Preços Mínimos e a Oferta de Produtos Agricolas" in Lopes, Mauro ed. *A Política de Preços Mínimos: Estudos Técnicos 1949-1979*. CFP—Coleção Análise e Pesquisa vol. 11, Brasília: CFP.

Carvalho, José L. 1987. "Aid, Capital Flows and Development: The Case of Brazil." Paper presented in a Conference on Aid, Capital Flows, and Development Organized by the International Center for Economic Growth, held at Talloires, France, September 13-17.

Carvalho Filho, J.J. de. 1977. "Politica Cafeira no Brasil: Seus Instrumentos, 1961-71," Serie Monografia, IPE, São Paulo: IPE, University of São Paulo.

Cruz, Elmar R.da, V. Palma, and Antonio Flavio Dias Avila. 1982. *Taxas de Retorno dos Investimentos Totais e Capital Físico.* Brasília, DF: EMBRAPA.

Da Matta, Milton. 1982. "Crédito Rural: Caracterização do Sistema e Estimativas dos Subsídios Implícitos." *Revista Brasileira de Economia,* 36 (July–September): 215–45.

Delfim Netto, Antonio. 1979. *O Problema do Café no Brasil,* Rio de Janeiro: Fundação Getulio Vargas.

Denslow, David Jr. and W. G. Tyler. 1983. "Perspectivas sobre Pobreza e Desiguldade de Renda no Brasil." *Pesquisa e Planejamento,* 13, no. 3 (December).

Dias, Guilherme Leite da Silva. 1974. "Avaliação do Serviço de Extensão Rural." *Estudos Económicos.* 4, no. 3: 7–52.

Doellinger, Carlos Von and Leonardo C. Cavalcanti. 1975. *Empresas Multinacionais na Indústria Brasileira.* IPEA—Coleção Relatório de Pesquisa. Rio de Janeiro, IPEA/INPES.

Duran, T.A. (co-ordinator), H.D.D.L. Lobato, V.L.V. Kottler, R.V. Neto, and R.M.S. Furtado. "Custos de Insumos *Versus* Rentabilidade na Agricultura." Projecto CECEX—Fundação Centro de Estudos do Comércio Exterior. Rio de Janeiro—CECEX (mimeo) undated.

Hayami, Yujiro and Vernon W. Ruttan. 1985. *Agricultural Development: An International Perspective.* Baltimore: Johns Hopkins University Press.

Hoffmann, Rodolfo. 1971. "Contribuição à Análise da Distribuição de Renda e da Posse da Terra no Brasil." *Livre Docência.* Thesis presented at Escola Superior de Agricultura Luiz de Queiroz—USP.

———. and Angela A. Kageyama. 1984. "Distribuição de Renda no Brasil entre Famílias e entre Pessoas em 1970 e 1980," in *XII Encontro Nacional de Economia, Anais.* São Paulo: AMPEC.

Homem De Melo, Fernando B. 1979. "A Política Econômica e o Setor Agrícola no Perio-do Pós-Guerra." Revista Brasileira de Economia, 33 (January–March): 25–63.

IBGE. *Crescimento e Distribuição da População Brasileira: 1940–1980.* 1981. Rio de Janeiro: Fundação Instituto Brasileiro de Geografia e Estatística.

Langoni, Carlos G. 1973. *Distribuição de Renda e Desenvolvimento Econômico do Brasil.* Rio de Janeiro: Expressão e Cultura.

Lattimore, Ralph. 1974. "An Econometric Study of Brazilian Beef Sector." Ph.D. diss., Purdue University. Processed.

Lattimore, Ralph and G.E. Schuh. 1976. "Un Modelo de Política para la Industria Brasileña de Ganado Vacuno." *Cuadernos de Economía,* 13, no. 3 (August).

Leff, N. 1979. "The Exportable Surplus Approach to Foreign Trade in Underdeveloped Countries." *Economic Development and Cultural Change* 17.

Levy, Fred (Chief of Mission), D. Graham, N. Rask, L. Reca, and D. Kyle. 1982. *Brazil: A Review of Agriculture Policies.* A World Bank Country Study. Washington, D.C.: World Bank.

Longo, Carlos Alberto. 1984. "Uma Política Tributária para o Setor Agrícola." São Paulo: FIPE/USP. Dezembro.

Lopes, Mauro de Rezende. 1978. ''The Mobilization of Resources from Agriculture: A Policy Analysis for Brazil.'' Ph.D. diss., Purdue University, 1977. Processed. Published in Portuguese as CFP—Coleção de Análise e Pesquisa vol. 8.

———. and G.L.S. Dias. 1986. ''The Brazilian Experience with Crop Insurance Programs,'' in P. Hazell, C. Pomareda, and A. Valdés. *Crop Insurance for Agricultural Development.* Baltimore: International Food Policy Research Institute–The Johns Hopkins University Press.

Malta, Mauro. 1985. ''Café-Intervenção Estatal, 1906–1985,'' Rio de Janeiro: Organisação das Cooperativa Brasileiras. *Cadernos Economicos* 22.

Martin, M.A. 1976. ''Modernization of Brazilian Agriculture: An Analysis of Unbalanced Development.'' Ph.D. diss. Purdue University. Processed.

Martone, Celso Luiz. ''A Expansão do Estado Empresário no Brasil,'' In *A Crise do ''Bom Patrão.''* Rio de Janeiro: CEDES/APEC, undated.

Mueller, Charles K. 1983. *Das Oliqarquias Agrárias ao Predomínio Urbano-Industrial: Um Estudo do Processo de Formação de Políticas Agrícolas no Brasil.* Rio de Janeiro: IPEA/PNPE.

Oliveira, João do Carmo. 1981. ''An Analysis of Transfers from Agricultural Sector and Brazilian Development, 1950–1974.'' Ph.D. diss. Cambridge: University of Cambridge. Processed.

Pastore, José, Guilherme Leite da Silva Dias, and Mancoel Cabral Castro. 1976. ''Condicionantes da Produtividade da Pesquisa Agrícola no Brasil.'' Estudos Econômicos 6, no. 3 (December).

Pelaez, C.M. 1972. História da Industrialização Brasileira. Rio de Janeiro: APEC.

Rabello de Castro, Paulo. 1977. *Agroanalysis: Retrospecto do Primeiro Semestre 1977.* Rio de Janeiro: Fundação Getúlio Vargas, July.

Ramos, Carlos Alberto. 1986. *Agricultura e Inflação: A Abordagem Estruturalista.* Rio de Janeiro: BNDES.

Roe, Terry and D. Green. 1986. ''The Estimation of a Shadow Equilibrium Exchange Rate: A Direct Method,'' *Staff Paper Series*, p. 86–45. Department of Agricultural and Applied Economics, October.

Santana, Carlos A.M. 1984. ''The Impact of Economic Policies on the Soybean Sector of Brazil: An Effective Protection Analysis.'' Ph.D. diss. University of Minnesota. Processed.

Sayad, João. 1977. ''Planejamento, Crédito e Distribuição de Renda.'' *Estudos Econômicos* 7, no. 1: 9–34.

Schuh, G. Edward. 1975. ''A Modernização da Agricultura Brasileira: Uma Interpretação.'' In CONTADOR, C.R. (ed) *Tecnologia e Desenvolvimento Agrícola.* Rio de Janeiro: IPEA/INPES.

Smith, G.W. 1969. ''Brazilian Agricultural Policy: 1950–67.'' In H.S. Ellis, ed. *Essays on the Economic of Brazil.* Berkeley: University of California Press.

Wright, C.L. and A.J.C. Rego. 1982. ''Política Agrícola, Estrutura Agráriae Produção Agropecuária''. *Revista de Economia Rural*, 30, no. 3 (July–September).

4 Chile

Alberto Valdés, Hernán Hurtado, and
Eugenia Muchnik

The objectives of this study are twofold. One is to measure the impact
of agricultural pricing policies as well as economywide policies on
relative agricultural prices. Considered also are the effects of such
policies on agricultural output, consumption, foreign exchange earnings, the government budget, income distribution, and transfers of
income between agriculture and the rest of the economy from 1960 to
1984 in Chile. The other is to explain the political and economic factors that led to the various types of price intervention. We seek to
answer questions such as: What political constraints influenced government decisions on agricultural prices? To what extent did economic constraints and market forces cause government policymakers
to change their policies on farm prices?[1]

One thesis of this paper is that agricultural prices in Chile were
strongly affected over the long run by developments in other sectors
of the economy, particularly through trade and macroeconomic policies. Because we are dealing with wage goods (food accounts for a
high percentage of the expenditures of urban consumers), the potential effect of changes in farm prices on urban real wages is a central
element in the analysis.

The study covers a twenty-four-year period marked by several radi-
cal shifts in national policies. Under President Alessandri (1960–64),
Chile followed traditional, and fairly conservative, policies. During
the next administration, that of President Frei (1965–70), Chile was
the scene of agrarian reform. That was followed by an attempt to
install a socialist system under President Allende (1970–73). Allende
was then overthrown by a military junta under General Pinochet,
which replaced the policies of the Allende administration with an
ambitious attempt to install a system of laissez-faire capitalism. Important changes that affected agriculture took place in 1982. Unfortunately, the data available did not allow the analysis to extend beyond 1984, when the effects of these changes were just beginning to
appear.

Chile and Its Agriculture

Chile is considered to have a comparative advantage in various economic activities related to natural resources, primarily mining, forestry, fisheries, and farming, especially the production of fresh fruits and vegetables for export. Measuring approximately 4,000 kilometers from north to south, but no more than 460 kilometers from east to west, Chile has no tropical areas. Its climate varies from arid zones in the north to areas in the far south where annual precipitation exceeds 2,000 millimeters.

Chile's population is predominantly urban. The last census in 1982 showed a total population of 11.3 million, approximately 82 percent of which lived in cities or towns, with a high concentration in the two largest cities—Santiago and Valparaiso-Viña del Mar. The urban population of Chile has seldom shown much interest in agricultural and rural life, a result of the social and geographic distance between the urban and rural classes, the relatively high degree of land concentration, and a belief that rural areas are dominated by an unprogressive landed aristocracy. The land reform of the late 1960s was undoubtedly inspired by inequality in land ownership and a general belief that the agricultural sector was inefficient—a belief that has changed drastically in the 1980s.

Chile is a middle-income country. In 1985, per capita GNP was US$1,430. Per capita gross domestic product (GDP) growth averaged 2.2 percent a year during 1960–70 but declined to 0.9 percent in 1970–80. Between 1981 and 1983, Chile suffered from the worldwide recession, but the economy began to recover in 1984. By 1986, the overall growth rate had risen to 5.5 percent.

Despite slow economic growth, there has been considerable improvement in the educational level in recent decades. The adult literacy rate is now approximately 95 percent, and between 1960 and 1980 the number of children enrolled in prebasic and primary school increased by 376 and 148 percent, respectively. Health status indicators also showed impressive improvement during those decades. For example, infant mortality declined from 120 per 1,000 live births in 1960 to 23 per 1,000 in 1980.

Agriculture has played a changing role in the Chilean economy since the 1930s, and especially since World War II. Until recently, it has not been a major factor in overall growth. Its share of GDP ranged from 5.5 to 10.2 percent during 1960–82. This sector, however, gave direct employment to more than 25 percent of the labor force in the 1960s and about 17 percent in the 1970s, and was perceived to have enormous growth potential. This potential has been confirmed in the 1980s. The country's agricultural (and forestry) trade deficit of US$420 million in 1975 evolved into a trade surplus of US$1,090 million in 1987 (figures in current dollars). Agricultural exports (with fresh fruits accounting for 80 percent) increased from US$24 million in 1973 (close to the average during 1960–73) to US$700 million in 1987, causing agricultural export revenues as a percentage of total export revenues to rise from 1.9 percent to 12.9 percent. Furthermore, domestic output of major import-competing crops, such as wheat, rice, and maize, has increased significantly since 1982.

Agricultural Production

Over 90 percent of agricultural production in Chile is classified as food, and it is estimated that more than 85 percent is tradable. The most important domestic products are wheat, milk, beef, sugar beets, corn, rice, tobacco, poultry, pork, and oilseeds. The principal farm exports are fresh fruits (grapes, apples, peaches), specialty fruits (prunes, apricots, and raspberries), pulses (beans, lentils, garlic, onions), wine, wool, and vegetables (asparagus and others).

Of Chile's total area of 75.7 million hectares (excluding territory claimed in Antarctica), some 27 percent (20.4 million hectares) are suitable for agriculture, livestock, or forestry. In 1985, some 1.8 million hectares were under irrigation. Wheat was planted on 41 percent of the area devoted to crops, while corn accounted for 10 percent and fruit trees 11 percent. The importance of the livestock sector has fluctuated substantially. In 1965, livestock accounted for 44 percent of total agricultural output. In 1975–77, that figure declined to 28 percent before increasing to 36 percent in 1979. Beef, milk, and poultry together account for more than 80 percent of the value of livestock production.

More than 95 percent of Chile's agricultural production takes place in the central and south-central provinces, starting approximately 300 kilometers north of Santiago (at Aconcagua), and extending down to Llanquihue, 1,200 kilometers south of Santiago. Areas outside this region are important only for a few products excluded from this study, such as mutton, wool, and the specialty fruits.

The bulk of Chile's agricultural output is produced on large commercial farms. Large, medium-size, and small farms coexist in Chile, but small farms (fewer than 5 hectares) are not a significant contributor to aggregate farm output, except for vegetables, potatoes, and pulses.

The pattern of land tenure changed drastically during the period under study, primarily as a result of land reform, whose objective was to give management of large farms to the workers. Over the period of the reform process, 1965 to 1973, about 48 percent of Chile's agricultural land was expropriated by the government.[2] Subsequently, 28 percent of this area was returned to its previous owners, and 56 percent was retained in the reformed sector, which was subdivided after 1974. The rest was sold at auction. In 1979, about 23 percent of Chile's cultivable land was owned by large farm producers, although they managed between 25 and 30 percent of all farmland. This was less than one-half of what they owned in 1965. Medium-size farms (between twenty-one and eighty basic irrigated hectare [BIH]) occupied about 22 percent of land area. The rest of the land area (53 percent) is in *minifundia*, which are plots of less than 20 BIH. The *minifundia*, which employ about 35 percent of the rural labor force, were largely unaffected by reform.

Overview of Economic Policies, 1960–84

One striking feature of the Chilean economy, particularly before the 1980s, was its one-sided export structure. During the period 1950–80, on average, exports of mineral products (mainly copper) accounted for 78 percent of total export revenues, making the economy very vulnerable to changes in world copper prices. As this study will show, the impact of foreign terms of trade on the exchange rate, and consequently on agricultural production incentives, is strong.

Another feature was Chile's low savings ratio throughout the 1960–84 period. This low rate of capital accumulation impeded the growth of agriculture and, as will be discussed later, had an impact on agricultural pricing policy.

Chile's imbalanced structure of exports, along with a relatively small proportion of trade to GDP, resulted from an import-substitution strategy adopted in the 1930s. As elsewhere in Latin America, Chile sought in various ways to encourage its industrial sector. Tariffs on imported industrial products were kept high, and the government did not hesitate to intervene in wages, prices, or the allocation of credit. The success of the drive toward greater industrialization, it was believed, depended to a great extent on keeping the prices of food low.

Moreover, the view dominant in Chile at that time was that farm production did not respond positively to higher prices. To put it another way, it was widely believed that output was inelastic and showed little response whether food prices went up or down. In short, low farm prices were not seen as having a negative effect on production.

The first law allowing the government to control agricultural prices was enacted in 1931. The law established an Agricultural Export Board with the authority to set the domestic prices of wheat, wheat flour, and bread, prohibit or limit exports of wheat, purchase Chilean or foreign wheat, and pay subsidies to wheat exporters. Then, in 1932, the government created a Comisariato de Subsistencias y Precios with broad authority over all "essential" goods and services (that is, items that were important in determining the cost-of-living index). Among other things, the Comisariato was given the power to set the prices of essential items, to limit or prohibit their export, and to import such items in the event of domestic shortages.

Fixing prices by government edict was resorted to again in 1953 in an attempt to tame the inflation that arose after World War II. In the language of one decree, "the prices of wheat, flours, and bread, in all forms in which they are sold, would be fixed by supreme decree of the Ministry of Economics and Commerce, according to the production and processing costs of these products." A second decree gave the Ministry of Economics and Commerce the authority to set the "prices for all the products and goods referred to in the earlier decree (of prime necessity, or essentials)."

The Alessandri Administration (1958–64)

When Jorge Alessandri became president of Chile in 1958, retail prices were rising at an average annual rate of 60 to 70 percent, and the new government took several steps to combat this inflation. Wage increases for public employees were limited to the amounts necessary to keep wages in step with the inflation rate, and the government urged private employers to impose similar limits on wage increases for their employees. In addition, a trade liberalization program was put into effect. The nominal exchange rate was fixed, tariffs were reduced, and quotas on imports, as well as import licensing, were eliminated. The hope was that these actions would reassure foreign investors and thus lead to a rise in foreign investment in Chile.

The government also attempted to reduce its budget deficit by raising taxes and cutting expenditures, but had little success. Meanwhile, Chile's current account deficit soon made it impossible to maintain a fixed nominal exchange rate, and in 1961 the government acknowledged that its trade liberalization program had not resolved the problem of a severe shortage of foreign exchange. Chile then reverted again to protectionism. Import quotas and licensing were revived, and the uniform equivalent tariff began to rise, ascending from 43 percent in 1960–61 to 94 percent during 1962–64.

As part of its attempt to stabilize domestic prices while improving foreign exchange earnings, the Alessandri government instituted policies to aid consumers, farmers, and exporters of agricultural commodities. The stabilization measures included fixing the prices of numerous wage goods (rice, wheat, oilseeds, sugar, milk, and so forth), setting up marketing boards to control fluctuations in wholesale commodity prices, and expanding commodity storage and processing facilities. To improve the agricultural trade balance, Chile simplified its export rules, intensified its promotion of exportable commodities (especially grapes and apples), and agreed to participate in a Latin American free trade zone. To compensate farmers for the lid on commodity prices, the government reduced the tariff on numerous imported agricultural inputs and directly subsidized commodity transportation costs and purchases of fertilizers and seeds. In addition, the supply of credit available at subsidized interest rates was increased.

The government also sought to help Chile's lagging livestock sector. Public financing was provided for imported breeding animals, slaughterhouses, and dairy operations, programs to create additional pasture land were devised, and meat imports were controlled to reduce competition from foreign suppliers.

These changes, however, did not add up to a change in Chile's development strategy. The Alessandri government, like its predecessors, still placed its chief hopes for economic growth on intensified industrialization.

The Frei Administration (1964–70)

Alessandri was succeeded in 1964 by Eduardo Frei, who was elected on a platform that advocated raising incomes and redistributing wealth in all sectors, including agriculture.

Initially, the government nationalized the major copper companies in Chile (all of them U.S.-owned) by assuming a 51 percent share in company ownership, which was followed by increases in miners' wages. Then, in 1967, the government initiated a wide-ranging program of agrarian reform, a popular desire in a country where roughly one-third of the population worked in agriculture and 55 percent of the arable land was in the hands of large landowners. Under an agrarian reform law approved by Congress, the government was authorized to expropriate uncultivated land and to limit holdings of 80 hectares. Progress under the reform law was slow, however, because the government sought not only to redistribute land but also to stimulate and modernize the agricultural sector. Extensive plans were made to provide new housing for Chile's agricultural workers, to mechanize agricultural activities, and to expand the amount of irrigated land. The goal of all this activity was to make Chile less dependent on imported agricultural products.

Aware of the problems caused in the past by balance of payments problems, the Frei government adopted a crawling peg system for adjusting the nominal exchange rate. By this means, the government hoped to avoid overvaluation of the peso. Meanwhile, the Frei administration conducted another experiment in trade liberalization. To promote exports, exporters were given tax refunds of up to 30 percent of the f.o.b. price of their exports. (Except for fresh fruit, this incentive did not apply to agricultural exports.) Furthermore, tariffs were relaxed. During the first years of the Frei administration, the uniform equivalent tariff was 94 percent. By 1970, it had fallen to 38.6 percent (see table 4-1).

Along with the pivotal 1967 land reform law, the government took several other steps related to agriculture. Farm prices were allowed to rise more quickly than nonagricultural prices, a larger share of all available credit was allocated to small and mid-size farms, and a single agricultural land tax (based on potential farm productivity) was substituted for the variety of existing taxes. Moreover, farms taken over by the government were exempted from the land tax—in effect, another form of redistribution of wealth. Also significant was the creation of a National Institution of Agricultural Research (INIA) at Santiago, and the beginnings (in 1966) of government investment in reforestation.

The Frei administration had also committed itself to supporting organized labor. However, real increases in urban wages during the 1965–70 period went far beyond existing government guidelines. The government then faced a tradeoff between the stated objective of raising farm prices and a need to restrain real wages in the non-agricultural sector and thus reassure investors in that sector. Exceptionally favorable terms of trade (caused by higher prices for copper), together with greater revenues from tax reform, allowed an expansion in government credit. The budget deficit began to rise quickly, however, and large real wage increases for both urban and rural workers again raised the specter of galloping inflation.

The Allende Administration (1970–73)

Frei's successor as president of Chile was Salvador Allende, a socialist who won election with about 37 percent of the vote. Supported by a left-wing coalition, Allende laid out a program to achieve socialism in Chile that included government expropriation of large industrial firms, farms, and private banks, intensified agrarian reform, and further redistribution of income to the poorest workers.

Prodded from the left, the Allende government moved ahead in ways that disrupted the economy. The attempt to nationalize industry caused industrial production to stagnate, the intensification of agrarian reform reduced farm output, and the sharp leftward tilt of the government produced a boycott of Chile by foreign investors. The government then tried to reactivate idle industrial plants by adopting a policy of monetary expansion. Meanwhile, faced with a high and rising rate of inflation, the government abandoned the crawling peg system. To protect Chile's floundering industrial sector, the Allende regime then reverted to protectionism.

With money plentiful and goods scarce, inflation accelerated, and the government attempted to curb it by instituting price controls on essential goods, including food. Predictably, the combination of intense inflation and official ceiling prices led to the formation of black markets and food shortages. The Allende government reacted to this situation by attempting to monopolize all sales and purchases of wheat, corn, and several other farm products, as well as fertilizer. This attempt to control farm markets, however, was no more successful than the regime's attempt to control industry. In 1973, the net losses of industrial firms directly controlled by the government amounted to more than US$500 million.

The Allende period was also a time of rising budget deficits. By 1973, the deficit amounted to almost 24 percent of gross domestic product, and inflation was out of control, running at an annual rate of more than 400 percent. By presiding over a descent into economic chaos, the Allende government lost the support of the middle class and had few defenders when it was toppled by a military coup in September 1973.

The Military Government (1973 to Present)

The new government, led by army general Augusto Pinochet, acted quickly to halt the economic turmoil. Most of the price controls imposed during the Allende years were lifted, wage increases were postponed, and strikes, collective bargaining, and political activity by labor unions were curtailed. The military government also did what it could to improve Chile's trade position. The peso was devalued, the crawling peg system was put back into place, and successful attempts were made to extend the schedule of repayments of foreign loans.

The new regime made it clear that its chief goal was to end Chile's flirtation with socialism and to reinvigorate the country's capitalist economic system. Spokesmen for the new government placed emphasis on such traditional views as letting private markets establish prices, reducing the role of government in the economy, liberalizing trade, and strengthening private ownership. Legal ceilings on interest rates were adjusted upward and then completely removed. Real interest rates, which had been negative because of inflation, turned positive. Furthermore, preferential interest rates for operators in certain sectors, including agriculture, were abolished. After relying on government loans with subsidized interest rates for many years, most farmers found the open market to be their only source of loan funds.

In 1975 the military government began a new experiment in trade liberalization. Together with the elimination of almost all nontariff barriers, tariffs on most imported goods were rapidly reduced. At the start of the new liberalization episode, the uniform equivalent tariff

Table 4–1. Agricultural Prices, Protection and Exchange Rate, Related Variables, 1960–86

Years	Prices[a]	Direct nominal protection[b] (percent)	Uniform equivalent tariff[c]	Real exchange rate[d]	Absorption relative to GDP[e]	Foreign terms of trade[f]	Rate of growth of agricultural GDP
Alessandri							
1960–64	100	17	94	100	1.03	100	−0.3
Frei							
1965	117	19	94	109	0.99	278	2.0
1966	120	22	76	115	0.99	202	21.2
1967	116	−7	76	118	0.99	151	3.0
1968	114	−11	76	128	0.99	161	4.7
1969	125	−12	39	134	1.02	187	−11.4
1970	135	1	39	144	0.99	170	3.6

Military government

1975	225	−14	95	245	1.02	80	4.8
1976	259	−8	33	317	0.97	87	−2.9
1977	238	44	20	295	1.02	75	10.4
1978	209	15	14	240	1.03	75	−4.9
1979	223	0	10	246	1.03	78	5.6
1980	216	8	10	233	1.04	71	3.6
1981	184	7	10	202	1.1	61	3.7
1982	162	7	10	177	1.02	54	−2.1
1983	186	8	18	206	0.97	58	−3.6
1984	162	35	25	229	1.01	54	7.1
1985	238	18	26	285	0.97	51	5.6
1986	306	33	20	295	0.96	54	8.7

a. Domestic agricultural to nonagricultural prices. Agriculture includes wheat, milk, and beef.
b. Measures weighted average of direct nominal protection on wheat, beef, and milk.
c. Methodology defined in Final Report.
d. Defined as E_o times the ratio of the U.S. Wholesale Price Index to the Domestic Price of Home Goods, where E_o is the official exchange rate.
e. From Banco Central.
f. International export prices divided by international import price.
Source: Hurtado, Valdés, and Muchnik (1990).

was 95 percent. Two years later, it had fallen to 20 percent (see table 4-1) and was used primarily to protect producers of certain essential agricultural products, such as wheat, sugarbeets, oilseeds, and milk and milk products.

Economic stabilization did not come quickly, however. By 1978, Chile's annual rate of inflation was still 50 percent, investment was still sluggish, and the working class was unhappy over lagging wages as well as the continued curb on union activity.

The regime removed a number of restrictions on the financial sector, and to deal with a low level of investment liberalized the rules on inflow of foreign capital. And to pacify wage earners, the government in 1979 indexed wage increases to the rate of inflation and relaxed the restrictions on the unions' right to strike.

The liberalization efforts had positive effects. Inflation was reduced and capital inflows in 1980 were doubled what they were in 1979. In 1981 they doubled again. Real wages increased substantially, and real gross domestic product grew by more than 7 percent in 1980.

This revival was shortlived, however. The worldwide recession of 1980–82 did not spare Chile, and in 1982 the government was forced to abandon both wage indexation and the fixed exchange rate adopted in 1979. Then in 1982, faced with an acute shortage of foreign exchange, the government decided to raise tariffs. Meanwhile, the steep rise in interest rates and a high level of private borrowing brought about an increase of 40 percent in Chile's external debt. Recovery from the recession began in 1984, and by 1987 the economic crisis had been overcome.

Measures of Intervention in Agricultural Prices

As described in the previous section, the prices of agricultural products in Chile have been subject to a wide array of interventions. Sector-specific interventions (that is, direct intervention in prices) have included government-mandated minimum and maximum prices, trade controls, and government allocation of agricultural inputs. Economywide policies have also affected agricultural incentives.

This section first presents measures of direct intervention in the prices of each of the five selected products. Wheat, beef, and milk are important import-competing products, while apples and grapes are important exportables. In 1969, a typical year, these five products accounted for approximately 43 percent of the total value of Chile's agricultural production Department of Agricultural Economies, Universidad Catolica (DEA-UC 1976). Wheat, moreover, has played a singular role in the establishment of prices, in the sense that other crop prices were fixed in explicit relation to wheat prices during the period of study.

Measuring Direct Intervention

To measure the direct nominal protection rate (NPR) and the effective protection rate (ERP), border and domestic prices must first be adjusted to make them comparable in terms of location, quality, time of comparison, and other differentials not resulting from policy intervention. The adjustments were as follows:

- Meat. In 1974, after establishing regulations on foot-and-mouth disease, Chile began to restrict imports of live cattle from Argentina. Although Argentinian cattle were cheaper than those from other countries, they often were afflicted by the disease. These restrictions can be viewed as trade distortions, or alternatively as optimal interventions in the presence of market failure caused by externalities. Consequently, two time series for the border prices of beef were prepared for this study—one for imports of live animals and one for imports of boneless meat.

Two adjustments were made to assure comparability under two scenarios analyzed with respect to foot and mouth disease. In the first case, the c.i.f. price of imported cattle was adjusted to make it comparable to the wholesale domestic price by including quarantine costs, sanitary inspection costs, other fees and commissions, the cost of transport to Santiago, and the profit margins of importers. In the second case, the c.i.f., price of imported boneless meat was adjusted only by the profit markup of importers, because c.i.f. quotations take into account the costs of moving the product to Santiago. The latter series was used to simulate the border price of live cattle.

- Milk. The border price of milk refers to the price of powdered milk, the product actually traded. Because the c.i.f. price does not specify the fat content of the traded product, adjustments were made to make domestic (fluid) milk and imported (dry) milk comparable. Other adjustments were made to make domestic and border milk prices comparable. These included adjustments to take account of transportation and other costs incurred between the port of Valparaiso and the capital of Santiago, and for seasonality. These two adjustments yielded the powdered milk price that would have prevailed under free trade in Santiago.

Because domestic producers react primarily to the price paid for fluid milk, we then assessed the impact of changes in the price of powdered milk on fluid milk. We began by assuming that changes in the price of powdered milk were fully transmitted to the price of fluid milk. We then found, however, that changes in the price of powdered milk were only partly transmitted because these changes led to a redistribution of regional milk output. These partial results are the results presented below.

- Wheat. The first adjustment was to include domestic transport costs and other costs required to transport imported wheat to Santiago. The second was to adjust prices on the basis of differences in quality (that is, the proportions of soft and hard wheat) in imported and domestic wheat. Our analysis indicated that differences in quality explained only about 2 percent of the 20 percent difference in the costs of domestic and imported wheat during the period 1960–64, and approximately 4 percent during the period 1971–84.

A third adjustment was to take account of seasonality in wheat prices. The standard practice in Chile in determining levels of protection is to compare average domestic wheat prices at harvest time with import prices at the time of import. The results of this comparison have led to claims that Chile's wheat mills behave as monopsonists because they pay lower prices for domestic wheat. Imports, however, only appear on the domestic market after domestic supplies have been exhausted. Meanwhile, the imported wheat is stored at the mills, and the costs of storing it must be taken into account. When this is done, the difference between the imported and the domestic price falls from 20 percent to about 2 percent. This seems to refute the allegations of monopsony. (Expected devaluations of the peso were taken into account in estimating the costs of imports.)

- Apples and grapes. The f.o.b. prices of these two products were adjusted by the amount of export subsidies for each year, and by exchange rate adjustments for those years during which a premium exchange rate prevailed. In addition, an adjustment for quality was necessary. The domestic prices of apples and grapes could not be used, since exports are of better quality than those sold domestically. Hence, the domestic prices of export-quality apples and grapes were estimated by generating f.o.b. price series at the packinghouse level.

Quantitative Results of Direct Intervention

The actual producer prices of wheat, beef, and milk during the period 1960–84 remained more stable than those of apples and grapes. This is not surprising, since the first three are products whose share of urban household expenditures is considerably larger than the share of the latter two. Although domestic wheat prices reflected the jump in world prices that occurred between 1973 and 1975, the stability of the real prices of the three products during most of the period is striking.

Table 4-2 presents direct nominal and effective rates of protection. Milk and beef show a contrast. There was consistent positive nominal protection for milk production throughout the period (between 16 and 186 percent), compared with persistent taxation of beef prior to 1975 (−10 to −26 percent). When cattle became less tradable owing to foot and mouth disease regulations (after 1975), it enjoyed a slight degree of protection. Nominal protection of wheat production was positive (between 5 and 44 percent), except during the years 1970–74, which was a period of exceptionally high world prices. Apples and grapes experienced positive protection before 1975, benefiting from export and exchange rate subsidies. They had no protection thereafter. Fluid milk production was highly protected until 1964. From then on, it received nominal protection of between 16 and 20 percent. The processing of domestic fluid milk into powdered milk, whose analysis is presented in *Trade, Exchange Rate, and Agricultural Pricing Policies in Chile*, was highly protected throughout the period.

It is commonly argued that input subsidies fully compensate farmers for lower output prices. Relative to most developing countries, Chilean agriculture makes intensive use of tradable inputs, and so one should expect a significant difference between nominal and effective rates of protection. Although several inputs were subsidized (such as credit), others were taxed (nitrogen fertilizers). Given differences in the share of tradable inputs in costs among farm products, one would expect that the difference between nominal and effective protection would vary across products.

The effective protection rates were based on direct comparisons between the domestic and border prices of inputs for some years, or according to tariffs on others, based on 1977 input-output coefficients. Intervention was computed for a broad range of tradable inputs, including tractors, fuel, fertilizer, seeds, herbicides, fungicides, insecticides, milking machinery, feed supplements, and breeding stock.

Table 4-2 shows that (except for beef before 1980, milk from 1965 to 1974, and fruits after 1975) effective rates of direct protection were positive. In some cases, input subsidies reinforced protection. The differences between nominal rates of protection and effective rates of protection were substantial during the 1960–75 period, but in later years the differences virtually vanished. Under both the nominal rate of protection and the effective rate of protection, beef cattle were taxed, the effective rate being negative except in the 1980–84 period. High support for milk, as measured by the nominal rate, is reduced drastically if the effective rate is used. Indeed, the positive nominal

Table 4-2. Average Annual Direct and Total Price Interventions to Agricultural Producers, 1960–84

(percent)

Period	Direct					Total				
	Wheat	Beef	Milk	Apples	Grapes	Wheat	Beef	Milk	Apples	Grapes
Nominal Rate of Protection										
1960–64	5	−10	186	11	12	−41	−49	61	−37	−37
1965–69	13	−26	39	27	28	−17	−45	2	−4	−4
1970–74	−11	−24	16	42	44	−28	−38	−4	14	16
1975–79	9	5	28	0	1	33	27	56	22	23
1980–89	15	8	16	0	0	2	−5	2	−7	−7
Effective rate of protection										
1960–64	25	−9	96	23	21	−37	−54	0	−36	−37
1965–69	17	−31	−23	34	14	−14	−47	−42	3	−5
1970–74	135	−30	−23	56	53	93	−33	−25	39	47
1975–79	20	−3	22	−11	−1	77	−16	28	32	47
1980–84	18	6	1	−25	−3	2[a]	3[a]	1[a]	−20[a]	−10[a]

a. The reported averages are for the period 1980–82.
Source: Hurtado, Valdés, and Muchnik (1990).

rate in the period 1965–74 becomes a negative effective rate. One unexpected result was the positive nominal rate and the higher positive effective rate for fruit production during the years 1960–74, followed by virtually zero direct (the nominal rate) protection for grapes during the period 1975–84; the effective rate was negative. This is paradoxical when one considers that Chile's boom in fruit production and fruit exports took place after 1975—that is, after protection ceased. Exchange rate misalignment (discussed in next section), the complex regulatory framework for exports, and the risk of expropriation under land reform were, we postulate, deterrents against investment in fruit production before 1975.

Overall, policy reforms implemented between 1974 and 1978 resulted in a significant decline in direct intervention, except in the case of wheat. Although they varied with world prices, rates of direct intervention were lower between 1975 and 1984 than they were between 1960 and 1974.

Measures of Total Intervention

Total NPRs and ERPs were both calculated. To obtain the ERPs, value added was estimated in the nonagricultural sector. We disaggregated that sector into twelve subsectors (three exportable, five importable, and four home goods sectors) for which effective protection rates were calculated.

To obtain measures of total intervention, the real exchange rate (RER) had to be adjusted to its equilibrium value. The RER was assumed to be a function of the foreign terms of trade (TOT), commercial policy, real wages in the public sector, domestic absorption relative to GDP (which generally depends on fiscal and monetary policies and permanent income expectations), and a variable to capture the change in the export share of the industrial sector relative to industrial output. Most of the variables in that equation are shown in table 4-1. This equation was estimated, and the results were used to obtain the equilibrium RER.

The year 1969 was selected as a base year when macroeconomic variables were considered to be sustainable in the long run. The current account was almost in balance, the government deficit as a percentage of GDP was relatively low (0.4 percent), the inflation rate (30 percent) was close to its trend for the period, the unemployment rate was low (4 percent), and gross investment was close to the historical average. The level of trade intervention that year was considered in calculating the equilibrium real exchange rate. In obtaining the equilibrium real exchange rate, fluctuations in the real exchange rate owing to changes in commercial policies (based on changes in the equivalent tariff) and "excessive" absorption and real wages (that is, above the levels in 1969) were eliminated, using elasticities obtained by the real exchange rate regression. As an illustration, the required devaluation to eliminate real exchange rate misalignment fluctuated from more than 100 percent in 1961–62 to 24 percent in 1968, 2 percent in 1970, −35 percent in 1977, and 9 percent in 1982.[3]

During the Frei administration, domestic agricultural relative prices were higher than during the Alessandri administration, particularly in 1966, 1969, and 1970 (table 4-1). This rise exceeded the increase in world prices. It is important to note that the higher domestic farm prices were mainly the result of a higher real exchange rate (column 5) and a reduction in the equivalent tariff (column 4) and not of higher direct (nominal) protection to agriculture, except in 1965–66 (column 3).

During the Military government, farm prices rose sharply compared with 1970 (column 1, table 4-1). International prices increased in 1975–76, which explains a fraction of the rise in domestic prices during those years, but then it declined drastically. Nominal (direct) protection to agriculture changed from negative in 1975–76 to 44 percent in 1977, followed by a low positive protection rate until 1984, when it rose significantly (column 2). This last rise coincided with years of low world prices.

Our analysis indicates that the Frei administration and the Military government improved incentives to farmers in comparison with the Alessandri administration. There was considerable fluctuation in farm prices relative to nonagricultural prices and in nominal protection for agriculture (except during 1980–83), but, as will be shown later, the farm price fluctuation was less than that of border prices. The analysis also indicates that the major determinants of higher farm prices under the Frei and military governments were the higher real exchange rate and lower industrial protection, which demonstrates that the effects of total intervention on relative agricultural prices were dominated by the effects of indirect intervention. This is shown in table 4-2. In several years, when direct intervention produced positive protection, indirect intervention led to lower or, often, negative total protection. In addition, wide variations were found in direct nominal and effective protection among the five products, which suggests that further thought should have been given to defining sectoral policies.

The Impact of Removing Price Intervention, 1960–84

This section presents the results of a simulated elimination of price intervention, showing what would have happened to agricultural output, consumption, trade, and the government budget if the government had not intervened in Chilean agricultural prices during the period being studied. The analysis is postulated on the view that sector-specific policies influence resource allocation within agriculture but that economywide intervention has a greater impact on the long-term growth of agriculture.

Which variables are to be taken as exogenous in analyzing the supply response to prices is a complex question. Exogenous factors are defined here to include certain production parameters (carrying capacity for livestock; labor requirements per hectare), the growth of the rural labor force, world prices, gross domestic product, the real interest rate, the economy's total stock of capital, and wages in the nonagricultural sector. In the short-run response analysis, it was assumed that total capital and labor supply in agriculture were given, and that nonagricultural prices have no impact on allocation within agriculture in the short run. The allocation of capital and labor to agriculture was assumed to reflect agriculture's profitability relative to the rest of the economy. The output model further assumes that changes in relative profitability are linked to relative effective rates of protection. Actual effective rates of protection were estimated for 13 sectors of the Chilean economy, and the undistorted value added for 1960–84 was computed. The investment and migration equations were provided by Coeymans and Mundlak. The estimate related to investment was then used to generate a new series on capital stock in agriculture in the absence of intervention, assuming a given level of total capital in the economy. This total capital turned out to be an influential constraint on the expansion of aggregate agricultural output.

Agricultural wages were estimated from a sector supply and demand model for labor, where nonagricultural wages were assumed as given. Given the labor requirements for each sector, as well as intrasectoral capital allocation, nonagricultural wages, and total supply of labor in agriculture, the model determines agricultural wages. These, in turn, are used in the migration equation to determine the next year's labor supply in agriculture.

An output supply model was used to determine changes in output in response to changes in relative prices (both products and inputs) and changes in the amount of capital allocated to each activity. The amounts of capital allocated to the production of beef, milk, fruit (including wine), and annual crops were estimated as a function of the relative prices of these products and of the lagged values of specific forms of capital.

An effort was made to incorporate explicitly the interdependence in supply when simultaneous changes occur in the prices of several commodities. Thus, acreage functions were estimated, including parameters to capture cross-effects—for example, how number of livestock affects the amount of crop acreage. Such cross-effects turned out to be quite significant in determining the combination of farm outputs that would have occurred without price intervention.

Another interaction is the one between productivity and price changes. Empirically, this is difficult to measure. The productivity of land used for wheat and fruit production (yield per hectare) was allowed to vary as a result of changes in the price of fertilizers and in the number of tractors, which in turn depends on crop prices. Productivity in livestock production, however, was treated as exogenously determined.

Effect on Output of Removal of Direct Intervention

The cumulative proportional output and input effects owing to removal of direct intervention are presented in table 4-3. The analysis postulates that sector-specific policies will mainly influence a reallocation of land, labor, and capital within agriculture to higher productivity activities through changes in the output mix without changing the total amounts of capital and labor devoted to agriculture. This contrasts with economywide intervention, which can have a greater impact on the long-term growth of agriculture as migration of labor and capital takes place between sectors in response to changes in agricultural terms of trade. Nonintervention in prices was assumed to start in 1960, and its effects are cumulative year by year. The main effects on output would have been as follows:

- During most of the period analyzed, beef production would have been reduced by 11 to 16 percent, and the supply of milk by 11 to 19 percent. As reported earlier, milk production during the period 1960–74 was systematically protected, whereas cattle production was not. Because the two activities are linked, the results suggest that milk production strongly influences the overall level of livestock production.
- The amount of land planted with fruit trees would have increased. The average cumulative effect would have been an increase of about 11 percent above the actual figure for fruit acreage for the period 1960–84. During the period 1963–74, however, the planted area would have been about 20 percent larger. This reflects the fact that fruit production was unprotected relative to other sectors despite the occasional existence of export subsidies.[4]
- Wheat output during the years 1960–69 would have shown little change, but output would have been substantially higher during the period 1973–84. After 1965, wheat acreage would have expanded because of a decline in the number of livestock.[5]

Table 4-3. Cumulative Change in Selected Agricultural Variables after Removing Direct Price Interventions, 1960–84

(percent)

Category	1960–64	1965–69	1970–74	1975–79	1980–84
Wheat production	0.3	3.9	17.9	33.0	32.8
Beef production	−2.6	−11.1	−16.9	−12.5	−13.5
Milk production	−19.3	−13.9	−6.2	−11.4	−12.1
Wheat acreage	2.9	4.4	18.0	32.9	29.7
Fruit acreage	8.3	20.4	21.0	−0.7	5.8
Beef livestock	−1.5	−4.2	−4.1	−14.0	−14.8
Tractors	−2.8	−6.7	−6.4	19.6	21.6
Agricultural labor force	0.2	1.9	6.4	7.1	2.2[a]
Agricultural wages	0.6	−0.4	3.0	−3.4	1.0[a]
Agricultural value added	−2.9	−2.2	−0.3	11.1	11.0[b]

a. Includes 1981 and 1982.
b. Includes 1980, 1981, and 1982.
Source: Hurtado, Valdés, and Muchnik (1990).

Effect on Output of Removal of Total Intervention

Simulation of total nonintervention consists of hypothesizing a policy of free trade, maintaining the real exchange rate at equilibrium (corrected for commercial policies, absorption and real wages in the public sector), and correcting for direct intervention. In analyzing total intervention, capital and labor in agriculture were assumed to be endogenous and to respond to their returns in agriculture relative to those in the rest of the economy. The results in table 4-4 are:

- Fruit, and wheat, and wine would have been the subsectors most favored by total nonintervention, particularly wheat and wine after 1974. Given a policy of free trade and an equilibrium real exchange rate, the amount of land planted in fruit (primarily table grapes) would have been approximately 15 percent higher in the 1965–74 period. This implies that the export expansion that has occurred since the late 1970s would have started at least ten years earlier if there had been no intervention. By 1982, the difference in output would have been considerably smaller (around 6 percent), because most types of price intervention had been removed by then.[6]

- Actual wheat production was consistently less than it would have been under a nonintervention scenario. It is interesting to note, however, that direct intervention had a greater impact on wheat production than total intervention did. During the period

Table 4-4. Cumulative Change in Selected Agricultural Variables after Removing Total Price Interventions, 1960–82

(percent)

Category	1960–64	1965–69	1970–74	1975–79	1980–82
Wheat production	1.5	2.6	15.1	28.9	30.8
Beef production	−1.7	−9.7	−13.5	−10.2	−11.2
Milk production	−14.5	−11.9	−1.8	−6.1	−8.3
Wheat acreage	2.9	1.5	12.2	26.1	23.5
Fruit acreage	3.1	16.0	18.9	−1.9	5.9
Beef livestock	−1.0	−2.7	−1.5	−11.5	−12.5
Tractors	1.7	1.6	2.9	29.9	32.4
Agricultural capital	0.8	3.4	6.0	7.6	7.2
Agricultural wages	0.5	1.6	6.7	7.4	3.1[a]
Agricultural labor force	0.5	−0.4	3.3	−3.4	1.3[a]
Agricultural value added	−1.9	−2.4	0.9	10.1	10.8

a. Includes 1981 and 1982.
Source: Hurtado, Valdés, and Muchnik (1990).

1974–82, wheat production in the absence of all intervention would have been around 30 percent higher than actual production (see table 4-4). Most of this increase in wheat output would have come from acreage expansion, resulting in part from a reduction in beef and milk production.

- Beef production in the absence of total intervention would have been very similar to its actual level until the late 1960s, and then would have fallen below its actual level by around 12 percent.

- The actual amounts of fluid milk produced during the study period were larger than what they would have been without intervention, particularly during 1960–69 (by about 13 percent). During the rest of the period, actual milk production was higher than what it would have been without any intervention by a range of 1.8 percent to 8.1 percent.

- Under the nonintervention scenario, total agricultural capital would have remained similar to actual agricultural capital during the 1960–69 period but would then have been 3.5 to 7.5 percent above the actual values.

- Agricultural GDP under nonintervention would have been relatively similar to actual agricultural GDP during 1961–74, but would have been approximately 7 to 17 percent higher during 1975–82. These increases would have been the result of removing direct intervention.

Overall, the farm output mix would have changed under a nonintervention scenario. Production of annual crops and fruit would have been larger, and beef and milk output would have been smaller, than they were. Wheat production would have expanded significantly, especially after 1973, even relative to overall annual crop production.

The results reported so far assume underemployment in agriculture. But since demand for agricultural labor would increase after the elimination of intervention, wage income per worker would rise as a result of more hours worked. However, one needs to measure whether the rise in wages is large enough to invalidate the assumption of underemployment. Analysis suggests that under a nonintervention scenario, real wages in agriculture would have been slightly higher than actual wages, particularly during the periods 1968–70 and 1973–75, and would have been less than actual wages in the years 1977–78. Overall, however, the differences are small, except in the period 1970–79. Agricultural employment under the nonintervention scenario (see table 4-4) would have been very similar to actual employment during the period 1960–69 and would have been increased during the years 1970–74 because of the expansion that would have occurred in wheat acreage. Labor availability in the absence of intervention would have not imposed a binding constraint on output. Two considerations are relevant here. One is that the reduction in rural/urban migration observed in the simulation would have prevented significant increases in rural wages. Second, wages outside of agriculture were assumed to be unaffected by the simulations.

Although indirect intervention in Chile had a greater impact on agricultural incentives than direct intervention did, the differences in the cumulative change in aggregate agricultural output predicted by the supply model are in general small, except for the large divergence predicted for 1970–74. The puzzle has important policy implications, to which we turn.

Output expansion from the removal of indirect intervention would have come from a higher share of capital and labor reallocated to agriculture, mainly from the home goods sector. The parameters used for the intersectoral migration and investment functions, for which the only source available at the time (1986) was preliminary estimates by Coeymans and Mundlak, had relatively low elasticities. More recent estimates by these authors (1988) obtained higher elasticities. Even so, we believe there are still unresolved questions in those econometric estimates, probably resulting in a systematic downward bias in the aggregate supply response to the removal of total price intervention. For example, 1965–73 was a period of drastic agrarian reform in Chile, which probably inhibited private investment in activities with long gestation periods, such as fruit trees, beef cattle, and land improvements. Furthermore, while the terms of trade did increase substantially in the 1970s and 1980s relative to the 1960s, this increase was not so much the result of higher sectoral prices but mainly the result of changes in the real exchange rate and reduction in industrial protection (table 4-1). Except for the new industrial policy since the late 1970s, the other determinants of indirect effects were highly unstable. This could affect the output effects, if one considers that the approach to aggregate agricultural supply response in this study postulates that incentives to agricultural production were also associated with policies in the nonagricultural sector and to foreign conditions, mainly terms of trade and supply of foreign credit. How the "elasticity" of response would have changed with lower price and exchange rate variability, and with more credible policies, is perhaps not captured adequately by the available econometric estimates.

We believe the potential aggregate agricultural response to higher agricultural terms of trade is higher than the one predicted in this study. But for this to take place, in addition to prices, three other determinants are influential. One is real interest rates. Farm output in Chile is highly sensitive to real interest rates and supply of credit. These rates were high during most of 1975–84, inhibiting output response. Second, the often undefined limits between the public and private sector in the 1960s and early 1970s created considerable uncertainty about property rights, and, hence, returns to private investments. Third, expectations about long-run economywide economic conditions are crucial for a sector in which a large part of the output expansion comes from highly capital-intensive activities (fruit, livestock) which take years before yielding profits, and are tradable. Only the first of the three determinants was treated explicitly in the supply model.

Effect on Foreign Exchange Flows of Removing Direct and Total Intervention

The foreign exchange flows that would have resulted from the removal of direct price intervention reflect the changes in production and input demand predicted by the supply model discussed above, and in final consumption. The variables in this computation are wheat, beef, and milk production, changes in fruit acreage, and changes in the quantities of tractors and agricultural machinery, both of which are assumed to be imported. Changes in domestic consumption of fertilizers and pesticides were also estimated, based on price elasticities of demand and the changes in retail prices that would have occurred as a result of eliminating protection. As part of the computation of consumption effects, the cost-of-living index was recomputed (using a simulated free trade CPI) to simulate the effect of removing price intervention. It is relevant to stress that the calculations on foreign exchange effects pertain to the agricultural sector only and do

Table 4-5. Foreign Exchange Effect of Removing Direct Price Interventions on Selected Agricultural Products and Inputs, 1960–84

(millions of U.S. dollars)

Category	1960–64	1965–69	1970–74	1975–79	1980–84
Wheat	0.3	2.3	41.1	62.0	41.2
Beef	6.5	18.1	13.9	−24.5	−38.6
Milk	−5.8	−4.3	−3.5	−9.3	−13.0
Fruits	0.3	1.4	2.6	−0.2	18.3
Nitrogen	0.0	−0.4	−0.4	−0.3	−0.6
Tractors	0.4	0.8	−0.3	−7.5	−2.6
Other machinery	−0.1	−0.2	−0.2	0.0	0.0
Total	1.6	17.7	53.2	20.2	4.7

Source: Hurtado, Valdés, and Muchnik (1990).

not indicate the overall effects on the trade balance or the current account.

Elimination of direct intervention would have induced an increase in net foreign exchange earnings in eighteen of the twenty-five years. However, the increase in foreign earnings resulting from the increase in agricultural net export revenues would have been only a small share of Chile's total export revenues between 1960 and 1970. The increase in farm export revenues would have been 2 to 7 percent during the years 1972–76, but after 1977 would have become insignificant because intervention had become much smaller (table 4-5).

The difference between what actually happened and what would have happened without intervention emerges with particular clarity when the effects of total intervention are considered (see table 4-6).

Table 4-6. Foreign Exchange Effect of Removing Total Price Interventions on Selected Agricultural Products and Inputs, 1960–82

(millions of U.S. dollars)

Category	1960–64	1965–69	1970–74	1975–79	1980–82
Wheat	11.5	7.5	36.1	50.9	51.7
Beef	52.1	25.4	27.6	−15.5	12.7
Milk	2.6	1.0	5.8	−2.5	−2.7
Fruits	0.1	0.9	2.2	−1.4	11.8
Nitrogen	0.9	0.6	0.8	0.1	0.4
Tractors	−0.4	0.1	−2.0	−9.1	−6.7
Other machinery	−0.2	−3.2	−3.8	−1.6	−1.0
Total	66.6	32.3	66.7	20.9	66.2

Source: Hurtado, Valdés, and Muchnik (1990).

Chile's agricultural trade earnings under a nonintervention scenario would have been much more substantial during 1960–64. That is, foreign exchange earned from agricultural trade as a percentage of total export earnings would have been 10 percent higher. During the period 1965–74 the earnings from agricultural exports would have ranged from 1 to 8 percent more. After 1977 the increase would have been less significant. In absolute terms, the estimated increment would have ranged from a high of US$166 million in 1974 to a low of US$24 million in 1979.

Wheat and beef would have been the principal products causing a change in the trade balance. If intervention had not occurred, their higher domestic prices would have resulted in greater domestic production and lower domestic consumption, thus resulting in a reduction of imports. Wheat in particular would have become an exportable during most years, especially during the period 1962–65 and in the years after 1974.

The substantial expansion in net farm exports that actually took place, beginning in 1983–84, is beyond what we would expect from extrapolating the model's projections. A reasonable hypothesis is that the regulatory framework and the economic policies of the early 1980s were drastically different from those in the 1960s and early 1970s. Thus, the econometrically estimated parameters could reflect a high inelasticity with respect to investments in products requiring a long gestation period (such as fruits) in the 1960s and 1970s. In contrast, guarantees against expropriation of land, a high real exchange rate (except during 1979–82), and a strong political commitment toward an outward-oriented trade policy probably gave investors different expectations after 1973.

Effect on the Government Budget of Removal of Direct Intervention

During the period under study, the government collected duties on imports of wheat, beef, milk, fertilizer, tractors, and agricultural machinery, and collected revenues from a tax on domestically produced wine.[7] Government expenditures included fertilizer subsidies, subsidized credit,[8] rail transport subsidies, forestry subsidies, and drawbacks on selected agricultural exports. The Food Marketing Board (ECA) generated revenues from its operations in some years and suffered losses in others, and was accounted for accordingly. Food consumption subsidies for preschool children and pregnant mothers in low-income families were also important.

The effects of direct agricultural pricing policies on the government budget during the period 1960–83 are summarized in table 4-7. The table shows that pricing policies had a negative effect on the govern-

Table 4-7. Summary of the Effect of Pricing Policies on the Government Budget, 1960–83

Period	Total revenues[a]	Total expenditures[b]	Net revenues[c]	Total budget[d]	Budget deficit[e]
	(annual average of millions of 1985 Chilean pesos)			(average annual percentage rate)	
1960–64	1,625	3,929	−2,304	−0.7	−3.4
1965–69	10,112	7,159	2,953	0.5	5.6
1970–74	14,144	8,883	5,261	1.4	5.1
1975–79	8,593	3,445	5,148	0.8	8.1
1980–83	6,256	2,755	3,501	0.5	−5.7

a. Includes tariff revenues, taxes on wine production and operational surplus of ECA, the parastatal. The period 60–64 does not include 1960. The period 80–83 does not include 1983.

b. Includes the milk program, subsidies on fertilizers and railway transport, credit subsidies from INDAP, CORA, and Central Bank, drawback on exports, and operational deficit of ECA.

c. Corresponds to (a)–(b).

d. Ratio between net revenues and total government expenditure. The period 60–64 does not include 1960. The period 70–74 only includes 1970 and 1974. The period 80–83 only includes 1980 and 1981.

e. Ratio between net revenues and government budget deficit. The period 60–64 does not include 1960. The period 70–74 only includes 1970 and 1974. The period 80–83 only includes 1980 and 1981.

ment budget between 1960 and 1964; thereafter, the government derived revenues because of direct intervention in agricultural prices. The effect during the years 1978–81 was not too different from the one observed for the years 1955–70. The last two columns of table 4-7 present estimated net revenue as proportions of the total government budget and the government budget deficit. Annual net losses owing to pricing policy during the years 1960–64 ranged from 0.5 to 1.1 percent of the government budget, which was equivalent to 2.0 to 5.7 percent of the total budget deficit. From 1965 onward, annual net revenues from direct intervention in agricultural pricing ranged from 0.3 to 2.8 percent of the total budget. Compared with other developing countries, including Argentina and Brazil, agricultural price intervention had only minor effects on Chile's budget.

Effect on Sectoral Income Transfers

The effects of direct intervention in farm prices on foreign exchange earnings and intersectoral income transfers were at the forefront of the debate on agricultural price policy in Chile during the 1950s and 1960s. At that time, the negative agricultural balance of trade was offered as evidence of the inefficiency of agriculture and a reason for land reform. Although there was some recognition of the possibility of transfers out of agriculture because of output price policies, the counterargument was that agriculture was subsidized by public investments and input subsidies. To measure the intersectoral transfers, we must include public investments, input subsidies, and revenues from direct taxation.

The level and the composition of public investment in Chilean agriculture varied significantly between 1960 and 1984. Between 1967 and 1969, outlays of the Development Corporation (CORFO) for new state companies involved in marketing farm inputs and farm products increased substantially. The late 1960s also saw a major rise in government expenditures on agrarian reform. By 1970, the last year of the Frei administration, government outlays for agrarian reform programs constituted more than 60 percent of total public investment in agriculture.

Under the Allende administration in the early 1970s, the government created numerous vertically integrated state enterprises to monopolize the processing and marketing of agricultural goods. These included ECA (cereals), ENAFRI (fruit), SOCAGRO (meat), CO-MARSA (oil seeds), SACOOP (vegetables), and SOCORA (exports from farm cooperatives). Meanwhile, expenditures for agrarian reform remained strong.

Under the military regime that assumed power in 1973, the aggregate level of government expenditures on agriculture declined, and there were shifts in spending priorities. Funding for agrarian reform came to a halt in 1979, after all the expropriated land had been assigned. The military government also reduced expenditures on farm parastatals by selling most of them to the private sector. Expenditures on forestation, however, increased substantially, and by 1983 such expenditures accounted for 25 percent of all government outlays on agriculture. What did not change under the military government—and what has remained stable ever since the creation INIA in 1964—has been the percentage of agricultural sector expenditures for research and development. These have remained at about 15 percent ever since 1964.

Three different estimates of government investment in agriculture were made for this study. The first estimate includes all expenditures, including those made to support land reform. This estimate includes appropriations for purchases of land and other assets, as well as subsidized loans not allocable to specific products. The second estimate is similar to the first, except that it omits the government outlays made to support agrarian reform. The third estimate is like the second, except that it omits subsidized loans to small farmers by Instituto Nacional de Desarrollo Agropecurario (INDAP). It is the second estimate that is used here.

Agricultural Credit Subsidies

Chile historically has shown a predilection toward using preferential credit to stimulate agricultural production. Estimates of the amount of credit granted by the Central Bank, the Banco del Estado, CORA, and INDAP during the period 1960–83 were used to estimate the annual subsidy, based on the London interbank offered rate (LIBOR) plus 6 percent—the latter being the estimated country risk. In general, short-term loans provided a larger absolute subsidy than longer-term loans, partly because of the smaller volume of longer-term credit and partly because the outstanding balances of the latter were adjusted for inflation.

Government Revenues

The sources were revenues from land and wealth taxes (the latter during 1964–74), sales taxes (later replaced by a value added tax), and the wine tax that was collected during 1960–83. The value added tax has become the major source of tax revenue from agriculture, despite a significant increase in land tax receipts.

The Change in Resource Transfers Resulting from Removal of Direct Intervention

The change in value added that would have occurred if government intervention in agricultural prices had been removed, measured at the actual level of agricultural production, is shown in table 4-8. The table indicates that:

- Beef production was taxed from 1960 to 1974 and subsidized from 1975 to 1984. Wheat production was mostly taxed during the years 1970–79 (especially 1970–76) and was subsidized in the other years of the study period. There was a consistently positive transfer of resources to milk producers throughout the period. Fruit producers also received a positive, albeit small, transfer.

- The domestic prices of nitrogen fertilizer, pesticides, tractors, and machinery were higher than border prices throughout the period 1960–84, which caused transfers of resources from agriculture for virtually the entire period.

- When both output and input prices are considered, we find that producers of the five agricultural products suffered a net transfer loss during the period 1965–79. However, they had net transfer gains during the years 1960–64 and 1980–84. We attribute this

Table 4-8. Resource Transfers into and out of Agricultural Sector Due to Removal of Direct Price Intervention, 1960–84

(millions of 1985 Chilean pesos)

Category	1960–64	1965–69	1970–74	1975–79	1980–84
Wheat	155	438	−426	−456	583
Beef	−687	−2,539	−2,467	343	658
Milk	884	528	321	585	362
Grapes	5	21	50	5	0
Apples	5	21	53	0	0
Nitrogen	−19	−209	−627	−95	−204
Phosphorus	235	−5	270	−102	−210
Pesticides	−1	−28	−68	−101	−103
Tractors	−30	−256	−255	−248	−43
Other machinery	−23	−135	−39	−76	−34
Total	524	−2,164	−3,188	−145	1,009

Note: (+ = in; − = out)
Source: Author's calculations.

latter gain to the implementation of a price bands scheme from 1982 to 1984. Producers of these five farm products received positive transfers during the Alessandri administration, suffered negative transfers during the Frei and Allende administrations, and suffered negative transfers during the first two or three years of the military regime. During the rest of the period, transfers were positive.

Table 4-9 shows the overall transfers after both direct and indirect intervention have been eliminated. Overvaluation of the exchange

Table 4-9. Resource Transfers into Agricultural Sector Due to Removal of Total Price Interventions, 1960–84

(average millions of 1985 Chilean pesos per year)

Category	1960–64	1965–69	1970–74	1975–79	1980–82
Wheat	−3,562	−1,209	−803	3,113	64
Beef	−6,366	−5,939	−3,170	4,851	−487
Milk	392	85	295	2,062	29
Grapes	−28	11	64	292	−99
Apples	−23	2	53	288	−44
Nitrogen	319	−35	−1,128	−861	270
Phosphorus	808	282	305	−1,116	−13
Pesticides	99	35	−59	−350	−22
Tractors	392	−64	−67	−978	−7
Other machinery	219	−20	−57	−303	91
Total	−7,750	−6,852	−4,567	6,998	−218

Note: (+ = in; − = out)
Source: Author's calculations.

rate changed the direct positive transfers to agriculture during the 1960–64 period into negative transfers out of agriculture and rein-forced the transfer of resources out of agriculture during the period 1965–74. Large transfers to agriculture during the years 1976–77 were the result of undervaluation, followed by small positive transfers un-til 1980. Transfers of resources to agriculture turned negative during the 1981–82, again reflecting overvaluation. Note that the years of overvaluation placed an implicit tax on the product prices received by farmers but reduced the implicit tax on the prices of inputs. The net effect was a substantial transfer of resources out of agriculture during the study period, except during the years 1975–79.

A summary of the resource transfers into and out of agriculture is presented in table 4-10. This table shows both the transfers caused by price intervention and those resulting from government expendi-tures. The last two lines of the table report absolute net values (in 1985 pesos) of direct and total price intervention. The table categories of taxes, subsidies, and price transfers show net transfers into agricul-ture before 1975 because of direct intervention and prior to 1980 be-cause of total intervention. After 1975, taxes increased substantially in real terms, while credit subsidies declined. An increase in transfers into agriculture from eliminating total intervention was observed dur-ing the period 1965–74, although the figures exclude expenditures on land reform. The first five listings in table 4-10 refer to all of agricul-ture, while the rest refer to the five products only. This probably

Table 4-10. Transfers in and out of Agriculture if All Intervention is Removed, 1960–84

(average millions of 1985 Chilean pesos per year)

Category	1960–64	1965–69	1970–74	1975–79	1980–84
Taxes	−3,637	−6,019	−6,833	−9,847	−19,581
Public investment	6,815	10,605	9,206	5,022	4,527
Research & extention	438	835	1,363	1,492	1,504
Credit subsidy	4,250	6,699	18,055	967	2,830
Transport subsidy	149	894	499	0	0
Subtotal	8,015	13,014	22,290	−2,366	−10,720
Direct price intervention	524	−2,164	−3,188	−145	1,009
Total price intervention	−7,750	−6,852	−4,567	6,998	−218
Net transfer (direct)	8,539	10,850	19,102	−2,511	−9,711
Net transfer (total)	265	6,162	17,723	4,632	−10,938

Note: In taxes, the first period does not include 1960, the period 1975–79 does not include 1978, and the last period includes only 1980 and 1981.

In public investment, the first period does not include 1960 and the period 1970–74 includes only 1970 and 1974.

In research and extention the last period does not include 1984.

The subsidy on railway transport applied only between 1964 and 1973.

(+ = in; – = out)

Source: Author's calculations.

Table 4-11. Net Transfers as Proportion of GDP, 1961–81

(average annual percentage)

Period	Removing direct distortions	Removing total distortions
1961–64	0.62	0.16
1965–69	0.59	0.33
1970–74[a]	0.53	0.63
1975–79[b]	−0.13	0.28
1980–81	0.32	−0.22

a. Includes 1970 and 1974.
b. Does not include 1978.
Source: Author's calculations.

exaggerates net transfers into agriculture because it excludes taxation on commodities other than the five included in this estimate. Table 4-11, on transfers relative to GDP, shows that total net transfers to agriculture through the elimination of all types of intervention would have been equivalent to approximately 5 percent of agricultural GDP (except during the years 1970–74), or less than one-half of 1 percent of GDP.

Income Distribution Effects of Removing Intervention

The price of food historically has been a sensitive issue in Chile, because urban lower-income households spend a much greater share of family income on food than do those with larger incomes. To the extent that higher prices to producers result in higher rural employment, however, price intervention can have profound repercussions on rural labor income. Because there have been no household budget surveys representative of rural areas of Chile, our analysis of the effects of price intervention on personal income covers only urban areas. Conversely, analysis of the effects of price intervention on functional income applies only to agriculture.

The analysis of household real income concentrates on changes in the cost of the food basket of low-income and medium-income urban families relative to the cost of the food basket for the high-income group.[9] The analysis is then broken down to show the impacts of direct and indirect intervention. Differences in the composition of household expenditures among income classes and in price intervention among commodities influence the personal income distribution effects.

On the basis of a 1977–78 survey of urban households in metropolitan Santiago, three income groups were specified—the lowest-income quartile, the upper-income quintile, and a medium-income category covering 55 percent of all households. Approximately one-

Table 4-12. Percentage Change in the Relative Cost of the
Consumers Basket for Low and Medium Groups with Respect
to the High Income Group, 1960–84

Period	Removing Direct Intervention		Removing Total Intervention	
	Low income	*Medium income*	*Low income*	*Medium income*
1960–64	−1.5	1.3	10.1	7.8
1965–69	−0.8	0.2	8.9	5.8
1970–74	3.0	2.1	12.1	6.5
1975–79	−0.1	0.5	−0.3	−1.5
1980–84	−2.4	−1.1	−0.3	−0.1

Source: Author's calculations.

third of expenditures by the three income groups were for home
goods. The consumption basket of the high-income families con-
tained more manufactured importables and nontradables, but the
share of food was lower. Among food imports, wheat derivatives
(bread and others) were the most important items, followed by milk,
cheese, and eggs, and then meats.

Table 4-12 presents the percentage changes in the annual cost of the
food basket of a typical low- and a typical medium-income urban
household as a result of removing all intervention. Because wheat
and milk were protected, removing direct intervention would have
slightly decreased the cost of food to low-income households (except
for the period 1970–74) but would have raised the cost of food for
medium-income families (except for 1980–84) relative to the cost of
high-income families. The taxation of beef would have affected the
high-income group more, given the lesser importance of beef in the
food basket of low-income families. Intervention in the price of milk
implicitly taxed the medium-income family less than the upper-
income family because of the smaller share of milk and milk products
in the medium-income diet.

Overall, direct intervention did not have a significant impact on the
food costs of low- and medium-income consumers relative to high-
income consumers. The change in the relative cost of the consumer
baskets of the first two groups that would have resulted from the
elimination of such intervention would have been less than 2.5 percent in most years.

Total intervention had a greater impact on income distribution before 1974. During the period 1960–74, removal of total intervention
raised the cost of living for low- and middle-income households by
between 6 and 12 percent relative to that of high-income households
because the richer households consumed more protected importables
and nontradables. After 1974, however, total intervention had no
effect on income distribution (except in 1977).

These results reflect the instantaneous effects of intervention on personal income, which are politically sensitive. The long-run effect, however, may be different as a result of changes in employment and wages in agriculture. Thus, there is a need to examine the effects on wages and returns to capital, which we do next.

Effect of Removing Direct and Total Intervention on Returns to Labor and Capital

We first determine the evolution of the total wage bill in agriculture when both direct and total intervention are assumed away. We then measure the impact of price intervention on labor's share of income. Agricultural wage and rural urban migration equations were used to estimate annual real wages per worker and employment of hired labor under two scenarios.

Table 4-13 shows the evolution of labor's actual share of agricultural income in real terms over the period 1960–81. During 1960–71 it increased by about 12 percent, but it then fell during 1972 and 1973, so that the share in 1975–79 was about 30 percent below that of 1970–74. By 1980–81, it had recovered to the level observed during 1970. Comparing labor's actual share of income with hypothetical evolution of the real wage bill under our two scenarios shows that the elimination of direct intervention would have caused no systematic difference in labor's share of the sector's income; eliminating all intervention would have lowered labor's share of sectoral income, relative to the actual, except during 1980–81.

Changes in the real wage bill arise from either changes in real wages or in employment. Taxing wheat production through exchange rate overvaluation and industrial protection reduced employment relative to a situation of no intervention. For example, removal of total intervention in 1974 would have raised the real wage rate by some 14 percent. Protection for wheat production, as in 1977, however, meant that labor demand would have been lower without intervention. In turn, this would have lowered the real wage rate by 13 percent during 1978.

Table 4-13. The Share of Labor Income in Agricultural GDP under Alternative Policies, 1960–81

Period	Actual	Removing direct	Removing total
1960–64	0.34	0.41	0.25
1965–69	0.36	0.34	0.23
1970–74	0.38	0.28	0.21
1975–79	0.27	0.23	0.18
1980–81	0.30	0.32	0.31

Source: Author's calculations.

These results reflect the importance of wheat in Chilean agriculture. Although wheat farming is not very labor-intensive in comparison with other commodities, such as fruit, the large amount of land in wheat suggests that more labor was employed in wheat production than in all other agricultural activities combined.

According to national account estimates, labor's actual share of agricultural income ranged from 22 to 45 percent during the 1960s and 1970s. It rose from 37 to 45 percent during the period 1971–72 but declined substantially in 1973. Between 1973 and 1984 it remained below the 35 percent of the 1960s.

Effects of Price Interventions on Domestic Price and Consumption Stabilization

One objective of agricultural price intervention is to reduce the transmission of border price variability into domestic markets. Given the wage-good character of some farm products, trade policy instruments are often used to try to reduce food price variability. This objective is distinct from those underlying the levels of nominal protection. In this section we first address the question of what domestic price variability would have been if there had been no price intervention, relative to the actual variability that prevailed during 1960–84. This is followed by an analysis of the extent to which fluctuations in domestic food production influenced aggregate domestic consumption and food prices.

We used several alternative measures of variability to capture variation in both prices and annual changes in prices, and they all indicated the same results. Our results indicate that the actual price variability of wheat, beef, and milk was substantially less than it would have been in the absence of direct intervention. For grapes and apples, however, there were no statistically significant differences between actual price stability and price stability in the absence of direct intervention. Domestic price stability (at the official exchange rate) was clearly sought for products with a large weight in total household expenditures. Wheat (and its derivatives), meat, and milk (and its derivatives) and weights of 10, 8, and 4 percent, respectively, in the consumer price index (CPI). In contrast, apples and grapes had a combined weight of only 2.5 percent. The same results (except for wheat) were found if it were assumed that all price intervention had been eliminated. We would expect direct intervention to be used to achieve price stability, of course, since macroeconomic policies are normally used to achieve other objectives, such as reductions in unemployment, deficits in the current account, and inflation.

Were fluctuations in production associated with fluctuations in domestic consumption (availability) or prices? We found a relatively high positive correlation between production and consumption of wheat (0.48), milk (0.50), and beef (0.81). In short, the analysis indicates that agricultural trade policy reduced the transmission of border price variability to the domestic prices of products that had significant weight in the cost-of-living index. This applies to direct intervention (that is, at the official exchange rate), and not to indirect intervention. But the policy did not eliminate all association between fluctuations in per capita production of tradables and consumption of wheat, milk, or beef.

The Political Economy of Price Intervention

This interpretation of Chilean economic policy involves the interpretation of motives, which is an exercise fraught with risk. Our model is offered as a framework for developing a number of scenarios consistent with the evidence examined. Alternative scenarios may also be consistent with that evidence. Intervention in agricultural prices can be seen as part of a set of policies that also include intervention in labor and capital markets. By intervening in farm prices, the government attempts to achieve a compromise among different pressure groups.

Given enough policy instruments, a government can have considerable effect on real wages and the sectoral distribution of income. Unquestionably, however, the policy changes described here were strongly influenced by events that could not be foreseen by policymakers.[10] Five pressure groups were identified: agricultural workers, agricultural capitalists, nonagricultural workers, nonagricultural capitalists, and retirees or pensioners.

During the period 1960–71, the price structure was significantly distorted, interest rates were generally subsidized, and the rate of inflation was usually high. During the period 1974–84, however, direct intervention was gradually reduced, tariffs were reduced to a uniform low rate, the capital market was liberalized, and foreign credits to private institutions were allowed. During the second period the annual rate of inflation decreased to around 20 percent.

Intervention during the 1961–70 period reflects the attempts of the government to effect a compromise between urban workers and agricultural and nonagricultural capitalists. In contrast, the process of economic reform during the period 1974–83 was much broader in scope. During the 1961–70 period the simple correlation coefficient between real wages and the real exchange rate was 0.77 whereas, for the period 1975–83 it was 0.67, while the real exchange rate was found to be strongly correlated with relative agricultural prices for the whole period (0.81). This suggests that the effect of agricultural price policies on real wages was asymmetric in both periods. This raises the question of whether farm prices could have been liberalized after 1974 if the activities of trade unions had not been curtailed.

Our model relates agricultural prices to real wages and labor costs in the nonfarm sector through

$$(1) \qquad W_{NA}/P_{NA} \equiv W_{NA}/P + \alpha \, (P_A/P_{NA})$$

where W_{NA}/P_{NA} represents the real wage as a cost to nonagricultural employers (that is, deflated by the nonagricultural price index), W_{NA}/P represents the real wages of urban workers (that is, deflated by a consumer price index), α is the share of income that urban workers spend on agricultural goods, and P_A/P_{NA} represents relative farm prices (all variables measured in logarithms).

Farm prices vary as a result of changes in the real exchange rate, changes in agricultural price policy, and changes in the prices of nonagricultural goods. Assuming that real urban wages (W_{NA}/P) remain constant, a rise in farm prices implies a rise in urban labor costs (W_{NA}/P_{NA}).

Even though agriculture's share of GDP was small, the share of agriculture in total consumption was large. Those in the lowest quintile spent 50 percent of their income on food, and food costs for all but the rich amounted to 40 percent of their income. Although transfers to agriculture as a share of GDP were small, that does not necessarily mean that agricultural pricing policy did not have an effect on real urban wages. Therefore, we focus on urban wages rather than on transfers to agriculture.

During 1960–71, Chile's labor unions became strong enough to win wage increases that exceeded government guidelines. In short, urban wages during the period were not much affected by government policy. After 1974, by contrast, the government was able to exert much more influence on urban wages. The data suggest that one government objective after 1974 was to maintain urban wages as a constant fraction of urban income. This implies that urban labor costs also remained constant.

Results of the Model

Given the level or real urban income, equation (1) shows a positive correlation of 0.67 between relative farm prices and labor's share of nonagricultural income (θ) for the period 1960–71. The correlation between the real exchange rate and θ was 0.60.

For the period 1975–83 θ was assumed to be determined by government policy, which implies a given W_{NA}/P_{NA}. This then produces a negative correlation between relative farm prices and urban wages (W_{NA}/P). Empirically, this association proved to be true, with a correlation coefficient of -0.73.

In summary, farm prices were set by the government between 1960 and 1971, whereas wages were determined by the labor market. Both prices jointly determined the urban cost of labor, and that affected the return to nonagricultural capital. In the period 1974–84, however, θ (and W_{NA}/P_{NA}) were set by government policy, so that policies affecting P_A/P_{NA} determined real urban wages.

Investment and employment are not fixed in the long run, however, and our long-run model shows the link between changes in farm prices and changes in nonagricultural investment. If real wages (W_{NA}/P) in the nonagricultural sector in 1960–71 were fixed exogenously (and therefore the labor market did not clear), increases in farm prices raised the θ and W_{NA}/P_{NA}, thus reducing returns to capital and, therefore, reducing nonagricultural investment as well.

To ameliorate this effect on nonagricultural investment, the government could have subsidized interest rates, and in this way compensated investors. In a world of downward wage rigidity like that of 1960–71, interest rates could be interpreted as the instrument that was used to prevent the higher labor costs resulting from higher farm prices from depressing nonagricultural investment. Alternatively, the government could have avoided raising farm prices to avoid depressing nonagricultural investment and partially compensated farmers by expanding cheap credit.

Thus, in the 1960–71 period, agricultural labor played the role of a slack variable for the government, given the strong labor movement in urban areas and the government's desire to avoid reductions in nonfarm investment. The losers in this situation were the agricultural laborers and the pensioners whose savings were used to finance subsidized credit programs.

Farm prices in each year of the period 1965–70 were higher than the average for the years 1960–64. This was the result of price-fixing policies, border regulations administered by an ECA, and the crawling peg exchange rate policy implemented in 1967. In public speeches, government officials insisted that land reform would be successful only if agricultural prices were attractive enough to induce new investments in agriculture.[11] In summary, the creation of powerful trade unions in agriculture, combined with land reform, raised farm prices substantially.

This increase in farm prices should have induced an increase in urban labor costs, thus adversely affecting nonagricultural investment. The fact that nonfarm capital accumulation did not decline significantly was a result of an expansion in subsidized credit. As a percentage of total nonagricultural capital, loans granted by the Banco del Estado were 74 percent larger in 1970 alone than in the entire 1960–64 period. This credit, usually at subsidized and often negative real interest rates, helped to increase the profitability of nonagricultural private investments. Indirect evidence suggests that retired workers paid for part of the subsidy, because pensions increased significantly less than urban wages.

The increase in farm prices to 1970 favored agricultural growth but depressed nonagricultural growth and capital accumulation. Because agriculture accounted for no more than 10 percent of total GDP, the costs of this strategy were more visible than its benefits. Yet, it should be recognized that wage increases were more responsible for the depressive effect on urban capital accumulation than the higher farm prices were. It is likely that real urban wages would have increased even if farm prices had remained constant. This could have been done without raising urban labor costs W_{NA}/P_{NA} only by decreasing farm prices. That was not a realistic alternative, however, given the agriculture's desire to aid agriculture.

Finally it should be noted that the rural–urban conflict created by the increase in farm prices also became a conflict inside the government. The following quotation is illustrative:

> (Ministries of) Ecomony and Agriculture consistently disagreed over the question of agricultural prices in relation to inflation. Dirinco prevailed upon its ministry to insist on the stabilization of food costs to the consumer. Delaying price increases until the very last minute, however, placed a financial squeeze on the agricultural sector and meant that the cooperatives under the supervision of the Ministry of Agriculture operated at a loss. When the costs of production of "asentamientos" were superior to revenues, CORA had to restrict new investment and appeal for deficit financing, and the Ministry of Agriculture argued that the lack of economic incentives for the "campesinos" detracted from the social goals of the program . . . (Cleaves 1974: 97).

At the end of 1973, the new military regime faced hyperinflation, low levels of foreign reserves, a disrupted productive structure, and a huge fiscal deficit. Subsidized credit was out of the question. The implementation of a drastic stabilization program and trade liberalization in 1975 led to a drastic decline in real urban wages. That decline helped to prevent a further fall in nonagricultural investment.

During the years 1974–77, farm prices rose sharply above the 1970 level as a result of both an increase in the real exchange rate and the implementation of trade liberalization. By 1976, relative farm prices were almost two times higher than in 1970. This increase in farm prices did not imply an increase in θ, however. Urban wages declined, and in 1975 were only 60 percent of wages in 1970. Because of the fall in real wages, the increase in farm prices did not impose many costs on nonagricultural capitalists. The rate of growth in industrial capital during these years was relatively low compared with historical values, owing mainly to the government's policy of severely restricting expenditures in an effort to reduce the deficit. Furthermore, foreign political constraints forced the government to generate a current account surplus in 1976. Between 1975 and 1977, agricultural output grew at rates substantially higher than the historical ones. Capital accumulation in rural areas during this period was negative, however, as a consequence of extremely high domestic real interest rates and reductions in the amount of credit available to small farmers.

Foreign credit inflows increased significantly during the years 1978–82, inducing a fall in the real exchange rate, which depressed farm prices. The foreign credit allowed increases in urban wages and greater investment in the nonagricultural sector, however. Urban real wages in 1981 surpassed the 1970 level for the first time, and θ reached the level of 1970. Both investors and laborers in the urban sector benefited, but net external debt increased and the agricultural sector grew at a slower rate.

Mainly because of an abrupt fall in external capital inflows, Chile's situation became critical in 1982. The government reacted by drastically increasing the real exchange. In the process, farm prices increased substantially. The new agreements favored capitalists (urban and rural) at the expense of workers. The increase in farm prices did not affect nonagricultural investment, mainly because urban real wages fell below the 1970 level.

Implications of Alternative Policy Options

The impact of agricultural prices on the urban wage rate and on the return to capital in the nonagricultural sector, as well as a non-agricultural investment equation was estimated. The empirical estimates should be interpreted with care because the underlying structure of the urban labor market changed over the period of estimation. The estimated short-run model (constant overall capital) and the long-run investment equations were econometrically quite robust. It is worth highlighting that the observed impact of changes in farm prices over the real cost of labor to employers (W_{NA}/P_{NA}) is high. We get an elasticity of 0.68, which is higher than the share of all agricultural products in the cost-of-living index.

Four dynamic simulations within the sample period were performed in order to test the model. In these simulations, discussed below, farm prices and the real exchange rate were treated as exogenously determined.

Absence of Total Intervention with Rigid Real Wages in the Urban Sector.

This scenario assumes an increase in farm prices while urban real wages remain in the same as those that actually prevailed during the period under analysis. An increase in farm prices has two effects. Resources (capital and labor) should flow into agriculture, and second, labor's share of urban income should increase, reducing the profitability of urban capital and, thereby, depressing urban capital investment. For the period 1961–70, a significant fall in urban capital investment is observed, especially when total price intervention is removed. In fact, under this scenario, nonagricultural capital investment in 1971 would have been only 79 percent of the actual figure. If only commercial and direct intervention are removed, this percentage becomes 90 percent.

Earlier it was shown that, as a consequence of removing all intervention, the stock of agricultural capital in 1982 would have been about 7 percent larger than it actually was. Because agricultural capital was only 10 percent of total capital in 1982, it suggests that, when urban real wages are rigid, nonintervention might have adverse consequences on capital accumulation in the economy as a whole, and on employment as well. Our simulation indicates that, assuming no intervention, nonagricultural employment would have been 94 percent of the actual figure in 1971, and 87 percent, assuming no direct and commercial intervention. However, it is difficult to believe that urban wages would have grown systematically while employment grew at a slower rate. Eventually, a rise in unemployment would debilitate the power of labor unions, allowing a decrease in wages.

For the period 1977–83, the analysis shows the consequences for nonagricultural capital of commercial nonintervention and total nonintervention in a context where urban wages remain at the levels that actually prevailed. If only commercial policy intervention in both agriculture and nonagriculture is removed, the level of nonagricultural capital remains quite similar to its actual value during the period 1976–83. This is the outcome when direct intervention has been used to protect some products but not others. The net effect is that for the period 1976–83, undistorted farm prices would have been quite similar to the prevailing ones, leaving the level of nonagricultural capital virtually unchanged. The above considerations suggest that when trade liberalization took place, the behavior of urban wages did not place binding restrictions on farm price policy.

Absence of Total Intervention with a Constant Fraction of Labor Income in Nonagriculture (θ)

Under this scenario, all intervention is assumed to be nonexistent and is set at the levels that actually prevailed during the 1960–71 period. Direct intervention in agricultural and nonagricultural prices is removed under two alternatives: one when θ is maintained at its prevailing level, and the other when industrial real wages are maintained at their prevailing actual values.

Absence of Total Intervention with Urban Real Wage at 1964 Level

This scenario indicates that industrial wages held at the 1964 level would have substantially reduced the adverse effects of nonintervention on industrial investment. In 1971, the level of industrial investment, assuming no direct intervention, would have been only 6 percent below the actual figure. Clearly, however, keeping wages constant would have caused difficulties with the urban labor unions.

Nonintervention and the Use of Subsidized Credit

It should be clear at this point that a policy of nonintervention in agricultural prices generates a conflict with nonagricultural capitalists and urban workers. Theoretically, at least, a policy of providing abundant subsidized credit would prevent this problem. The model was used to estimate the amount of public credit that would have been required to keep urban real wages and nonagricultural investments at the actual levels, assuming no intervention of any kind. This alternative did not seem to be feasible, however. The additional credit that would have been required to compensate the urban sector, assuming no intervention, would have been between 6.7 and 32.6 percent of total public expenditure in each selected year.

Summary and Implications

These results suggest some important considerations with relation to the feasibility of agricultural price liberalization policy. A combination of a "cheap credit" policy and a wage policy oriented to the control of excessive wage demands will reduce the cost of agricultural price liberalization in terms of capital accumulation in urban sectors. Then, it is easier to liberalize agriculture during a period when the country enjoys a stronger situation in its external accounts, such as favorable terms of trade, foreign exchange reserves or access to external borrowing, so as to ease the burden of adjustment for those sectors who will lose in the short run. Finally, the liberalization process should be implemented within a macroeconomic framework that should be considered "feasible" by the economic agents. To be feasible, this framework should include compensation mechanisms designed to share the costs of agricultural liberalization between different pressure groups in the country. If these costs are not shared, the conflict with urban workers (in the case of a too restrictive wage policy), nonagricultural capitalists (in the case of exaggerated wage demands), or nonvoluntary savers (in the case where an excessive credit subsidy is required), will be inevitable. If economic agents foresee the commercial policy reform as a feasible project they may believe in the success of the experiment, allowing capital and labor to flow faster, which, in turn, would allow the benefits of the reform to be captured earlier.

The approach suggests that: (a) The analysis of a farm price policy reform is enriched if it is analyzed in conjunction with other related policies. In Chile, it is difficult to understand agricultural price policy if the analysis fails to consider urban wage and credit policies, and (b) The approach highlights the importance of capital accumulation in the economy. In an economy where agriculture is a small fraction of GDP, implications of other policies on capital accumulation in the nonagricultural sector acquire importance.

The analysis of the Chilean economy suggests a tradeoff between (1) agricultural terms of trade; (2) real wages in the urban sector; (3) return to capital in the nonagricultural sector; (4) foreign borrowing; and (5) the supply of domestic subsidized credit. Raising farm prices (1), and maintaining the levels of (3), (4), and (5) implies a drastic decline in urban real wages (2).

The policy simulation examined in this study consists of moving from actual (distorted) agricultural prices to border prices after correcting for exchange rate misalignment and elimination of industrial protection. An implication of (a) above is that these policies have potential effects on variables such as wages, functional distribution of income, and others, which could differ significantly according to what is assumed about other related policies (that is, credit, urban wages, foreign capital flows, and so forth).

Furthermore, (b) implies that agricultural price policy could affect not only the intersectoral allocation of capital, but also overall capital accumulation in the economy. This effect will vary according to which related policies prevail. The effect on overall capital accumulation may be particularly important in middle-income countries where food is an important share of consumer expenditures, and where the nonagricultural sector is relatively large and could be negatively affected by an increase in farm prices. Conversely, in lower-income countries where the agricultural sector is large relative to GDP, increases in capital accumulation in agriculture and the probable increase in agriculture's demand for nonagricultural goods and services may offset the direct effects of higher P_A/P_{NA} on investment in the nonagricultural sector.

Three findings of this study are especially notable. First, indirect intervention in agricultural prices in Chile had a much greater impact on the agricultural sector than direct intervention. That is, Chile's macroeconomic policies (including its policy of protecting domestic industry) led to overvalued real exchange rates that adversely affected the agricultural sector.

The reason that agricultural producers ignored these types of intervention until the 1980s is unclear. One explanation may be that the effects of indirect intervention are, by nature, less visible than the effects of direct intervention in prices. Another possible explanation is that agricultural producers believed that they had little influence on macroeconomic policies (which were unstable in any case) and that they consequently paid more attention to direct intervention, over which they had much more influence.

Then, our study indicates that in assessing the impact of eliminating intervention in agricultural prices, government intervention in other markets (for example, factor markets) cannot be ignored. Specifically, the operations of the labor market may have a strong effect on what happens to the economy when intervention in agricultural prices is halted.

Finally, an end to agricultural price intervention will lead in the short run to losses of income for certain groups. The chances that the reform will succeed—that is, persist over time—will depend on the political power of those groups and the size of the losses they suffer. The availability of additional resources to compensate those groups for their losses during the transition period (for instance, through an increase in terms of trade) will make the reform more likely to succeed.

Notes

1. Our special thanks go to Maurice Schiff and Anne O. Krueger for their suggestions, and to Juan Eduardo Coeymans and Yair Mundlak for providing us with investment and migration functions and some time series on capital. We would also like to thank Jorge Cauas, Sebastian Edwards, Yair Mundlak, Larry Sjaastad, and the participants at project workshops for constructive comments. We are greatly indebted to Jorge Quiroz and Pablo Barahona for helping us plan the study and doing the laborious computations required.

2. All figures for area are expressed in hectares of equal productive capacity measured in basic irrigated hectare (BIH) units.

3. The exchange rate misalignment was calculated using both the regression analysis used for the simulations, and an elasticity model similar to the one used in the other country studies in this volume. The misalignment was similar regardless of the method used.

4. Wine production during 1974–84 would also have increased. A relatively small increase in vineyard acreage would have been complemented by higher yields per hectare, resulting from lower nitrogen fertilizer prices.

5. We should warn that the output effects are based on estimates of protection at the official exchange rate, which are quite different from previous estimates of the protection for wheat and livestock, owing mainly to discrepancies in the adjustment made here to compensate for border prices.

6. The actual area planted in vineyards was consistently less than it would have been in the absence of all intervention, particularly after 1975, when the acreage would have been approximately 14 percent larger than the actual. The increase would have been the result of nonintervention in vine grape prices and a cross-price effect with competing crops.

7. Tariff revenues are overestimated because scheduled import tariff times import values was used instead of actual tariff revenues. State agencies such as ECA, Banco del Estado, and CORA were exempted from import tariffs. Unfortunately, no information was obtained on tariff revenues on these items.

8. Subsidized credit from CORA and INDAP, but not credit from Banco del Estado because the later represents a transfer from savers.

9. The methodology did not allow calculation of the proportional income gain or loss by income group but only of one income group relative to another income group. To calculate the former, one needs to know whether the adjustment in the real exchange rate is from adjustment in the nominal exchange rate or from the price of home goods. This was not determined from the model.

10. Under this approach, the focus is on interventions affecting the relative prices of agricultural and nonagricultural products (P_A/P_{NA}), rather than in explaining those sectoral policies affecting prices within agriculture, the latter reflecting direct price interventions. The intersectoral approach was chosen because (a) economywide policies had a bigger impact on prices than direct policies (particularly during 1960–75); (b) the output mix in most farms is quite diversified, particularly in central Chile; (c) agriculture represents a small fraction of GDP and food represents a high share in urban consumer's expenditures (half of CPI basket). Thus, food prices influence real wages.

11. See Corvalán (1969) for a speech by the Minister of Economics offering a social justification for raising farm prices.

References

Cleaves, P. 1974. *Bureaucratic Politics and Administration in Chile.* Berkeley, Los Angeles: University of California Press.

Coeymans, J.E. and Y. Mundlak. 1984. Un Modelo Econométrico para el Analisis del Crecimiento del Sector Angrícola Chileno. *Documento de Trabajo* 90. Instituto de Economía, Universidad Católica de Chile.

Corvalán, Rene. 1969. *Documentos Económicos.* Año IV, no. 3. Santiago, Chile.

Departamento de Economía Agraria. 1976. *Chile: Agricultural Sector Overview, 1964–74.* Facultad de Agronomía, Universidad Católica de Chile.

De Vylder. S. 1974. *Allende's Chile: The Political Economy of the Rise and Fall of the Unidad Popular.* Cambridge Latin American Studies.

Diario Oficial (various issues), Republica de Chile. Santiago.

Ffrench-Davis, Ricardo. 1973. *Políticas Económicas en Chile: 1952–1970.* Centro de Estudio de Plantificación, Ediciones Nueva Universidad, Universidad Católica de Chile.

Hurtado, Hernán, Alberto Valdés, and Eugenia Muchnik. 1990. *Trade, Exchange Rate, and Agricultural Pricing Policies in Chile.* A World Bank Comparative Study. Washington, D.C.

Sjaastad, Larry A. 1981. ''La Protección y el Volumen del Comercio en Chile: la Evidencia,'' *Cuadernos de Economia* no. 54–55. Universidad Católica de Chile.

5 Colombia

Jorge García García

This chapter analyzes the impact of government intervention on Colombian agricultural prices during 1960–83, the factors that determined the extent of that intervention, and its variations over time. The analysis covers direct intervention in agricultural prices at the product and input levels, and indirect intervention resulting from macroeconomic and exchange rate policies.

The first section introduces the main characteristics of the Colombian economy and its agricultural sector, and describes the types of government intervention in agricultural prices. The next sections present the effects of intervention on relative producer and consumer prices, agricultural output, net foreign exchange earnings, net government revenues, price stability, real transfers into and out of agriculture, and income distribution. The final section offers a brief history of agricultural pricing policies during the twentieth century and analyzes the factors that motivated reform of those policies.

Four products—coffee, cotton, rice, and wheat—were selected as representative of Colombian agriculture. Altogether, these four products account for about 45 percent of the value of Colombia's annual crop output. Colombia is the world's second largest producer of coffee, exports of which generate around 40 percent of Colombia's foreign exchange earnings. Cotton is also economically important; cotton production has a large impact on agricultural employment as well as on economic activity at the regional level. Wheat was selected because it is an important food commodity that is perennially imported by Colombia, even though the country's domestic wheat producers are regularly protected in their efforts to compete with foreign suppliers. Rice was also selected for analysis because of the government's intervention in Colombia's rice market. Intervention here has taken two forms—prohibition of rice imports when the price of domestic rice was not competitive internationally, and prohibition of exports when domestic rice did become competitive, chiefly because of production of new, high-yield varieties.

An Overview of the Colombian Economy and the Agricultural Sector

Colombia's 1985 census showed the total population to be about 28.5 million. The annual rate of population growth accelerated from 2 percent in the 1940s to almost 3.4 percent in the 1950s, fell to 2.8 percent in the mid-1960s to early 1970s, and fell again to 2.0 percent in the 1973–83 period. Rural–urban migration was the main factor in increasing the urban share of total population from less than one-third in 1938 to almost two-thirds in 1982.[1]

- Evolution of the Economy. Total gross domestic product (GDP) expanded at an annual average rate of 5.1 percent a year between 1960 and 1983, while per capita income increased 2.7 percent a year during the same period. Between 1960 and 1967, the economy grew at a rate of 4.7 percent a year. Diversification and expansion of noncoffee exports, together with increased domestic savings and investment, induced more rapid growth during 1967–74, when the rate reached 6.4 percent a year. The rate slipped to 5.4 percent during the 1974–78 period, and then tapered off to 2 percent between 1979 and 1983 because of stabilization measures and the world recession.

  Agriculture, manufacturing, and trade were Colombia's major growth sectors during the study period. Agricultural expansion picked up sharply in the late 1960s and continued throughout most of the 1970s when the country benefited from high coffee prices and an increase in coffee exports. In 1970–78 agricultural GDP grew at a rate of 4.3 percent a year, but the rate dropped to 3.2 percent a year in the period 1979–83. Manufacturing growth was most pronounced during the period 1967–74, when the annual average rate of growth was 8.9 percent. The rate of increase decelerated markedly in subsequent years.

  These differing rates of growth caused the relative importance of the sectors to shift over the period. Between 1960 and 1983, agriculture's share of GDP fell from 32 to 18 percent, while that for manufacturing rose from 16.5 to 18 percent, and that for trade increased from 16 to 19 percent.[2]

- Investment and Savings. During the 1960–83 period, the rate of investment ranged from 17.0 to 21.5 percent of GDP, with an average value for the period of 19 percent. The rate of investment declined during the 1970s and particularly after 1975, even though the rate of savings was the highest of the study period. In the early 1980s, a substantial reduction in government savings reduced the overall rate of savings, but the rate of investment was kept fairly high through foreign borrowing.

- Trade Policy. The period from 1960 to 1967 was marked by a continuation of Colombia's postwar policy of import substitution. In March 1967, however, the magnitude of foreign trade began to increase as the government reduced the antiexport bias. Moreover, management of macroeconomic policy became more consistent. The value of exports, in real terms, increased at an average annual 4.3 percent in 1967–83, while imports grew at an average 7.2 percent a year. That does not mean that external trade became a high proportion of GDP. The ratio of exports to GDP did not exceed 15.2 percent, while the ratio of imports to GDP only reached a high of 16.4 percent.

The Agricultural Sector

Agriculture is the most important sector of the Colombian economy; it generated close to 55 percent of exports of goods and services in 1983. Coffee, the principal export product, accounted for 40 percent of all exports (in value) in 1983, while noncoffee agricultural exports constituted 14.7 percent. Imports of agricultural products were relatively small at 5.7 percent of all imports of goods and services.

Colombia's agricultural output is roughly divided into equal proportions among coffee production (32 percent), other agricultural production (35 percent), and animal production (33 percent). Agricultural output is 62 percent exportable, 13 percent importable, and 25 percent nontraded.

PHYSICAL ASPECTS. Colombia has approximately 1,138,868 square kilometers (113.8 million hectares). Approximately 12 percent of the country's land (14 million hectares) has soils with agricultural potential, while 18.7 million hectares can be used for cattle raising. Much of the rest is forested. In 1983 the country used 4.1 million hectares for growing crops. In the case of agriculture, 7.5 million of the 14 million hectares of arable land are on the slopes of the Andean mountains and can be used only for perennial crops. Of the remaining 6.5 million hectares, 3.0 million are rainfed, and 3.5 million could be irrigated.

In 1960, the 76.5 percent of farms with fewer than ten hectares occupied 8.8 percent of Colombia's land, while the 0.5 percent of farms with more than 500 hectares constituted 40.5 percent of the land. Most of the large farms, however, were located in the Orinoquian and Amazon regions, and were characterized by poor soils, water problems, and locations far away from consumption centers. According to figures from Colombia's Departamento Administrativo Nacional de Estadistica (DANE) and Sociedad de Agricultores de Colombia (SAC), intermediate farms (those with ten to 500 hectares) grew at a faster rate than farms of zero to nine hectares. Thus, their share in the total number of farms went from 23 percent in 1960 to 40 percent in 1983, while in terms of area their share rose from 50.8 to 59.7 percent.

Government Intervention in Agricultural Prices

Government management of overall commercial policy led to taxation of exports in general, and agricultural exports in particular, during the period studied. During the first half of the 1960s, chronic over-valuation of the Colombian peso more than offset any subsidies granted to agricultural exports. Trade reforms initiated in 1967 then caused the peso to depreciate substantially. As a result, the net rate of taxation of agricultural exportables fell during 1967–78.[3]

- Coffee Policy. All proceeds from exports of coffee must be sur-rendered to the Central Bank, which sets a surrender price (*rein-tegro*) for coffee based on the international price. This surrender price has usually been lower than the world price, with the difference (usually small) between them accruing to the Central Bank.

  Permission to export is granted to private exporters after evi-dence of payment of the retention quota is presented. The reten-tion quota is payment in kind (or the equivalent in cash) of a quantity of *pergamino* (parchment) coffee equivalent to a propor-tion of the green coffee to be exported. The retention quota varies directly with variations in the international price of coffee, and is paid to the Fondo Nacional del Café (FNC), or National Coffee Fund. The retention quota (*impuesto de retención*) has ex-isted since 1958.

  Until 1967, coffee was also taxed by a lower rate of exchange for coffee exports. This differential was abolished in 1967 and replaced by an ad valorem tax, initially set at 26 percent of the minimum surrender price. Over the years, the ad valorem tax has declined, and by 1983 it was 6.5 percent, of which 2 percent went to the central government and the rest to the National Coffee Fund, whose chief purposes are to stabilize prices, pro-mote coffee production, and develop and retain foreign markets for Colombian coffee. Between 1977 and 1980, a discount on currency exchange certificates was introduced for coffee and some other exports.

- Cotton Policy. The prices of cottonseed and cotton fiber were originally controlled by the Ministry of Economic Development and later by the Ministry of Agriculture. In 1973 internal prices were freed and, since then, domestic prices have been set by agreement between cotton growers and textile producers for cotton fiber, and between cotton growers and producers of fats and oil in the case of cottonseed. The government, however, must sanction the agreements reached.[4]

- Wheat Policy. The wheat market in Colombia is controlled by the Instituto de Mercadeo Agropecuario—IDEMA—(Institute for Agricultural Marketing), an autonomous public agency whose objectives are, among others, to facilitate agricultural production and to import and export agricultural and food products.[5]

  When acting as an importer, IDEMA collects customs revenues that would otherwise go to the central government. As a result, IDEMA has developed an import bias in its operations. Because IDEMA has been the sole importer of wheat, and is exempt from paying import taxes, the selling price of imported wheat is usually higher than the international price by an amount equal to legislated import surcharges.

- Rice. The principal interventions of the government in this product have been to prohibit imports of rice when the price of domestic rice was not competitive, to prohibit exports when the price of domestic rice became competitive with the international price, and to extend substantial support to the development of new rice varieties.

Intervention in Agricultural Input Prices

Policymakers in Colombia have used subsidized credit to compensate the agricultural sector for the price discrimination caused by macroeconomic and commercial policies. Other traditional arguments put forward by farmers' associations to justify government intervention in the cost of agricultural credit have been the scarcity of alternative sources of funds for small farmers, the stimulus to innovation, and the need to support farmers while they are in the process of learning how to use modern inputs. The evolution of agricultural credit institutions in Colombia has been determined by the effort to reach these goals. Money created through rediscount facilities in the Central Bank and commercial bank funds allocated by law are the sources of funds for agricultural credit. The interest rate charged on agricultural loans is less than market rates of interest.

Imports of urea and compound fertilizers are subject to a prior licensing regime. Tariffs are 1 percent for urea and 10 percent for compound fertilizers. In addition, import surcharges other than tariffs are close to 9 percent, raising the total cost of importing by 10 and 19 percent for urea and compound fertilizers, respectively.

The price of fungicides is controlled by the Ministry of Agriculture. Pesticides are subject to the prior licensing regime, and tariffs on the product are about 34 percent.

The Effects of Price Intervention on Relative Prices

The prices of the four selected agricultural products were measured relative to prices in the nonagricultural sector. To compare prevailing producer with prevailing border prices, adjustments were made for transportation, storage, and production costs. For an export or import product, the divergence d between prevailing and border prices at a Colombian port is given by

$$(5\text{-}1) \qquad d = [p(1 + c) - p']/p' = [p(1 + c)/p'] - 1$$

where p = prevailing relative producer price at farmgate; p' = relative price in the absence of direct intervention; and c = handling costs (transport, storage, insurance).

If d is negative, direct price intervention placed a tax on production of the commodity in question. If d is taken to represent the divergence between prevailing and border consumer prices, a positive value for d means that consumption is taxed.

The border-adjusted relative price (p^*) is the relative price of a commodity in the absence of direct and indirect price intervention—that is, the price measured at the nominal equilibrium exchange rate (E^*) relative to the adjusted price level for the nonagricultural sector (P_{NA}^*). Therefore, the divergence d^* between prevailing and border-adjusted relative prices is given by

$$(5\text{-}2) \qquad d^* = [p(1 + c) - p^*]/p^* = [p(1 + c)/p^*] - 1.$$

If d^* is negative, total (direct plus indirect) price intervention placed a tax on production of the product. If d^* is the divergence between prevailing and border-adjusted consumer prices, a positive value for d^* means that consumption was taxed.[6]

Calculation of the equilibrium nominal exchange rate used to measure the impact of price intervention on relative prices was based on the assumption that there were no trade restrictions and that the current account deficit was zero. The latter is a particularly restrictive assumption, because a current account deficit can often be financed by external borrowing.

P_{NA} was adjusted as follows. Letting P_{NAT} and P_{NAH} denote, respectively, the price of traded and nontraded goods in the nonagricultural sector, and b the share of the traded goods in P_{NA}, then P_{NA} is given by

$$(5\text{-}3) \qquad P_{NA} = bP_{NAT} + (1 - b)P_{NAH}, \text{ and}$$

the adjusted P_{NA} (P_{NA}^*) will then be

$$(5\text{-}4) \qquad P_{NA}^* = b(E^*/E_O)P_{NAT}/(1 + t_{NA}) + (1 - b)P_{NAH}$$

where t_{NA} is the tariff equivalent of all trade restrictions in the nonagricultural sector. Actual and equilibrium nominal exchange rates during five-year periods are shown in table 5-1 for the period 1960–83.[7]

Table 5-1. Actual and Alternative Equilibrium Exchange Rates (E*), 1960–83

(pesos per US$)

| | | Equilibrium Exchange Rate: Alternative Values | | | | | Divergencies from original E* | | |
| | | Equilibrium in current account | Sustainable deficit in current account (2 percent of GDP) | | | | | | |
Period	Actual E (1)	Base E* (2)	Dollar value of imports and exports (3)	Peso value of imports and exports (4)	Dollar value of imports and exports (5)	E*/E (1)/(2) (6)	(2)/(3) (7)	(2)/(4) (8)	(2)/(5) (9)
1960–64	7.5	9.2	9.4	9.2	9.2	1.2	1.0	1.0	1.0
1965–69	14.0	16.5	18.3	16.6	17.4	1.2	0.9	1.0	0.9
1970–74	22.3	27.6	28.8	26.7	27.6	1.2	1.0	1.0	1.0
1975–79	36.8	43.7	41.6	42.8	42.3	1.2	1.0	1.0	1.0
1980–83	57.4	82.1	84.1	78.7	80.7	1.4	1.0	1.0	1.0

Source: García García and Montes Llamas (1989), appendix tables A2.2 and A2.4.

Because our original calculations showed that indiret price intervention had a particularly great impact on relative prices, especially in
the late 1970s, it was considered useful to calculate alternative values
of the equilibrium exchange rate to determine the extent of any over-
estimation of the effects. E^* was then computed using the dollar
value of imports and exports, and the sustainable deficit in the current account was assumed to be equivalent to 2 percent of GDP. It is
estimated that illegal drug activities in Colombia may account for as
much as 4 to 6 percent of GDP, but that the foreign exchange inflow
from the drug trade is less than 2 percent of GDP.[8]

Column 1 of table 5-1 shows the prevailing exchange rate and column 2 shows the equilibrium exchange rate originally used to calculate the indirect effects. Column 3 shows the exchange rate calculated
on the basis of dollars instead of pesos. Columns 4 and 5 show the
equilibrium exchange rate under the assumption of a 2 percent current account deficit, for peso and dollar values, respectively.

Given E^* derived from the dollar value of imports and exports
(column 7), it can be said that the original E^* underestimates the true
value of the equilibrium exchange rate for almost all of the study
period but 1964 and 1976–80.

Column 8 shows the original equilibrium exchange rate with the
alternative values of E^* calculated under the assumption of a 2 percent deficit in the current account. From this information it can be
said that the original E^* underestimates the true value of the equilibrium exchange rate in the 1960s, and overestimates it in the 1970s and
1980s.[9]

Comparing the original values of E^* with those values of E^* obtained using dollars, it is found that the original exchange rate tends
to underestimate the true equilibrium exchange rate from 1960 to
1975, and overestimate it from 1976 to 1982. On average, for the
period 1960–83 there is no divergence between the original E^* and the
alternative calculated value of E^*.

Because the divergences found between the original and the alternative calculated values of the equilibrium exchange rate are relatively small, we can feel confident about our overall results. Nevertheless, the current account surpluses of 1964 and 1976–80 suggest
that the effects of indirect intervention were overestimated when calculated with the original exchange rate.

Relative Producer Prices

The divergence between actual producer prices and producer prices
in the absence of intervention (border and border-adjusted prices) is
presented in table 5-2. The following conclusions can be drawn with
respect to direct intervention:

Table 5-2. Divergencies between Prevailing Producer Prices and Prices in the Absence of Direct and Total Price Interventions, 1960–83

(percent)

Period	Wheat Bogota		Adjusted Pergamino coffee f.o.b. Manizales		Rice New Orleans c.i.f. Colombian port		Cotton fiber f.o.b.					
							Costa-Meta		Interior		Country	
	Direct	Total	Direct	Total	Direct	Total	Direct	Total	Direct	Total	Direct	Total
1960–64	19.5	−11.5	−5.6	−29.9	48.0	10.1	3.6	−22.9	6.3	−21.3	3.7	−23.1
1965–69	29.9	−0.7	−17.4	−36.7	42.6	8.6	8.4	−17.1	1.0	−17.4	4.6	−20.0
1970–74	−3.4	−28.7	−10.7	−33.8	−25.9	−45.6	−5.3	−30.0	−9.6	−32.7	−4.7	−29.4
1975–79	4.4	−19.7	−11.6	−31.5	−16.0	−35.8	2.8	−20.5	−4.0	−25.7	0.6	−22.1
1980–83	14.6	−25.3	−7.1	−39.1	25.4	−18.8	21.7	−20.6	4.1	−31.9	7.4	−29.7

Source: García García and Montes Llamas (1989), tables 4.3–4.6.

- In nineteen out of twenty-four years, direct government intervention in prices protected wheat production.
- Except for 1961 and 1962, coffee production was taxed, and the peak of this taxation occurred in the second half of the 1960s.
- For rice production the pattern is clear: protected between 1960 and 1970; and taxed after 1971, except in 1977, 1982, and 1983.
- There was no pattern for cotton. Cotton production was both taxed and protected during the period, but more often than not it was protected rather than taxed. Thus, for sixteen out of twenty-four years, the nominal rate of protection for cotton fiber was positive.

The following conclusions can be drawn with respect to total intervention in prices:

- Production of all four products was taxed. The negative effect of direct intervention in coffee and rice prices was compounded by the negative effect of indirect intervention. The positive effect of direct intervention in rice prices was sometimes offset by the negative effect of indirect intervention. The positive effect of direct intervention in wheat prices was more than offset most of the time by the negative effect of indirect intervention. The negative effects of indirect intervention on cotton prices swamped the positive effects of direct intervention and reinforced the negative effects of such intervention.
- On average, the most heavily taxed commodity during the period was coffee, at 34 percent. Cotton was the second most heavily taxed, at 24.6 percent. The third most heavily taxed commodity was wheat, at 16.8 percent. The least taxed commodity was rice, at 16.2 percent.

Relative Consumer Prices

The behavior over time of the divergence between prevailing relative consumer prices and consumer prices in the absence of intervention is presented in table 5-3. The following conclusions can be drawn:

- Consumers were penalized by direct intervention in the price of wheat for twenty-two of the twenty-four years during the period.
- Consumers were penalized by direct intervention in rice prices between 1960 and 1967, but were then favored in all succeeding years except for 1982 and 1983.
- Consumers of cotton were usually favored by direct intervention; only in eight of the twenty-four years did they pay more than the border price.

Table 5-3. Divergencies between Prevailing Consumer Prices and Prices in the Absence of Direct and Total Price Interventions, 1960–83

(percent)

| Period | Wheat Bogota | | Coffee Bogota | | Rice New Orleans c.i.f. Bogota | | Cotton fiber | | | | | |
| | | | | | | | Costa-Meta | | Interior | | Country | |
	Direct	Total	Direct	Total	Direct	Total	Direct	Total	Direct	Total	Direct	Total
1960–64	25.6	−7.0	−43.7	−58.1	19.5	−10.9	4.0	−22.5	2.9	−23.6	1.6	−24.5
1965–69	38.1	5.5	−26.9	−43.8	11.4	−15.1	1.1	−22.9	−4.6	−22.0	−1.8	−25.2
1970–74	−4.2	−29.4	−31.5	−49.3	−37.2	−53.8	−20.4	−41.1	−20.6	−41.0	−17.8	−39.1
1975–79	26.4	−2.3	−64.9	−72.3	−22.9	−41.1	0.4	−22.4	−9.9	−30.1	−2.7	−24.6
1980–83	9.8	−27.9	−40.9	−52.3	16.2	−24.7	19.6	−21.9	1.0	−34.0	5.0	−31.2

Source: García García and Montes Llamas (1989), tables 4.8–4.11.

- Consumers were favored by direct intervention in the price of coffee.
- The effects on consumers of total price intervention were as follows. Consumers of cotton were favored during all years of the period. Consumers of wheat were favored in nineteen of the twenty-four years, and consumers of rice in twenty-two of the twenty-four years. The effect of total intervention on domestic coffee prices would also favor consumers.

Other studies have examined the effect of macroeconomic policies on incentives to the agricultural sector. These include García (1983), Montes (1984), and Thomas (1985). In the study of Thomas, macroeconomic policies are seen to affect agricultural incentives through their impact on the real exchange rate (RER). To measure that impact, the RER was estimated as a function of a number of variables, including the budget deficit and the terms of trade (where coffee plays an important role). The study found that over the period examined macroeconomic policies (as well as a rise in the price of coffee) led to an appreciation of the RER and to a fall in the incentives to agriculture.

In the present study, we examine both the impact of economywide policies on the RER and thus on the price of agriculture relative to nontradables, as well as their impact on industrial prices (through industrial protection policies) and thus on the price of agriculture relative to nonagricultural tradables. We found that agriculture is taxed on both counts.

Thus, despite using different approaches, both Thomas's study and the present one found that macroeconomic policies resulted in significant discrimination in agriculture.

The Effect of Intervention on Agricultural Output

The calculated values for the short-term and cumulative effects of intervention on output are presented in table 5-4, and the following conclusions on the impact of direct price intervention on output are drawn from the information presented there.

- Over the short term, direct intervention in prices increased cotton output most of the time. The cumulative effect of direct intervention was an increase in output between 1968 and 1974, and a reduction between 1975 and 1982.
- Over both the short term and the long term, direct intervention increased rice output in the 1960s and reduced it in the 1970s.
- Both the short-term and cumulative effects of direct price intervention on wheat output were positive. These effects were more pronounced in the 1960s than in the 1970s.

Table 5-4. Estimated Short Term and Cumulative Effects on Output of Direct and Total Price Interventions, 1961–83

(percent)

	Short run								Cumulative							
	Cotton		Rice		Wheat		Coffee		Cotton		Rice		Wheat		Coffee	
Period	Direct	Total	Direct	Total	Direct	Total	Direct	Total	Direct	Total	Direct	Total	Direct	Total	Direct	Total
1961–64	2.2	−11.4	31.8	12.4	10.4	−1.5	−0.6	−3.6	n.a.	—	—	—	—	—	—	—
1965–69	7.6	−11.7	23.4	7.9	16.1	2.8	−3.5	−6.5	n.a.	n.a.	136.7	9.6	145.4	−3.8	−10.7	n.a.
1970–74	0.5	−13.2	−9.1	−14.5	−0.7	−9.1	−2.2	−5.5	13.7	−42.0	2.7	−24.4	106.7	−11.8	−9.3	−21.4
1975–79	−0.4	−13.3	−5.8	−12.0	2.2	−6.9	−1.8	−4.9	−6.8	−44.4	−21.6	−34.2	16.3	−22.4	−7.4	−19.4
1980–83	26.4	−11.5	15.2	−4.1	7.6	−7.9	−2.2	−6.6	13.3	−46.7	14.2	−25.3	10.4	−27.9	−7.5	−21.3

— Not available.

Note: The proportional differences in output were estimated as $(Q - QNI)/QNI*100$ where QNI is output in the absence of intervention and Q actual output.

Source: García García and Montes Llamas (1989), tables 5.2 and 5.3.

- For coffee, both the short-term and cumulative effects of direct intervention were negative with respect to output.

Total intervention in prices had a negative effect on the output of all four products. Over the short term, the largest average decline in output occurred in cotton, -12.3 percent, followed by coffee, -5.4 percent. The smallest decline occurred in rice, an average -2.6 percent.

As for cumulative effects, the largest fall in output during the period 1970-83 occurred in cotton (-44 percent), followed by coffee (-20.6 percent), rice (-18.2 percent), and wheat (-15.9 percent).

The Effect of Intervention on Foreign Exchange Earnings

The effect of price intervention on gross foreign exchange earnings was derived from the impact of intervention on output and consumption.[10] For cotton, wheat, and rice, the gross foreign exchange effect was calculated as the difference between absolute changes in production and consumption times average export or import price. For coffee, a different procedure was followed. The International Coffee Agreement (ICA) places a ceiling on the total volume of coffee that can be exported by Colombia to other ICA members, meaning that not all increases in output can be exported. For this reason, several assumptions were made. The first was that when Colombia's quota was binding, any increase in coffee output that was not exported was used to enlarge coffee stocks. When there was no export quota, the ratio of stocks to output was assumed to be equal to the observed ratio. Therefore, estimated stocks were calculated as estimated output times actual ratio of stocks to output. The effect of price intervention on exports was then calculated as the difference between the effect on output and the effect on stocks. Because the market was not free between 1962-63 and 1971-72, all increases in coffee output were assumed to go into stocks. The ICA then freed the market in 1973, and it is assumed here that the accumulated stocks were all exported that year, subject to the constraint that the estimated stock–output ratio in 1972-73 was equal to the actual ratio for that year.

The net foreign exchange effect was calculated by taking into account any changes in imported inputs. The preemergents, pesticides, insecticides, and fertilizers used in production of cotton, rice, and wheat were all assumed to be imports. Tractors, combines, and other machinery were omitted from this calculation because it was not possible to assess their effect on changes in output.

Fertilizer was the only imported input considered for coffee. The fertilizer–output ratio in the absence of intervention was assumed to be equal to the actual fertilizer–output ratio, which was then multiplied by the change in output induced by intervention. If the fertilizer–output ratio was sensitive to price changes, the effect of changes in coffee prices on foreign exchange expenditures for fertilizer is underestimated.

The annual peso cost of imported inputs per hectare or per unit of output was converted to its U.S. dollar equivalent, using the average actual exchange rate. The total cost is the average dollar cost of inputs times the change in the number of hectares or in output brought about by the elimination of intervention. The effect of intervention on net foreign exchange earnings is presented in table 5-5. The following conclusions can be drawn.

Direct intervention in the prices of the four farm products had, on average, very small effects (either positive or negative) on foreign exchange earnings. In some years, however, the short-term and cumulative negative effects were large for rice, especially in the mid-1960s and in the first half of the 1970s. The cumulative negative effects of direct intervention in coffee prices on foreign exchange earnings were also large when quotas were not binding.

Total intervention in wheat prices had a very small impact (either positive or negative) on foreign exchange earnings. For cotton, the short-term effects were very small, but the cumulative effect was large (on average, -4.1 percent in foreign exchange earnings for the period 1970–83). The largest impact occurred in rice, a change of -3.4 percent over the short term and -11.7 percent cumulatively. This result is surprising, given the importance of coffee in generating foreign exchange, but it is explained by the low supply response of coffee and the high supply response of rice to price changes.

The Effects of Intervention on the Government Budget

REVENUES. Tariffs on imports of agricultural inputs and on wheat imports provide some government revenues, as do taxes on exports of coffee. A distinction is drawn here between central government export revenues from tariffs on imported inputs and IDEMA's revenues from tariffs on imports of wheat. For coffee, a distinction is made between central government export revenues and National Coffee Fund (NCF) revenues.

EXPENDITURES. The main government expenditures are production credit subsidies, research and development costs, and export subsidies (tax credit certificates and guaranteed minimum export prices). Expenditures on research and development for rice, wheat, and cotton were assumed to come from the central government budget. Expenditures on research, development, and extension for coffee were assumed to come from the NCF budget. Expenditures for credit and

Table 5-5. Estimated Short Term and Cumulative Effects on Net Foreign Exchange Earnings of Direct and Total Price Interventions, 1961–83

(percentage of total commodity exports or imports)

| | Short run | | | | | | | | Cumulative | | | | | | | |
| | Cotton | | Rice | | Wheat | | Coffee | | Cotton | | Rice | | Wheat | | Coffee | |
Period	Direct	Total	Direct	Total	Direct	Total	Direct	Total	Direct	Total	Direct	Total	Direct	Total	Direct	Total
1961–64	0.1	−0.8	4.0	0.8	0.7	−0.0	−0.3	−0.6	n.a.	n.a.	n.a.	n.a.	n.a.	n.a.	n.a.	n.a.
1965–69	0.4	−1.1	4.6	0.4	1.1	0.3	0.0	0.0	n.a.	n.a.	n.a.	n.a.	n.a.	n.a.	n.a.	n.a.
1970–74	−0.3	−1.7	−7.8	−10.5	−0.3	−1.1	−3.1	−4.3	−0.0	−6.3	−6.5	−18.0	−0.2	−1.0	−11.8	−10.2
1975–79	−0.1	−0.7	−3.4	−5.3	0.4	0.0	−0.9	−2.5	−0.5	−3.3	−7.2	−12.8	0.5	−0.2	−4.2	−12.5
1980–83	0.4	−0.4	1.8	−1.2	0.2	−0.4	0.0	0.1	0.2	−2.8	1.4	−4.4	0.2	−0.5	0.1	0.3

Note: For cotton, rice, and coffee the effect is measured on total commodity exports. The effect on foreign exchange for wheat is calculated as a proportion of total commodity imports.

Source: García García and Montes Llamas (1989) table 5.7.

Table 5-6. Estimated Net Revenues Due to Direct Price Interventions on Output and Inputs of Cotton, Rice, Wheat, and Coffee, 1963–83

(percentage of central government revenues)

Period	Central government	NCF	IDEMA	Total
1963–64	13.7	−0.4	0.7	14.0
1965–69	9.5	0.1	0.9	12.9
1970–74	9.1	0.6	1.2	13.0
1975–79	12.8	2.2	1.0	14.5
1980–83	4.8	5.2	0.5	14.5

Source: García García and Montes Llamas (1989), table 5.8.

export subsidies were attributed to the central government. Subsidies arising from public investments (irrigation, drainage, and so forth) were omitted because of lack of information.

Subsidies for wheat consumption were imputed to IDEMA. The subsidized cost of fertilizer for coffee was imputed to the National Coffee Fund, as were the costs of holding stocks of coffee.

RESULTS. Net revenues as a proportion of central government revenues are presented in table 5-6. These revenues are differentiated as central government, NCF, and IDEMA revenues.

Direct price intervention tended to increase central government revenues, sometimes by large amounts.[11] Large increases were observed in the mid-1960s and in 1977–80, chiefly owing to export taxes on coffee. For the period 1963–83, price intervention resulted in a net annual average increase in central government revenues of 9.7 percent. The contribution of price intervention to net government revenues declined drastically during the period 1981–83, mainly because of a reduction in export taxes on coffee.

Net government revenues from direct price intervention were usually negative and very small for cotton, and positive and very small for rice (see table 5-7). Net revenues from intervention in coffee were rather large—an average of 10.2 percent of the f.o.b. price if only the central government is considered, and 19 percent if the National Coffee Fund is added (not shown). Net central government revenues from intervention in wheat prices were small, but they were very large when IDEMA's are added. The average of the ratio of net revenue (IDEMA plus central government) to the c.i.f. import price of wheat was 80.8 percent for the period 1960–83—113.0 percent when 1973 and 1974 are excluded (two years when wheat consumption was heavily subsidized).

Table 5-7. Estimated Net Government Revenues per Unit of Output and of Border Price from Direct Price Interventions on Output and Inputs of Cotton, Coffee, Rice and Wheat, 1960–83

	Net Revenues Per Unit of Output (pesos per ton)			Wheat		Net Revenues–Border Price (percent of f.o.b. or c.i.f. price)			Wheat	
Period	*Coffee*	*Cotton*	*Rice*	*Central government*	*Central government plus IDEMA*	*Coffee*	*Cotton*	*Rice*	*Central government*	*Central government plus IDEMA*
1960-64[a]	43.5	−23.3	16.9	22.2	200.8	8.6	−0.5	1.0	3.5	29.7
1965-69	94.8	−411.9	17.6	7.2	518.1	10.6	−4.8	0.5	0.6	49.3
1970-74	254.7	−599.2	21.1	−151.5	−4665.4	13.7	−2.9	0.6	−4.8	−84.7
1975-79	936.5	−742.3	17.2	−52.1	10257.7	10.9	−0.7	0.2	−0.8	181.2
1980-83	877.8	−11258.9	−177.6	152.8	27528.9	7.7	−11.1	−1.2	1.4	291.7

a. For cotton is 1961-64.

Source: García García and Montes Llama (1989), table 5.9.

The Effect of Intervention on Price Variability

This section analyzes to what extent intervention increased or reduced the variability of domestic prices relative to the variability of
border and border-adjusted prices. To determine the impact of intervention on price variability, the variance and variability of each relative price were computed. Variability is defined as

(5-5)
$$Z_x = [\sum_{t_o}^{t_o+N} (X_t - X_{t-1})^2]/(N-1)$$

where,

t_o = starting year of sample period
N = number of observations
X = relative price.

A value higher than one means that price intervention reduced
variability in domestic prices. Our calculations showed that the value
of the ratio was higher than one for all cases but one. Only for consumers of wheat did direct price intervention increase price variability, but the increase was very small. We found that price variability would have been larger in the absence of total intervention
than in the absence of indirect intervention. Therefore, if reduction in
price variability was an important policy objective, the policy was
quite successful.

The largest reduction in the variability of producer prices occurred
in rice; the smallest occurred in coffee. In the case of rice, only 20
percent of the variability in international prices was transmitted to
domestic prices; in the case of coffee, close to 70 percent of that
variability was transmitted to domestic prices. The small reduction in
the variability of coffee prices seems surprising because coffee is a
product for which a clear and explicit policy of producer price stabilization existed.

Note also that direct intervention reduced price variability more in
goods where the direct impact of price changes on consumer welfare
is very visible, such as wheat and rice, than in goods where that
impact is less visible, such as coffee and cotton.

Another point is that the impact of direct price intervention on
price stabilization was more powerful in rice than in wheat. There are
two reasons for this: one was the relatively large share of rice in food
expenditures compared with wheat's share, and the other is that
IDEMA did not have the financial resources to carry on for a long
period of time a policy of price stabilization in wheat, a commodity
whose domestic consumption is supplied in large part by imports.
When IDEMA tried to subsidize the price of wheat in the early 1970s,

it practically went bankrupt within three years, thereby obliging the central government to cover its losses.

Direct intervention reduced the variability of cotton prices in the Costa-Meta region more than in the Tolima region. The variability of domestic prices in Costa-Meta was less than half the variability of border prices, while in Tolima the variability was only 30 percent less. Because the Costa-Meta region is the largest producer of cotton, and prices for corporate consumers of cotton were lower than border prices, the effect of this intervention would benefit consumers (that is, textile producers) rather than cotton growers. This fact can be corroborated by noting that the reduction in the variability of prices for consumers of cotton was greater than the reduction in the variability of producers' prices.

Simple correlation coefficients between output and consumption per capita, and prevailing relative consumer prices, also were calculated (see table 5-8). They show that the variance of per capita output was larger than the variance of per capita consumption for cotton, rice, and wheat. Thus, these data indicate that an important policy consideration was to ensure that domestic production of cotton, rice, and wheat was sold primarily to the domestic market. If there were a surplus, exports of cotton and rice were permitted. For wheat, an imported commodity, the lower variance of consumption relative to output shows that wheat was imported to guarantee an adequate and stable supply of wheat.

The simple correlation coefficients between output and relative consumer price show that there was very little relationship between cotton production and the relative consumer price. This absence of relationship is a strong indication that direct price intervention fully

Table 5-8. Correlation Coefficients and Variance of Output, Consumption, and Relative Prices

| | Cotton | | | |
| | Costa- | | | |
Item	Meta	Tolima	Rice	Wheat
Variance				
Output per capita	2.06	1.07	311.05	13.56
Consumption per capita	0.46	0.37	285.11	11.10
Correlation Coefficients				
Between output and				
consumption	0.63	0.76	0.97	−0.08
Between output and relative				
price of consumers	−0.01	−0.12	−0.61	0.37

Source: García García and Montes Llamas (1989), table 5.12.

protected cotton consumers from variations in output. This was possible because there was always a considerable exportable surplus that could be denied an export permit if the controlled price was unacceptable to textile producers.

The high (almost one) positive correlation between output and consumption of rice shows that variations in rice consumption resulted from variations in production. In the same way, because there was no direct control over the price of rice to consumers, variations in rice production are reflected quite strongly in diametrically opposed variations in price. Self-sufficiency and price stability were both important considerations in rice policy. The large reduction observed in price variability was the result of the pursuit of self-sufficiency and stable growth in the production of rice.

For wheat, the correlation between output and consumption was practically zero, indicating the small role of domestic production in satisfying domestic consumption and the important role of imports. As wheat output declined and the ratio of imports to production increased, it became easier to offset variations in domestic production with small changes in imports. Moreover, the positive correlation between output and relative consumer price should not be surprising, because wheat is an imported commodity. This means that changes in the price paid by consumers, which is linked to the international price, changed output in the same direction.

Measuring Transfers into and out of Agriculture

A distinction is made here between transfers directly related to price intervention at the product and input levels and transfers unrelated to price intervention (nonprice transfers). Total transfers are price plus nonprice transfers.

Transfers from price intervention. Denoting gross real producer income at prevailing, border, and border-adjusted prices by y, y' and y^*, real transfers into or out of agriculture owing to direct and total intervention on an instantaneous, short-run, and cumulative basis are given by

Effects	Real transfers due to direct price intervention	Real transfers due to total price intervention
Instantaneous (i)	$yi - yi'$,	$yi - yi^*$
Short-run (s)	$ys - ys' + (dP'dQ's)/2$,	$ys - ys^* + (dP^*dQ^*s)/2$
Long-run (l)	$yl - yl' + (dP'dQ'l)/2$,	$yl - yl^* + (dP^*dQ^*l)/2$

where

$$dP' \quad = P_A - P_A'$$
$$dP* \quad = P_A - P_A*$$
$$dQ's \quad = Q_A - Q_{SA}$$
$$dQ'l \quad = Q_A - Ql_A$$
$$dQ*s \quad = Q_A - Q_{SA}*$$
$$dQ*l \quad = Q_A - Ql_A*$$
$$Q_A \quad = \text{actual output}$$

Q_{SA} = estimated short-run output in the absence of direct price intervention

$Q_{SA}*$ = estimated short-run output in the absence of total price intervention

Ql_A = estimated long-run output in the absence of direct price intervention

Ql_A* = estimated long-run output in the absence of total price intervention.

Denoting gross real expenditures on inputs at prevailing, border, and border-adjusted prices by v, v', and $v*$, real transfers due to intervention in input prices were:[12]

Effects	*Real transfers due to direct price intervention*	*Real transfers due to total price intervention*
Instantaneous (*i*)	$vi - vi'$,	$vi - vi*$
Short-run (*s*)	$vs - vs'$,	$vs - vs*$
Long-run (*l*)	$vl - vl'$,	$vl - vl*$

Input transfers were calculated on the urea used in the production of coffee and cotton, and the urea plus compound fertilizer used in the production of rice and wheat. Transfers that occurred because of credit subsidies were computed on the actual volume of credit used. No attempt was made to calculate credit in the absence of intervention because it was not possible to establish a stable relationship between input and output. Total real transfers arising from intervention in output and input prices were then added together to obtain total real price transfers into or out of agriculture (see table 5-9).[13]

COFFEE. The instantaneous, short-term, and long-term effects of direct intervention in the price of coffee transferred resources out of agriculture in most years during the period. Moreover, increases in these transfers seem to be associated with increases in the international price of coffee or with fiscal problems.

Indirect intervention in coffee increased the transfer of resources out of agriculture produced by direct intervention. Transfers owing to indirect intervention were more numerous than those owing to direct intervention, and they were strongly correlated with overvaluation of

Table 5-9. Estimated Real Transfers Due to Direct and Total Price Interventions by Product, 1960–83

(percentage of agricultural GDP)

Period	Direct interventions			Total interventions		
	Instantaneous	Short Run[1]	Cumulative	Instantaneous	Short Run[1]	Cumulative
Coffee						
1960–65	−3.7	−3.3	n.a.	−15.4	−15.9	n.a.
1966–70	−6.0	−6.1	n.a.	−15.4	−15.9	n.a.
1971–75	−2.0	−2.0	−2.1	−7.4	−7.7	−8.4
1976–80	−6.7	−6.8	−7.0	−20.0	−20.6	−22.4
1981–83	−3.1	−3.1	−3.2	−13.9	−14.3	−15.8
Average	−4.4	−4.3	−4.4	−14.5	−14.9	−15.7
Cotton[2]						
1960–65	−0.1	−0.2	n.a.	−1.5	−1.8	n.a.
1966–70	0.2	0.2	0.1	−1.0	−1.1	−1.7
1971–75	−0.1	−0.2	−0.2	−1.2	−1.3	−1.7
1976–80	0.2	0.2	0.3	−0.7	−0.7	−0.9
1981–83	0.2	0.2	0.2	−0.3	−0.3	−0.5
Average	0.1	0.1	0.1	−1.0	−1.1	−1.2

Rice						
1960–65	4.0	3.5	n.a.	1.1	0.7	n.a.
1966–70	2.3	2.1	1.6	−0.5	−0.6	−0.5
1971–75	−8.1	−8.8	−9.1	−12.2	−13.7	−15.1
1976–80	−1.3	−1.3	−1.5	−4.5	−5.1	−5.6
1981–83	3.1	2.6	2.6	−0.8	−1.1	−1.0
Average	−0.1	−0.7	−1.7	−3.4	−4.2	−5.5
Wheat						
1960–65	0.4	0.3	n.a.	0.1	0.0	n.a.
1966–70	0.2	0.1	0.1	−0.0	−0.0	0.0
1971–75	0.0	0.0	0.0	−0.1	−0.1	−0.1
1976–80	0.0	0.0	0.0	−0.0	−0.0	0.0
1981–83	0.1	0.0	0.0	−0.0	−0.0	−0.0
Average	0.1	0.1	0.1	−0.0	−0.0	−0.0

1. For short-run effects the 1960–65 period corresponds to the 1961–65 period.
2. For the cumulative effects on cotton the 1966–70 period corresponds to the 1968–70 period.
Source: García García and Montes Llamas (1989), tables 6.1–6.4.

the peso. Transfers increased in the 1960s and remained fairly high until 1968. Except for 1970, transfers then declined continuously until 1975, but increased sharply in 1976–79 because of higher export taxes induced by large increases in international coffee prices. Transfers then declined, but they were still high compared with their levels in the first half of the 1970s.

COTTON. The record on transfers owing to direct intervention in cotton prices is mixed prior to 1975, when it became consistently positive. Total intervention transferred resources out of agriculture in all but two (1975 and 1982) years of the period. The average size of the instantaneous transfer was 1.1 percent of agricultural GDP, that of the short-run transfer was 1.2 percent, and that of the long-term transfer was 1.4 percent.

RICE. Direct intervention in prices favored rice producers between 1960 and 1969, but the positive effect tended to be smaller in the short term and cumulatively than it was instantaneously. Between 1970 and 1981, however, direct intervention in rice prices led to a transfer of resources out of agriculture. Positive transfers to agriculture occurred again in 1982 and 1983 because of strong government intervention intended to prevent large reductions in the real income of rice producers in regions that had an abundant harvest.

Indirect intervention in rice prices reduced, but did not eliminate, positive transfers into agriculture for virtually all the 1960–69 period. In the 1970s, however, the negative impact of indirect intervention strengthened that of direct intervention. It is important to highlight the 1973–75 years, when instantaneous effects produced transfers out of agriculture equivalent to 16.7 percent of agricultural GDP. Transfers out of agriculture owing to short-run and cumulative effects of total price intervention over the period were larger than the transfers from instantaneous effects.

WHEAT. Wheat producers were net recipients of resources owing to the instantaneous effects of direct intervention in output and input prices in all but four years of the period. But the transfer was very small as a proportion of agricultural GDP because the contribution of wheat to agricultural production was very small. Transfers resulting from short-term and cumulative effects were smaller than transfers owing to instantaneous effects. The instantaneous effects of indirect intervention offset the positive effects of direct intervention in eleven years and strengthened the negative effects in four other years. Transfers out of agriculture were more frequent for instantaneous than for short-run and cumulative effects.

A summary of the results on estimated real transfers into or out of agriculture can be found in table 5-9. The instantaneous effects of direct price intervention produced a net transfer of resources out of agriculture in twenty out of twenty-four years. There was a net transfer out of agriculture in nineteen out of twenty-three years (1961–83) for short-run effects, and in twelve out of nineteen years for cumulative effects (1965–83). On average, during the relevant period for each length of run, price transfers out of agriculture owing to direct instantaneous, short-term, and cumulative effects were equivalent to 4.3, 4.8, and 4.8 percent of agricultural GDP, respectively.

Total price intervention increased the transfers out of agriculture already produced by direct intervention. Transfers owing to instantaneous, short-run, and cumulative effects reached a peak of 34, 35.2, and 38.5 percent of agricultural GDP in 1977. The average transfers out of the sector were 18.9, 20.3, and 18.2 percent of agricultural GDP for instantaneous, short-run, and cumulative effects, respectively. Thus, comparing average transfers resulting from direct or total price intervention, about 25 percent of the transfers out of agriculture were attributable to direct intervention and about 75 percent to indirect intervention. Therefore, transfers out of agriculture were mainly the result of below-equilibrium exchange rates.

TRANSFERS DUE TO NONPRICE INTERVENTION. Transfers due to nonprice intervention were calculated only for the agricultural sector as a whole. The nonprice transfers considered in this monograph were government expenditures for research and extension, NCF expenditures, and the subsidy for agricultural credit.

Adding nonprice transfers to transfers from direct price intervention varies our conclusions on the effects of intervention. Because of nonprice transfers, the number of years in which agriculture transferred resources to the rest of the economy because of direct price intervention falls from nineteen out of twenty-four years to ten out of twenty-four years for short-run effects, and from twelve out of nineteen years to seven out of nineteen years to seven out of nineteen years for cumulative effects. Transfers into agriculture were very similar for instantaneous, short-run, and cumulative effects, and their average size was 1.0, 0.6, and 1.3 percent of agricultural GDP (table 5-10).

Adding nonprice transfers to transfers from total price intervention changes the above results dramatically, as table 5-10 shows. In that case, the agricultural sector transfers resources to the rest of the economy every year for instantaneous and short-run effects and in all but four years for cumulative effects. The average transfer out of agriculture was a substantial fraction of agricultural GDP—13.7, 14.8, and 12.1 percent, respectively, for instantaneous, short-run, and cumulative effects. Transfers from instantaneous effects declined after reach-

Table 5-10. Estimated Real Transfers into (+)-out (−) of Agriculture Due to Price and Nonprice Interventions, 1960–83

(percentage of agricultural GDP)

| | Price transfers[1] | | | | | | Non-price transfers[3] | Total transfers[4] | | | | | |
| | Instantaneous | | Short run[2] | | Cumulative | | | Instantaneous | | Short run[2] | | Cumulative | |
Period	Direct	Total	Direct	Total	Direct	Total		Direct	Total	Direct	Total	Direct	Total
1960–65	0.5	−15.7	0.3	−16.9	n.a.	n.a.	2.8	3.0	−13.3	3.2	−14.2	n.a.	n.a.
1966–70	−3.4	−16.9	−3.7	−17.6	0.5	−5.2	4.6	0.7	−12.6	0.3	−13.4	5.0	−0.7
1971–75	−10.2	−20.9	−10.9	−22.8	−11.4	−25.3	8.0	−2.3	−13.1	−3.1	−15.0	−3.5	−17.5
1976–80	−7.8	−25.2	−7.9	−26.4	−8.2	−28.9	6.6	−1.5	−19.0	−1.7	−20.1	−2.0	−22.6
1981–83	0.3	−15.0	−0.2	−15.8	−0.3	−17.3	7.5	7.3	−8.0	6.9	−8.8	6.8	−10.2
Average	−4.3	−18.9	−4.8	−20.3	−4.8	−18.2	5.6	1.0	−13.7	0.6	−14.8	1.3	−12.1

1. Transfers on inputs comprise urea and credit for cotton and coffee, and fertilizers (urea and compound) and credit for rice and wheat.
2. The 1960–65 period corresponds to the 1961–65 period.
3. Nonprice transfers comprise public expenditure in agriculture, research and extension and subsidy on credit to the entire agricultural sector.
4. Transfers from credit for each individual product were not included in total transfers.
Source: García García and Montes Llamas (1989), tables 6.5 and 6.6.

170

ing a peak of 20 percent in 1964, but took a sharp upward turn in 1972, 1973, and 1974, mainly because the domestic prices of rice were not allowed to adjust to high and rising international prices. Transfers increased again between 1975 and 1979, but this time as a result of indirect price intervention. Transfers out of agriculture in the 1970s were the result of both direct and indirect price intervention, while in the 1960s they were essentially the result of indirect price intervention.

The Effects of Intervention on Income Distribution

The impact of price intervention on real producer income was calculated by dividing real transfers due to price intervention by real producer income. The instantaneous, short-term, and cumulative effects of price intervention on the incomes of producers of coffee, cotton, rice, and wheat are summarized in table 5-11.

COFFEE. Direct price intervention reduced the real income of coffee growers by an average annual 21.1 percent during the study period. The real income loss owing to direct price intervention was especially large relative to the average in 1966, 1967, 1976, 1977, and 1979 (these individual years are not shown in table). The large losses in 1966 and 1967 resulted from an increase in taxes caused by the change from a differential exchange rate for coffee to an ad valorem export tax, while the 1977 and 1979 results were because of reintroduction of a lower exchange rate for coffee. The reintroduction of a differential exchange rate for coffee in 1977 was an attempt to reduce the effects of the large accumulation of international reserves induced by a rise in the international price of coffee.

COTTON. Direct price intervention increased the real gross income of cotton growers by an average 3.1 percent instantaneously, 3 percent over the short term, and 4.6 percent cumulatively. In general, the increase was small except in 1966, 1975–76, and 1980–82, when direct intervention increased real income by more than 10 percent. The peak occurred in 1982, at 40 percent. It is worth pointing out that the most favorable income effects occurred during years when it was claimed that the sector was going through a crisis. This claim was correct in a sense, because area and output declined as a result of losses caused by bad harvests in previous years. However, cotton growers were able to extract large transfers from the rest of the society via government intervention, which permitted them to reduce their losses or even to be fully compensated for them.

Indirect price intervention, however, had an altogether different effect. Indirect intervention reduced the real income of cotton

Table 5-11. Estimated Real Income Effects of Price Interventions on Producers of Coffee, Cotton, Rice, and Wheat, 1960–83

(percentage of estimated real producer income)

Commodity	Direct effects			Total effects		
	Instantaneous	Short run[1]	Cumulative	Instantaneous	Short run[1]	Cumulative
Coffee						
1960–65	−15.3	−13.9	—	−63.1	−66.0	—
1966–70	−32.1	−32.7	—	−81.8	−84.6	—
1971–75	−12.1	−12.1	−12.8	−46.1	−47.5	−52.3
1976–80	−27.1	−27.4	−28.2	−81.0	−83.4	−90.8
1981–83	−19.1	−19.3	−19.9	−86.5	−89.6	−98.4
Average	−21.1	−21.2	−21.1	−70.1	−72.9	−78.5
Cotton[2]						
1960–65	−3.3	−4.8	—	−41.6	−49.8	—
1966–70	5.5	5.7	2.1	−23.8	−25.4	−35.8
1971–75	−2.6	−3.0	−2.8	−25.0	−27.5	−35.1
1976–80	5.8	5.9	6.1	−19.1	−20.7	−26.9
1981–83	17.0	17.1	17.2	−18.3	−18.5	−26.8
Average	3.1	3.0	4.6	−26.9	−29.2	−31.1

Rice						
1960–65	31.2	26.7	—	8.0	4.2	—
1966–70	16.7	15.2	11.6	–6.1	–7.3	–6.8
1971–75	–58.0	–63.1	–65.1	–90.5	–101.3	–111.0
1976–80	–11.1	–11.6	–12.7	–38.2	–42.9	–46.9
1981–83	22.0	18.9	18.7	–8.8	–11.3	–10.8
Average	–0.3	–4.7	–12.9	–27.2	–33.5	–43.9
Wheat						
1960–65	23.6	20.5	—	2.1	–0.9	—
1966–70	18.8	17.7	12.9	–0.9	–0.9	–0.3
1971–75	2.0	2.4	1.3	–15.1	–14.9	–12.3
1976–80	12.8	12.3	11.3	–2.1	–1.5	3.1
1981–83	19.8	18.7	16.9	–6.9	–6.6	–4.1
Average	15.4	13.9	10.7	–4.1	–4.8	–2.2

—Not available.

1. For short-run effects the 1960–65 period corresponds to the 1961–65 period.
2. For the long-run effects on cotton the 1966–1970 period corresponds to the 1968–1970 period.

Source: García García and Montes Llamas (1989), tables 7.1–7.4.

growers in all but two years of the period (1975 and 1982). The instan-taneous effect, on average, was a reduction of 27 percent in real income, the short-run effect was a 29 percent reduction, and the cumulative effect was a 31 percent reduction. Real income losses were very large in the 1960s and in 1970–74. The losses became somewhat smaller in 1977–81. The real income effects of direct and total inter-vention on cotton growers are presented by region in table 5-12.

RICE. The overriding policy consideration with respect to rice was self-sufficiency. Direct intervention in price increased the real income of producers in the 1960s by 27.4 percent, but decreased it in the 1970s, by 34 percent on average. These losses were particularly large between 1972 and 1976 because of a sharp increase in the interna-tional price of rice and a slow adjustment of internal to external prices. This may have been a result of the government's desire to combat inflation.

Indirect intervention reduced the real income of rice growers over the period. During the 1960s, the negative effects of indirect interven-tion were insufficient to offset the positive effects of direct interven-tion. In the 1970s, on the other hand, both direct and indirect inter-vention worked to depress the real income of rice growers, to such an extent that in 1973 and 1974 their real income losses were equivalent to 130 percent of the gross value of rice output.

WHEAT. Direct intervention increased the average real income of wheat producers by 15.4 percent instantaneously and 10.7 percent cumulatively during the 1960–83 period. Reductions of 30 percent in real producer income occurred in 1973 and 1974, however, induced by an insufficient adjustment of domestic to high and rising interna-tional prices. Domestic sales were subsidized during those years with the idea that keeping the prices of certain foodstuffs and crops stable would be sufficient to control inflation.

Total intervention reduced the real income of wheat growers in-stantaneously by an average of 4.1 percent over the period. The short-run and cumulative results were decreases in real producer income of 4.8 and 2.2 percent, respectively.

Effects on Consumer Income

The instantaneous and short-run effects of intervention in the prices of rice and wheat on the distribution of consumer income were calcu-lated by income group.[14] The instantaneous effects were obtained by multiplying each price divergence times the share of each commodity in total household expenditure. The short-run effects were calculated by multiplying each price divergence times the share of each commodity in total household expenditure times $(1 - nj)$, where nj is the total price elasticity of demand for that commodity in income group j. Instantaneous and short-run real income effects were calculated for a group of five cities (Bogota, Cali, Barranquilla, Bucaramanga, and Pasto) in the case of rice, and for a group of four cities (all but Pasto) in the case of wheat. The results are shown in table 5-13.

Direct intervention in prices hurt rice consumers in the 1960s but benefited them in the 1970s, while total intervention benefited consumers in all but two years (1961 and 1982) of the period. The size of the benefits owing to direct intervention in rice was rather small and never increased consumers' average real income by more than 1 percent. For low-income consumers (Group I, with household expenditure of less than 18,000 pesos per year), real income gains never exceeded 2 percent.

The short-term effects had the same pattern as instantaneous effects: consumers lost in the 1960s and gained in the 1970s, but total intervention in rice prices produced a net consumer gain in all but two years of the period. The gains and losses from direct and total intervention were not very large and never exceeded 3.5 percent for the lowest income group.

The direct and total effects of price intervention on the real income of consumers of wheat was approximated by assessing their effects on wheat flour. In calculating the real income effect on consumers, it was assumed that the percentage change in the costs of producing bread and pastry were transferred to the consumer in the same proportion.

The instantaneous effect of direct intervention was a decline in the real income of consumers in all but two (1973 and 1974) years of the period. The loss in real income, however, never exceeded more than 2.1 percent for the lowest income bracket. The short-term real income effects of direct intervention were negative in all but the same two years and were larger than the instantaneous effects.

The instantaneous effect of total price intervention on real income was a benefit for consumers in twenty-one of the twenty-four years. The largest increase in the real income of the lowest income bracket was 1.6 percent in 1974. The short-term income effect of total price intervention was positive for nineteen of the twenty-four years but was very small on average.[15]

In conclusion, the gains and losses in consumers' real income owing to direct and total price intervention were fairly small for all of the period. In the case of rice, the small gains in consumer real income do not seem to justify the large losses in real producer income that were induced by intervention.

Table 5-12. Estimated Real Income Effects by Region on Cotton Producers Due to Direct and Total Price Interventions on Output and Fertilizers, 1960–83

(percentage of estimated real producer income)

Period	Direct effects			Total effects		
	Instantaneous	Short run[1]	Cumulative[2]	Instantaneous	Short run[1]	Cumulative[2]
Costa-Meta						
1960-65	−5.3	−8.5	—	−44.8	−55.6	—
1966-70	5.4	5.5	1.9	−22.6	−23.6	−33.1
1971-75	−5.0	−4.9	−4.5	−27.7	−30.0	−37.5
1976-80	2.9	2.9	3.0	−21.8	−23.4	−30.5
1981-83	12.9	12.8	12.4	−22.5	−21.8	−29.1
Average	1.0	0.6	2.2	−29.0	−31.7	−32.9
Tolima						
1960-65	−1.9	−2.5	—	−39.8	−46.0	—
1966-70	−2.8	−2.7	−6.1	−33.2	−36.2	−49.6
1971-75	−10.2	−10.7	−9.7	−35.2	−39.5	−51.0
1976-80	1.1	1.5	1.7	−24.4	−26.0	−32.2
1981-83	14.9	14.8	14.6	−19.4	−18.3	−24.3
Average	−1.1	−1.2	−0.9	−31.7	−34.5	−39.8

Valle[3]						
1960–65	—	—	—	—	—	—
1966–70	8.8	9.4	10.5	−16.4	−17.5	−18.9
1971–75	13.5	11.6	9.4	−5.4	−5.6	−7.4
1976–80	4.3	4.7	4.9	−20.2	−21.5	−23.1
1981–83	5.3	7.1	11.4	−33.3	−43.1	−63.1
Average	8.2	8.3	8.6	−17.3	−19.7	−24.9
Total Country						
1960–65	−3.8	−5.4	—	−42.5	−50.8	—
1966–70	3.7	3.8	0.8	−24.9	−26.5	−35.6
1971–75	−3.9	−4.2	−4.1	−26.6	−29.1	−36.8
1976–80	2.6	2.7	2.9	−22.2	−23.8	−30.0
1981–83	12.9	13.0	13.1	−22.4	−22.5	−30.9
Average	1.2	1.0	2.2	−28.8	−31.2	−33.3

—Not applicable.
1. For short-run effects the 1960–65 period corresponds to the 1961–65 period.
2. For the long-run effects the 1966–70 period corresponds to the 1968–70 period.
3. The 1966–70 period corresponds to the 1967–70 period.
Source: García García and Montes Llamas (1989), tables 7.7 and 7.8.

Table 5-13. Real Income Effect on Urban Consumers of Price Interventions in Rice and Wheat by Income Groups, 1960–83

(percent)

	Instantaneous effects						Short run effects					
	Income level					Total	Income level					Total
Commodity	I	II	III	IV	V	average	I	II	III	IV	V	average
Rice												
Direct interventions												
1960–65	0.6	0.5	0.3	0.2	0.2	0.3	0.9	0.7	0.4	0.3	0.3	0.4
1966–70	−0.2	−0.2	−0.1	−0.1	−0.1	−0.1	−0.3	−0.2	−0.1	−0.1	−0.1	−0.1
1971–75	−1.6	−1.3	−0.9	−0.6	−0.6	−0.8	−2.3	−1.8	−1.2	−0.8	−0.7	−1.0
1976–80	−0.7	−0.5	−0.3	−0.2	−0.2	−0.3	−0.9	−0.7	−0.5	−0.3	−0.3	−0.4
1981–83	0.7	0.6	0.4	0.3	0.3	0.3	1.0	0.8	0.5	0.3	0.3	0.5
Average	−0.3	−0.2	−0.1	−0.1	−0.1	−0.1	−0.4	−0.3	−0.2	−0.1	−0.1	−0.2
Total interventions												
1960–65	−0.5	−0.4	−0.3	−0.2	−0.2	−0.3	−0.8	−0.6	−0.4	−0.3	−0.2	−0.3
1966–70	−1.0	−0.8	−0.5	−0.4	−0.4	−0.5	−1.4	−1.1	−0.7	−0.5	−0.4	−0.7
1971–75	−2.0	−1.6	−1.1	−0.8	−0.7	−1.0	−2.8	−2.2	−1.5	−0.9	−0.9	−1.3
1976–80	−1.3	−1.0	−0.7	−0.5	−0.5	−0.6	−1.8	−1.4	−1.0	−0.6	−0.6	−0.8
1981–83	−0.6	−0.5	−0.3	−0.2	−0.2	−0.3	−0.8	−0.6	−0.4	−0.3	−0.3	−0.4
Average	−1.1	−0.9	−0.6	−0.4	−0.4	−0.5	−1.6	−1.2	−0.8	−0.5	−0.5	−0.7

Wheat

Direct interventions

1960–65	0.9	0.7	0.5	0.4	0.3	0.5	1.5	1.1	0.7	0.5	0.3	0.6
1966–70	0.8	0.7	0.5	0.4	0.2	0.4	1.3	1.0	0.6	0.4	0.2	0.6
1971–75	−0.2	−0.1	−0.1	−0.1	−0.0	−0.1	−0.3	−0.2	−0.1	−0.1	−0.0	−0.1
1976–80	0.8	0.6	0.5	0.3	0.2	0.4	1.3	1.0	0.6	0.4	0.2	0.6
1981–83	0.1	0.1	0.0	0.0	0.0	0.0	0.1	0.1	0.1	0.0	0.0	0.1
Average	0.5	0.4	0.3	0.2	0.1	0.3	0.9	0.7	0.4	0.3	0.1	0.4

Total interventions

1960–65	−0.3	−0.2	−0.2	−0.1	−0.1	−0.2	−0.5	−0.4	−0.2	−0.2	−0.1	−0.2
1966–70	−0.2	−0.2	−0.1	−0.1	−0.1	−0.1	−0.3	−0.2	−0.1	−0.1	−0.1	−0.1
1971–75	−0.8	−0.6	−0.5	−0.3	−0.2	−0.4	−1.3	−1.0	−0.6	−0.4	−0.2	−0.5
1976–80	−0.1	−0.1	−0.1	−0.0	−0.0	−0.1	−0.2	−0.1	−0.1	−0.1	−0.0	−0.1
1981–83	−1.0	−0.8	−0.6	−0.4	−0.3	−0.5	−1.6	−1.2	−0.8	−0.5	−0.3	−0.7
Average	−0.4	−0.3	−0.2	−0.2	−0.1	−0.2	−0.7	−0.5	−0.3	−0.2	−0.1	−0.3

Note: A positive sign indicates the amount of real income that would have to be given to the consumer to maintain its actual consumption of the commodity. A negative sign indicates the amount of real income that would have to be taken off the consumer to maintain its actual consumption of the commodity. Thus, a negative sign indicates that the price intervention has favored the consumer, while a positive sign indicates that the price intervention has damaged the consumer. Income levels per year. I means less than $18,000, II between $18,001–42,000, III between $42,001–72,000, IV between $72,001–120,000, and V more than $120,001.

Source: García García and Montes Llamas (1989), tables 7.9–7.12.

Real Wages in Agriculture

A large, although declining, proportion of the Colombian population lives in the rural sector. Therefore, an important element in the analysis of income distribution is analysis of the factors that determined real wages in agriculture.

Let L^S and L^D denote the supply and demand for agricultural labor, W_A the real wage in agriculture, W_U the real urban wage in the sector in which migrants from agriculture are more likely to find employment, U the rate of urban unemployment, P_A/P_{NA} the price of agricultural output (P_A) relative to the price of output in the non-agricultural sector (P_{NA}), N_R the size of the rural population, and K_A the capital stock in the agricultural sector. The capital stock and the state of technology in agriculture determine the marginal physical product of labor in agriculture. The supply of and demand for labor in agriculture are given by

(5-6) $$L^S = L^S (W_A, N_R, U, W_U)$$

and

(5-7) $$L^D = L^D (W_A, P_A/P_{NA}, K_A).$$

The relationships between labor supplied and its determinants are

$$dL^S/dW_A > 0;\ dL^S/dN_R > 0;\ dL^S/dU > 0;\ \text{and}\ dL^S/dW_U < 0$$

and the relationship between labor demanded and its determinants are,

$$dL^D/dW_A < 0;\ dL^D/d(P_A/P_{NA}) > 0;\ \text{and}\ dL^D/dK_A > 0.$$

In equilibrium,

(5-8) $$L^S (W_A, N_R, U, W_U) - L^D E (W_A, P_A/P_{NA}, K_A) = 0.$$

From (4.3), W_A can be derived as a function of U, W_U, P_A/P_{NA}, N_R and K_A to obtain equation (4.4) below.

(5-9) $$W_A = W_A (P_A/P_{NA}, K_A, U, N_R\ W_U).$$

From the signs of the partial derivatives of the supply and demand functions for labor, it results that

$$dW_A/d(P_A/P_{NA});\ dW_A/dK_A;\ dW_A/dW_U > 0$$

and

$$dW_A/dU\ \text{and}\ dW_A/dN_R < 0.$$

Thus, the real wage in agriculture was a positive function of the relative price of agricultural output, the capital stock in agriculture, and the urban real wage, while it was a negative function of rural population size and the rate of urban unemployment.

The equation used in estimating real agricultural wages is:

(5-10) $\qquad \log W_A = a + b\log(P_A/P_{NA}) + c\log K_A$
$\qquad\qquad\qquad + g\log W_U + hU + j\log N_R + U$

where

log stands for the logarithm of the variable;
W_A = index of the real agricultural wage rate;
P_A/P_{NA} = price of agricultural value added/price of nonagricultural value added;
K_A = capital stock in agriculture;
W_U = index of real wage in the urban sector represented by the index of the real wage in the construction sector;
U = unemployment rate in the urban sector;
u = a random term.

The sign for the coefficients b, c, and g is expected to be positive, while that for h and j is expected to be negative. The estimation period is 1968–83.

The estimated equation used to generate real wages in the absence of direct and total intervention is:

$$\log W_A = 32.80 + 0.5395\log P_A/P_{NA} + 1.46\log K_A + 0.2686\log W_u$$
$$- 0.9399U - 4.2474\log N_R$$
$$R^2 = 0.995 \text{ Durbin-Watson } 2.29.$$

All the estimated coefficients are significant at a level of 99 percent.

The following paragraphs examine the impact of direct and indirect price intervention on real wages in the agricultural sector. Denote by prime (') the value of the variable in the absence of direct intervention and by an asterisk (*) the value of the variable in the absence of total intervention. Let

(5-11) $\qquad\qquad \hat{W}_a = \hat{W}_a (P_A/P_{NA}, OV)$

where $\hat{W}_a$ stands for the fitted value of real agricultural wages at prevailing relative prices P_A/P_{NA}, and for the actual value of all the other variables (OV) in equation (4.5). Then, W_A', W_A'', W_A^*, and W_A^{**} will be given by

(5-12) $\qquad\qquad W_A' = \hat{W}_A (P_A/P_{NA}', OV)$

(5-13) $\qquad\qquad W_A'' = \hat{W}_A (P_A'/P_{NA}', OV)$

(5-14) $\qquad\qquad W_A^* = \hat{W}_A (P_A^*/P_{NA}, OV), \text{ and}$

(5-15) $\qquad\qquad W_A^{**} = \hat{W}_A (P_A^*/P_{NA}^*, OV).$

The results of this exercise are reported in table 5-14, which shows indices of actual real wages, of real wages in the absence of direct and total intervention, and their respective divergences.

Direct intervention in agricultural output prices (Column 6) produced a small gain to rural laborers, because it increased the relative prices of agricultural output above what they would have been in the absence of intervention. Direct intervention, however, in both agricultural prices and other prices in the economy (columns 3 and 7) hurt agricultural workers considerably. On average, real wages in agriculture fell 18 percent for the period 1966–83 owing to direct intervention in agriculture and in the rest of the economy. This estimated loss is a lower bound, because higher relative agricultural prices would have increased the profitability of agriculture and induced a larger capital accumulation, thus raising labor productivity and, hence, real wages.

Agricultural workers also lost owing to the existence of disequilibrium exchange rates. Column 8 shows the divergence between actual real wages and real wages calculated in the absence of direct intervention in agriculture but measured at the equilibrium exchange rate, and prices in the nonagricultural sector measured at their prevailing values. This measure captures the impact on real wages of simultaneous elimination of direct intervention in agriculture and adjustment of the exchange rate to its equilibrium value.[16] The losses to agricultural workers owing to a lower exchange rate were great but not as great as those induced by direct intervention in nonagricultural sector prices. Wage losses attributable to a lower exchange rate, however, increased sharply in the late 1970s and early 1980s. Losses in the 1980s owing to a low exchange rate were larger than the losses attributable to direct intervention in the nonagricultural sector.

Column 9 shows the divergence between actual real wages and the real wages that would have prevailed in the absence of intervention. This column shows that real wages fell by an annual average of 14.8 percent because of direct and indirect intervention during the period.

In summary, agricultural workers seem to have been large losers because of the policy of import substitution. The principal cause of these losses was the protection provided for the nonagricultural sector, and not direct intervention in agricultural prices. Because the impact of indirect effects is not visible and is not felt directly, however, agricultural producers and their associations did not try to counteract the negative impact of this intervention.

The Political Economy of Agricultural Pricing Policies

Colombian agricultural policy during the twentieth century has had two primary goals: (1) to resolve balance of payments problems through self-sufficiency in the production of food and nonfood agri-

Table 5-14. Prevailing and Estimated Rural Wages and Divergences in the Absence of Direct and Total Price Interventions, 1966–83

Period	Index of Rural Wages					Divergences			
	Prevailing W_A	In absence of direct intervention W_A'	In absence of direct intervention W_A''	In absence of total intervention W_A*	In absence of total intervention W_A**	$W_A - W_A'$	$W_A - W_A''$	$W_A - W_A*$	$W_A - W_A**$
1966–70	75.6	73.4	93.6	80.9	84.4	2.2	−18.1	−5.3	−8.8
1971–75	90.9	88.9	110.5	98.0	102.2	2.0	−19.6	−7.1	−11.2
1976–80	110.3	110.1	129.4	123.2	128.9	0.2	−19.1	−12.8	−18.6
1981–83	106.9	102.9	122.1	126.3	131.2	4.0	−15.2	−19.4	−24.3

Note: W_A is observed agricultural wage, W_A' is estimated agricultural wage using P_A'/P_{NA}, W_A'' is estimated agricultural wage using P_A*/P_{NA}, W_A** is estimated agricultural wage using P_A'/P_{NA}', W_A* is estimated agricultural wage using $P_A*/P_{NA}*$.

Source: García García and Montes Llamas (1989), table 7.14.

cultural commodities; and (2) to maintain price stability.[17] The evolution of these and lesser priorities over time, and the weights attached to each, are presented in table 5-15. The evolution of Colombia's agricultural policies during the century is sketched below.

The 1900–1925 Period

At the end of the nineteenth century, Colombia was a backward country. During the first years of the twentieth century, however, Colombia began to develop as coffee production expanded, new land was settled, and the transportation system was improved.

Agricultural policy during the first twenty-five years of the century had three main elements: (1) incentives to grow and export coffee (and, on occasion, tobacco, rubber, and cotton) through specific subsidies and through reductions in transportation costs; (2) import substitution of wheat, rice, sugar, and oils and fats, mainly by protection; and (3) tariff exemptions for such agricultural inputs as fertilizer, machinery, tools, and barbed wire. Economic policy favored agricultural production because of the strong political power of landowners, the relatively small urban population, and the substantial share of the rural population involved in the production of coffee.

Emergency Law—1926–1931

The increasing importance of manufacturing after World War I, as well as urban population growth, began to erode the alliance between the government and the farmers. Gradually, the government's emphasis shifted toward cheap food policies. A steep rate of inflation during the period was attributed to a low agricultural supply response rather than to substantial increases in the money supply, and the government reduced tariffs on agricultural products through a so-called emergency Law (Law 3 of 1926). As a result, food imports almost doubled between 1926 and 1928, and domestic production of wheat, rice, sugar, and other import-competing agricultural products was undermined.

The Great Depression—1930–1940

The negative effects of the Great Depression on the Colombian economy led to stronger government intervention. The Emergency Law of 1926 was repealed in 1931, and a generalized and substantial increase in protection took place. A 100 percent devaluation of the peso in 1931–32, as well as direct subsidies to producers, stimulated coffee production. These steps were complemented by increases in subsi-

Table 5-15. **Relative Weight (WI) of Objectives of Agricultural Policy, 1900–85**
(percent)

Objectives	1900–25	1925–30	1930–40	1940–50	1950–67	1967–75	1975–85
Consumer welfare	—	0.20	0.10	—	—	0.10	0.15
Farmer income	0.10	—	—	0.30	0.10	0.10	0.10
Government revenue	—	—	—	—	0.10	—	—
Foreign exchange	0.20	0.20	0.20	0.10	0.20	0.20	—
Self-sufficiency	0.40	0.20	0.30	0.30	0.30	0.20	0.15
Regional equity	—	0.30	0.10	0.10	—	0.20	0.25
Nutrition	—	—	—	—	—	—	0.10
Support of domestic industry	0.10	—	0.20	0.20	0.30	0.20	0.25
Support of processing industry	0.20	0.10	0.10	—	—	—	—
Total	1.00	1.00	1.00	1.00	1.00	1.00	1.00

— Negligible.
Source: Author's calculations.

dized agricultural credit and a three-year moratorium on loan payments.

Debate on agricultural policy during this period had two sides. The government and the industrial bourgeoisie pressed for agrarian reform, arguing that skewed distribution of land and high land rents were the cause of rising food prices. But the Agricultural Society argued for increasing the supply of productive land through additional settlements. The Society also promoted railroad and highway building, irrigation projects, and an enlarged supply of agricultural credit. In 1936 the government passed a law whose goal was to shift large tracts of land from cattle raising to crop production by decreeing that large, privately owned land parcels would revert to the state if they were not used for crop production within five years.

But the new law did not break the political power of the landowners or break up large ranches. Instead, tenants and sharecroppers working on the large ranches were evicted. Furthermore, large landowners who raised cattle got the support of many coffee growers. Moreover, those in favor of import substitution and industrialization could not risk an open collision with the coffee sector, the provider of most of the country's foreign exchange.

World War II and Afterward—1938–1950

By the end of the 1930s, Colombia's agricultural policy objectives were clearly contradictory. On the one hand, there was a desire to increase agricultural production and thus achieve self-sufficiency in food and agricultural raw materials. On the other hand, though, there was the desire to obtain food and other raw agricultural products at the cheapest possible price. The conflict, as before, was between rural landowners and the rising bourgeoisie.

However, the economic realities imposed by World War II compelled the two groups to seek an accommodation with each other. In 1938 the government proposed the following objectives: (1) the achievement of self-sufficiency in the production of food crops (corn, rice, sugar, potatoes) and in the production of raw materials used in clothing manufacture (cotton, hides, furs); (2) intensified production of tropical exports (coffee, cocoa, bananas, rubber, and others). These objectives, similar to those of the 1920s, also included new funds for agricultural research and extension, credit, storage, and the creation of new farmers' association.

Quotas on the use of domestic import-competing crops were established to promote self-sufficiency, and price controls were introduced to achieve price stability. In addition, a law was placed in 1944 to modify the system of land tenancy. Because of wartime difficulties in obtaining agricultural commodities, the government created the National Institute of Food Supplies (INA) in 1944 to facilitate the exportation of Colombia's food commodities and internal distribution of imported commodities.

The postwar period in Colombia was characterized by rapid industrial growth (9.4 percent per year between 1945 and 1950), heavy rural-urban migration, substantial monetary growth, and increases in imports, mainly of machinery and equipment. Agricultural production also increased rapidly. An increase in food prices, and renewed access to world markets, then led the government to devise a system of "contracts" between the public and private sectors. These "contracts" included the concession of import quotas to industrial firms using imported agricultural raw materials as long as they also purchased a designated amount of domestic production at a fixed price, which was usually higher than the international price, and transferred a portion of their domestic crop purchases to INA. Furthermore, the final product had to be sold at a government-designated price.

The Modernization Drive—1950–1967

The 1950–67 period was characterized by a strong effort to develop an industrial sector through import substitution and by intensified rural-urban migration. The design of economic policy in general, and agricultural policy in particular, was again influenced by the need to solve balance of payments problems. The policy of import substitution in agricultural products persisted, and an attempt was made to promote agricultural exports through direct subsidies.

Because of the overvaluation of the peso and a specific commercial policy for each product, the various agricultural activities fared differently. However, it should be noted that overvaluation of the peso reduced the relative price of imported inputs, mainly tractors, thus causing a shift from cattle-raising to crop production that led, in various regions, to expansion of the agricultural frontier.

This period was also notable for consolidation of the system of subsidized credit under Law 26 of 1957. The new law obliged banks to allocate about 15 percent of their loans to agricultural enterprises at below market rates of interest. Government investment in agricultural research and extension was strengthened as well. However, an agrarian reform law issued in 1961 weakened the land expansion drive of the 1950s.

The substantial rural-to-urban migration that occurred during this period raised the political stakes of maintaining the scheme of import substitution. Landowners as a group were replaced by an agricultural bourgeoisie with enough political power to obtain a certain amount of compensation for the country's discrimination against agricultural producers.

Export Promotion—1967–1974

In 1967 a major effort to rationalize macroeconomic policy management was begun. It was evident by then that the strategy of import substitution was exhausted, and Colombia began to adopt a policy of freer trade.

A leading policy issue during this period was the relationship between trade in agricultural products and the impact of such trade on inflation. Exports of food products such as rice and beef were subjected to quotas and other restrictions to ensure that more of the products remained in the country, and price controls were placed on other basic items, such as milk. Imported wheat, meanwhile, was sold at a loss. In short, food policy was consumer-oriented.

Although Colombia's new macroeconomic policies were more favorable to agricultural development, specific policies on agriculture fluctuated frequently. The Liberal-dominated regime of 1966–70, insisting upon the difference between "latifundio" (large landholdings) and "minifundio" (small landholdings), reinforced the application of the agrarian reform law of 1961, and introduced some changes to it. The 1970–1974 government (Conservative) returned to a policy of increasing agricultural productivity through subsidized credit and expanding the agricultural frontier through fiscal incentives. In addition, it revised the agrarian reform law, making it more favorable to landowners. Under the following Liberal government, the fiscal incentives for land expansion were abolished, and the credit subsidy was weakened.

The Coffee Boom—1975–1983

In this period the world price of coffee substantially increased, and Colombia's export earnings multiplied. But the balance of payments surplus arising from the coffee boom was accompanied by serious inflation. To ease inflationary pressures, restrictions were placed on the allocation of credit to the private sector, and imports were allowed to increase. Public investment was severely curtailed, including investment in agriculture. Export subsidies were reduced. As a result of these developments, interest rates climbed, and the real exchange rate and relative agricultural prices declined. These developments, in combination with rising real wages and land prices, squeezed profits in agriculture.

An Analysis of Change

Colombia's 1960s goal of self-sufficiency in food and nonfood agricultural production favored small-scale producers of wheat and medium-size producers of rice. In the 1970s, however, and particularly between 1972 and 1976, the government's chief concern was the welfare of consumers. Thus, despite sharp increases in the world prices of rice and wheat, domestic prices were kept below the international level.

Coffee was the only product whose producers were consistently taxed by direct price intervention during the study period. Direct intervention in the prices of rice and wheat, which benefited producers, was sometimes strong enough to overcome the negative effects of indirect intervention—that is, overvaluation of the peso. In most years of the study period, however, indirect intervention depressed relative agricultural prices, reduced real wages in the rural sector, and helped urban consumers, who paid lower prices for agricultural products. The industrial sector also benefited from indirect intervention, since industrial firms paid lower prices for agricultural raw materials and received higher prices for their products than they would have if there had been no intervention.

The Political Economy—Some Hypotheses

Colombia's politics in recent times have been notable for the strength of civilian rule. Since 1958, Colombia has been governed by two political parties (Liberal and Conservative), dominated by modernizing elites, with few ideological differences in economic matters.[18] Populism, often a strong force in other Latin American countries, has not been an important force in Colombian politics. As a result, the country has not had extreme fluctuations in economic policy. Economic policy during the study period was characterized by an export tax on coffee that was justified by the "optimal tariff" argument, moderate protection for rice, wheat, and cotton, and high tariffs in combination with quantitative restrictions on imports of manufactured consumer goods. Tariffs on intermediate and capital goods, on the other hand, were low.

Taxation of the Coffee Sector

An important element in taxation of the coffee sector until the 1960s was the absence of other good sources of government revenue. The size of the export tax on coffee has always been a cause of debate between the Federation and the government. Although the Federation cannot prevent the taxation of coffee exports, it often succeeds in having the tax reduced. More importantly, most of the time it is able to establish the transitory nature of different taxes.

Equity considerations also play a role in explaining coffee taxation and the slow adjustment of the exchange rate. Entry into the coffee export market is restricted to the Federation and to certified private exporters, who must export "Federation quality" coffee. Given the surrender price on coffee exports, the maximum price paid by exporters for coffee at the farmgate is determined by the tax level, along with normal profit taking. If world coffee prices or the exchange rate increase (and the minimum surrender price remains constant), private exporters may make extraordinary profits. If world prices fall, on the other hand, private exporters may withdraw from the market, thereby forcing the Federation to buy the entire crop. Because changes in the retention quota and minimum surrender price are negotiated between the government and the coffee growers, peso devaluation has sometimes given substantial windfall profits to exporters.

Taxation of agricultural activities resulting from indirect intervention reduced rural wages and increased rural poverty. These then became the source of several agrarian conflicts over the years. In the coffee zone, though, the conflicts were tempered by the dominance of smallholders and by the existence of social service programs operated by the Federation of Coffee Growers. As of 1980, about 300,000 farms in Colombia produced coffee.

Policies on Cotton, Rice, and Wheat

COTTON. The process of industrialization via import substitution began with the textile industry. The Institute for the Promotion of Cotton (Instituto de Fomento Algodonero, or IFA) was established in 1947, and minimum prices were established to stimulate cotton production. During the subsequent decade, domestic cotton was not competitive internationally, but the country's textile producers were forced to absorb this production at prices exceeding the international prices.

Colombian cotton became competitive in international markets in about 1959. Because internal prices were below foreign prices, cotton growers had an incentive to export cotton fiber. But the government wanted to help the textile industry, and cotton growers were allowed to export cotton only after domestic textile producers had satisfied their needs.

In 1972, after lobbying by cotton growers, the government agreed to end its direct control of cotton prices. Henceforth, prices would be set under agreements negotiated between the textile sector and cotton growers (for fiber), and between oil and fat producers and cotton growers (for cotton seeds).

Although the ability of Colombia's cotton growers (who numbered 10,572 in 1987) to influence economic policy has been increasing, they are still at a disadvantage with respect to the textile industry. The textile industry has dominated the National Association of Industrialists (ANDI) to the point that it has felt no need to form an association for the textile sector (all the large textile firms have a representative on the national board of ANDI).

ANDI and the National Federation of Coffee Growers are the two more influential producer associations in Colombia. Both of them have close ties with Antioquia (all the presidents of ANDI except one have been from that department) and with the region of Antioqueno colonization (Quindio, Caldas, Risaralda), and the impact of the department on economic policy is substantial. This regional element is an additional reason that cotton growers are at a disadvantage with respect to the textile industry.

RICE. The overriding policy consideration toward the rice sector has been the achievement of self-sufficiency.[19] During the period 1950–69, rice production increased, mainly because of an increase in cultivated area, from 133,000 hectares in 1950 to 250,000 in 1969. Domestic prices were higher than international prices during this period, but rice imports were sporadic.

The period 1969–78 was characterized by an enormous jump in production as a result of the introduction of high-yield varieties. Cultivated area under new varieties increased during the period from 5 to 96 percent of total area, and annual rice yields per hectare leapt from 2.7 to 4.2 tons. Rapid technological change then slowed.

The rice producer association, FEDEARROZ, was created in 1947 and had about 6,000 members in 1984. It has been a highly successful association in providing inputs and in promoting technological change. In terms of its influence on economic policy, however, even sectoral policies, FEDEARROZ has not been so successful. FEDEARROZ's limited attention to lobbying and its scant political power are reflected in the small influence it exerts over the price of rice. FEDEARROZ has been ineffective in breaking the system of export quotas and prohibitions.[20]

What explains the relative weakness of FEDEARROZ? Two factors seem salient. As productivity increased significantly, the rice sector became accustomed to expanding prosperity. Moreover, rice is very important in the diet of low-income groups. Expenditures on rice accounted for 6.1 percent of the total expenditure of all consumers on food, and 9.7 percent for urban consumers in the lowest income quintile. Thus, an increase in the price of paddy rice implies higher prices for consumers. The government opposes such an outcome.

WHEAT. In the early 1950s, Lauchlin Currie observed that Colombia had been following an incorrect policy on wheat—that is, striving to achieve self-sufficiency in wheat production without regard to comparative advantage.[21] Largely as the result of this lack of comparative advantage, wheat production has been in decline since the mid-1950s. This decline cannot be blamed on the negative influence of economic policies, as a recent study suggests.[22] The drop in wheat production has occurred despite protection and subsidies for Colombia's 17,000 wheat farmers.

Beginning in 1954, the government's agricultural marketing agency was granted a monopoly on wheat imports. The marketing board's imports of wheat are duty free, which has often led to revenue-maximizing behavior. As a result of heavy financial losses because of the amounts of wheat imported in the period 1966–1974 (close to 8,000 million pesos, or around US$ 300 million), there was a move toward profit maximization. Although IDEMA does not pay import tariffs on wheat, it can increase the price it charges by the amount of the tariff when it imports wheat on behalf of third parties. The income thus obtained has become an important financial resource for IDEMA.

Why did total intervention in the wheat sector cause a transfer of resources to producers? The answer is mainly because they are small peasants using traditional technology.

Producer Associations and Economic Policymaking

Students of policymaking in Colombia disagree about the strength and influence of the associations of agricultural producers. Bagley believes that they have significant and increasing power. Urrutia, on the other hand, has argued that their influence on policymaking is limited because they are economically weak and have a hard time in mobilizing political support among the producers they claim to represent.[23] Hartlynn says that they have ". . . considerable, but not unlimited, capacity for influence."[24] In a sense, these evaluations are not contradictory because they are based on different aspects of that impact. Perhaps it would be useful to divide the influence of these pressure groups into two dimensions—between sectoral and macroeconomic policies and then initiating and vetoing policies.

Agricultural producer associations in Colombia tend to have considerable influence in initiating policies that directly affect their sector and the ability to veto policies that directly hurt their affiliates. Their influence, however, seems to be much more modest on macroeconomic policies. The main reasons for this are:

· The relative institutional weakness of the associations.

- The way long-term economic agendas are designed by the central government.
- The logic of collective action.

The relative institutional weakness of most producer associations forces them to concentrate on trying to either influence sectoral policies (vetoing or proposing) or veto macroeconomic policies that directly harm their members. Because the lobbying services they provide are a public good, when there are many producers, the incentive to contribute to providing for the public good is minimal.[25]

There is a general consensus among the leaders of producer associations, policymakers, and researchers, that associations representing the industrial and service sectors have a greater influence on general economic policy than those representing the agricultural sector. Several factors explain this. One is the larger number of agricultural producer associations. This proliferation has gradually eroded the strength of the once relatively powerful SAC. Currently, producers of all of the major agricultural products have their own associations.

What has happened in the agricultural sector seems to fit Olson's discussion of the logic of collective action and its application to the rural sector.[26] His explanation is based on the following arguments. First, there is a great difference in the spatial diffusion of agriculture in comparison with most urban activities. Because of the difficulties of supervision and coordination when vast distances are involved, the optimal size of agricultural units is smaller than in industry. Then, because the optimal size of agricultural units is relatively small, there are many agricultural producers. Because there are so many producers, the benefits of collective action are not great enough to provide a strong incentive to associate. In industry, where the number of producers is much smaller, most (if not all) will get a significant share of the benefit resulting from collective action. Finally, in underdeveloped countries, the costs of transportation and communications in rural areas are very high.

The two fundamental policy variables affecting the relative prices of agricultural products are overall macroeconomic and commercial policy and sectoral policies toward agriculture. Colombian agricultural producer associations have concentrated on trying to influence sectoral policies. There are several reasons for this.

The first, and perhaps the most important, reason is that a change in sectoral policy may bring a significant benefit to the members. To bring about a change in macroeconomic policies, on the other hand, the many producer associations would have to cooperate with each other.[27] Another important reason that agricultural associations concentrate on influencing sectoral policy is that they lack the technical staff to engage in debates on longer-term policy.

Sectoral policies toward agriculture have been an important source of distortion of relative agricultural prices. The influence of producers on sectoral policies depends, to a great extent, on the strength of their associations. Their strength depends on the amount of positive inducements they can offer (technical assistance, marketing) and the capacity to be coercive (for example, through compulsory membership or state-created taxes).

The strength of producer associations in Colombia is also influenced by the country's abrupt topography. As a result of its topography, Colombia has at least five distinct cultural and economic regions, and the relative political weight of the different regions is quite varied. This regional dimension is important because crop production is often specialized by region (cotton on the Caribbean coast and in Tolima, rice in Tolima and Huila, wheat in Cundinamarca, Boyaca, and Narino).

Another important determinant of sectoral policies is the ideological attitude of policymakers. Many of those who design policies for the agricultural sector come from urban areas and are negatively inclined toward large agricultural producers, whom they see as the embodiment of backwardness.[28] Thus, products dominated by small producers (like wheat) tend to be overpriced, while a product where larger producers are the rule (like cotton) may be underpriced. Whether the product is food or nonfood may influence the attitude of policymakers. Thus, for products that are basic food (such as rice), policymakers prefer to see the incomes of producers drop rather than allow them to export. Also, policymakers may decide to freeze the price of basic foods if inflation threatens.

The economic interests of the state agencies dealing with agriculture are also a factor. IDEMA, with its inherent desire to survive as a bureaucratic entity, directs its efforts to maximizing its revenues rather than to accomplishing other objectives.

Determinants of Agricultural Prices: A Regression Analysis

A simple regression analysis corroborated the arguments presented here. We performed an OLS regression analysis with the logarithm of the real producer price as the dependent variable to explain the factors that affect its determination. One key explanatory variable was the real border price, while the other was the rate of inflation or the acceleration in the rate of inflation. The results of the analysis are presented in table 5-16.

For wheat, cotton, and coffee, the real border price was highly significant. For cotton and coffee, the estimated coefficient for the border price was less than one, implying that only part of the changes in international prices was transmitted to the domestic price. Because 90 percent of the domestic consumption of wheat is supplied through imports, that the real border price lagged one year is highly significant. Only in the case of rice was the border price not significant.

Acceleration in the rate of inflation was also significant. It has a positive sign in the case of coffee, showing that the coffee growers are strong enough politically to defend the real price of their product in the face of an acceleration in the rate of inflation. In the case of wheat and cotton, acceleration in the rate of inflation had a negative sign, reflecting the peculiarities of these two markets. The price of wheat clearly depends on IDEMA's policies. When inflation accelerates, the government often tries to reduce inflationary pressure by slowing the increase in the price of basic foods. Something somewhat different occurs in the cotton market. Although the price has not been regulated by the government since 1973, the existence of a monopsony (DIAGONAL) prevents an immediate increase in the price when inflation accelerates.

In the case of the real producer price of cotton, the rate of increase of textile output is also statistically significant and has a negative sign, probably reflecting the influence of textile producers on the cotton export quota. When the rate of growth of textile output accelerates, domestic producers want to absorb a larger share of domestic output of cotton fiber, and they pressure the government to reduce the export quota. This had a negative effect on the domestic price of cotton, because foreign prices have been generally above domestic consumer prices.

In addition to real border prices, the percent of imports in total supply is a variable that affects the real producer price of wheat negatively. This result is to be expected because domestic consumption is largely supplied by imports, and domestic production is highly protected. Another significant variable is the acceleration in the rate of inflation. It is important to mention that purchases of domestic production of wheat by IDEMA do not appear to affect its price significntly.

The main independent variables that affect the real producer price of coffee are the real border price, the rate of inflation, and the deviation of the border price from its trend value. Together, these variables explain 89 percent of the variance in the real producer price. The border price by itself explains 84 percent of the variance. The central government's deficit, as a percent of GDP, is marginally significant and has the expected negative sign. Thus, the argument, which has frequently been advanced by finance ministers that they could not reduce taxes on coffee in the short run because of the fiscal deficit, seems corroborated.

Table 5-16. Determinants of Real Producer Prices

Period	Constant border price/P_{NA}			Rate of acceleration of inflation			Fiscal Deficit	Change in textile output
		t	t-1	t	t-1	t-2	GDP	t-1
1963–83 Cotton	1.357	0.765			−0.0003			−0.0023
	(4.413)	(13.927)			(−3.004)			(−2.573)
1964–83 Cotton	1.461	0.745			−0.0003			
	(4.542)	(13.042)			(−4.509)			
1961–83 Wheat	2.873		0.417					
	(8.666)		(5.186)					
1961–83 Wheat	2.914		0.391					
	(8.464)		(4.620)					
1961–83 Wheat	2.81		0.415					
	(8.735)		(5.390)					
1962–83 Wheat	2.922		0.415	−0.0003				
	(9.281)		(5.494)	(−2.091)				
1961–83 Coffee	1.182	0.530						
	(4.836)	(7.554)						
1964–83 Coffee	1.211	0.526					−0.026	
	(4.738)	(7.581)					(−1.465)	
1964–83 Coffee	1.762		0.366				−0.026	
	(7.320)		(5.594)				(−1.454)	
1963–83 Coffee	1.780		0.358			0.0003	−0.021	
	(10.582)		(7.783)			(2.327)	(−1.584)	
1963–83 Coffee	1.657		0.386			0.0003		
	(10.652)		(8.717)			(2.261)		
1963–83 Rice	4.618	−0.019						
	(6.654)	(−0.123)						
1963–83 Rice	7.064							
	(8.415)							
1963–83 Rice	16.45							
	(4.993)							

1. The dependent variable is the producer price /P_{NA} for each product.
2. t-statistics in parentheses.
Source: García García and Montes Llamas (1989), table 8.1.

The econometric results for the real producer price of rice are consistent with it's being domestically a competitive market, and with the government's policy keeping it isolated from the international market. The two significant independent variables in the case of rice, output and per capita GDP, reflect the interaction of supply and demand.

Conclusions

The main conclusion that can be drawn is that agricultural producers had significant influence on direct government intervention in their

IDEMA purchases of wheat/output		IDEMA imports of wheat/ Output t-1	GDP per capita t-1	Output of rice t-1	Deviations around border price of coffee	R²	D.W.	RHO
t	t-1							
						0.906	1.616	
						0.907	1.644	
		−0.093 (−5.280)				0.729	1.711	
−0.001 (−0.941)		−0.080 (−3.637)				0.709		
	−0.001 (−1.102)	−0.079 (−4.159)				0.747		
		−0.100 (−5.430)				0.742	1.971	
						0.840	2.143	0.581
						0.891	2.090	0.305
					0.545 (6.835)	0.886	2.097	0.273
					0.559 (7.911)	0.898	1.973	
					0.613 (9.448)	0.889	1.956	
						−0.05	0.407	
				−0.362 (−3.045)		0.695	1.785	0.560
			−1.202 (−3.621)			0.679	1.835	0.426

specific markets, but not on overall economic policy. Representatives of the producer associations (FEDERACAFE, FEDEARROZ, FEDER-ALGODON, and FENALCE) said during interviews that their influence on sectoral policies is significant, but that the same thing was not true for overall economic policy.

In the case of coffee, an overvalued peso significantly increases the negative effect of direct intervention. The case of coffee is interesting, because it is the only product in which the effect of direct intervention was to reduce the income of producers. That this occurred, despite the enormous political influence of the National Federation of Coffee Growers, is paradoxical. The central role of coffee is total exports and the relatively low cost involved in the collection of export taxes seem to explain part of this situation. The desire by government and the Federation to "rationalize" the coffee market and to have some type of optimal tariff to maximize foreign exchange earnings also has some explanatory power. The government also uses some of the taxes as a tool to regulate the "rent" of coffee growers.

As the results on the effects of government intervention illustrate, the transfer of resources out of agriculture did not occur mainly through direct government intervention, but through the existence of an overvalued peso. Because implicit taxation is relatively covert and does not require budgetary outlays, it has fewer political costs. That the representatives of the producer associations interviewed do not perceive the negative impact of commercial and exchange rate policies on their product in the last three decades, indicates the relative ease with which a development model, based on policies that transfer resources out of agriculture, could be implemented. Price stability and equity rationales were also examined to explain why devaluations were not used more often to obtain an equilibrium exchange rate.

Agricultural producer associations concentrate their lobbying resources on influencing sectoral and not general policies because the large number of producers involved in agriculture debilitates their coalitional strength. In contrast, industrial production is concentrated in a small number of firms that, therefore, can easily organize to influence both direct and overall economic policy.

Notes

1. See World Bank (1984), table II.3; Departamento Administrativo Nacional de Estadística (DANE), Censo de Población, 1964 and 1985; Rueda et al. (1982).

2. World Bank (1984), tables I.1 and I.2.

3. García García (1981), ch. 6.

4. García García, (mimeograph, IFPRI, 1979) and DNP-UEA, *El Cultivo del Algodón* (mimeo), Bogotá, 1982.

5. See on IDEMA's functioning and policies FEDESARROLLO, *Manejo de Existencias, Comercio Exterior y Precios Agricolas: El Papel del IDEMA*, (Bogotá: February 1976), and Eduardo Sarmiento (1981).

6. The procedure and adjustments done to compare prices for coffee, cotton, rice, and wheat are presented in Jorge García García and Gabriel Montes Llamas, *Trade, Exchange Rate, and Agricultural Pricing Policy in Colombia*, (1989), appendix 1.

7. The procedure to obtain the equilibrium exchange rate is explained in detail in García García and Montes Llamas, (1989), ch. 4. The values of the elasticities of the demand for imports and supply of exports are assumed to be equal to one.

8. See Hernando J. Gomez, ''The Colombian Illegal Economy: Size, Evolu-

tion, Characteristics and Economic Impact,'' in B. Bagley, F. Thoumi, and J. Tokatlian (eds.), *State and Society in Contemporary Colombia: Beyond the National Front* (Boulder, Colorado: Westview Press, 1989).

9. The different values of imports, exports, current account imbalances, and the sustainable deficit used to calculate the alternative values for the equilibrium exchange rate are presented in García García and Montes Llamas, (1989), appendix 2.

10. For details on the procedure followed to calculate the foreign exchange effect on inputs see García García and Montes Llamas, (1989), ch. 5.

11. A description of the way these effects were calculated is present in García García and Montes Llamas, (1989), appendix 4.

12. For more details on the methodology used to measure these transfers see García García and Montes Llamas, (1989), ch. 6.

13. The credit subsidy on individual products has been left out to avoid double counting.

14. A detailed presentation of the way the effects of price intervention on the real income of consumers was calculated can be found in Garcia García and Montes Llamas, (1989), appendix 4.

15. This section is based on parts of chapter 6 of Jorge García García and Gabriel Montes Llamas, IFPRI, (1988).

16. Using the equilibrium exchange rate to calculate real wages in agriculture implies that direct interventions in the rest of the economy have been eliminated. Calculating W_A'', however, can be interpreted as what would be the impact of simultaneously eliminating direct interventions in agriculture and devaluing the peso to the equilibrium exchange rate.

17. This section owes a great deal to two studies, one by Jesús Antonio Bejarano (1985), and one by Absalón Machado (1981).

18. Robert Dix (1967).

19. Based on interview with Rafael Posada, Director of Economic Research of FEDEARROZ, March 2, 1987.

20. Exports of rice were prohibited in 1966, 1967, 1971, 1974, 1977, and 1980, and subject to quotas in 1965, 1976, and 1979 (only in 1973 were there no restrictions). A recent study done by the Central Bank on nontraditional agricultural exports, concludes that one of the main reasons for their poor performance in the 1980s has been the regime of export quotas, and suggests that they be abolished. See Gabriel Montes Llamas, et al. (1985) and Banco de la República, ''Los Obstáculos a las Exportaciones Menores Agropecuarias'', *Revista del Banco de la República*, No. 711, Enero 1987, Separata, p. 13.

21. Ricardo Candelo (1986), p. 137.

22. Mejia, Millán y Perry (1986), p. 3.

23. Miguel Urrutia (1983), p. 16.

24. Jonathan Hartlynn (1985), p. 111.

25. Mancur Olson (1982).

26. Mancur Olson (IFPRI, 1985), p. 229.

27. In the interviews with members of agricultural associations representing specific products (FENALCE, FEDERALGODON, FEDEARROZ) all of them expressed their desire that Sociedad de Agricultores de Colombia (SAC) could serve agriculture by concentrating its efforts on influencing the direction of overall macroeconomic policy (leaving sectoral policy to them). The

problem here, however, is who would be willing to provide SAC with the resources it requires (for example, a staff of highly trained economists) to do this effectively.

28. Former president Alfonso Lopez Michelsen believes that part of the reason that agriculture was stagnant during the 1960s was that the agricultural price policy of the Superintendencia de Industrial y Comercio was implemented by bureaucrats recruited from the political class who had very little contact with the rural sector. See Alfonso Lopez Michelsen, "Prologo," in Jesús A. Bejarano (1985), p. 25.

Bibliography

Banco de la República. *Cuentas Nacionales de Colombia 1950–1972.* Bogotá: Departamento de Investigaciones Económicas.

Banco de la República. 1987. "Los Obstáculos a las Exportaciones Menores Agropecuarias," *Revista del Banco de la Republica.* 711, (January) Separata.

Bejarano, Jesús Antonio. 1985. *Economia y Poder: La SAC y el Desarrollo Agropecuario Colombiano: 1871–1984,* Bogotá: Fondo Editorial CEREC.

Candelo, Ricardo. 1986. "Análisis y Perspectivas del Cultivo del Trigo." *Revista Nacional de Agricultura* 877 (December).

Departamento Administrativo Nacional de Estadística (DANE) 1974. *Censo Agropecuario 1960, 1970–1971.* Bogota: DANE.

DANE, *Colombia Estadística,* Bogotá, 1985 and 1986.

DANE, *Cuentas Nacionales de Colombia 1970–1984,* Bogotá, 1986.

DANE, *Cuentas Nacionales de Colombia 1970–1983,* Bogotá, 1985.

DANE, *Cuentas Nacionales de Colombia 1970–1984,* Bogotá, División de Edición del DANE, 1985.

Departamento Nacional de Planeación. 1982. Unidad de Estudios Agrarios (DNP-UEA), *El Cultivo del Algodón.* Bogotá: Departamento Nacional de Planeacion, Unidad de Estudios Agrarios. Processed.

Díaz-Alejandro, Carlos, 1976. *Foreign Trade Regimes and Economic Development: Colombia.* New York: Columbia University Press for the National Bureau of Economic Research.

Dix, Robert H. 1967. *Colombia: The Political Dimensions of Change.* New Haven: Yale University Press.

Dudley, L. and R. Sandilands. 1975. "The Side Effects of Foreign Aid: The Case of Public Law 480 Wheat in Colombia." *Economic Development and Cultural Change* 23, no. 2.

Echeverri, Fabio. 1981. "El papel de los Gremios en la Democracia Colombiana." *Revista Andi* 54.

Elías, Victor J. 1981. *Government Expenditures on Agriculture in Latin America,* International Food Policy Research Institute—IFPRI, Research Report 23, (May).

Federación Nacional de Cultivadores de Cereales (FENALCE). 1984. *El Cerealista* 10 (October).

———. 1986 *El Cerealista* 23 (November–December).

FEDERALGODON, *El Algodonero*, several issues.

FEDESARROLLO. 1976. *Manejo de Existencias, Comercio Exterior y Precios Agrícolas: El Papel del IDEMA*, Bogotá. (February).

FEDEARROZ, *Arros*, several issues.

García García, Jorge. 1979. *Aspectos Económicos del Cultivo del Algodón en Colombia: Politicas de Precios, Comercio Exterior y Crédito entre 1953 y 1978*. Washington, D.C.: International Food Policy Research Institute. Processed.

———. 1981. *The Effects of Exchange Rate and Commercial Policy on Agricultural Incentives in Colombia: 1953-1978*. IFPRI Research Report 24. Washington, D.C.: International Food Policy Research Institute.

———. 1983. "Aspects of Agricultural Development in Colombia, 1970-1982," Bogota: World Bank (Colombia division). Processed.

———. 1987. *The Timing and Sequencing of Trade Liberalization: The Case of Colombia: 1967-1982*. Processed.

García García, Jorge, and Gabriel Montes Llamas. 1986. *Second Report of The Political Economy of Agricultural Pricing Policies: Colombia*. World Bank, Washington DC. Processed.

———. 1987. *Final Report on The Political Economy of Agricultural Pricing Policies: The Case of Colombia: 1960-1983*. World Bank, CECSS, Washington DC.

———. 1988. *Coffee Boom. Govern26x71.11ment Expenditure and Agricultural Prices: The Colombian Experience*. Washington, D.C.: IFPRI. Research Report 68.

———. 1989. *Trade, Exchange Rate, and Agricultural Pricing Policies in Colombia*. A World Bank Comparative Study. Washington, D.C.

Hartlynn, Jonathan. 1985. "Producer Associations, The Political Regime, and Policy Processes in Contemporary Colombia." *Latin American Research Review* XX, 3.

Hertford, Reed. 1978. "Government Price Policies for Wheat, Rice, and Tractors in Colombia." In Theodore Schultz, ed., *Distortions of Agricultural Incentives*. Bloomington: Indiana University Press.

Mudassar, Imran, and Ron Duncan. 1988. *Optimal Export Taxes for Exporters of Perennial Crops*. International Commodity Markets, Policy, Planning and Research, Working Papers WPS 10. Washington, D.C.: The World Bank.

Instituto Colombiano Agropecuario (ICA). 1980. *Sector Agricola Colombiano: Diagnóstico Tecnológico Colombiano*, Bogotá.

Krueger, Anne O., Maurice Schiff, and Alberto Valdés. 1987. *Introductory Chapter for Volumes 1 and 2 of Country Studies*. Washington, D.C.: World Bank, CECSS.

Krueger, Anne O., Maurice Schiff, and Alberto Valdés. 1986. *Memo #12 to Country Authors Note 1*. World Bank, CECSS.

Liévano, Aguirre Indalecio. 1973. "Speech defending Law 5 of 1973 on Land Reform." In *Diario Oficial*. (March).

López Michelsen, Alfonso. 1985. Prólogo to Jesus Antonio Bejarano. *Económia y Poder: La SAC y el Desarrollo Agropecuario Colombiano: 1871-1984*. Fondo Editorial CEREC. Bogota.

Lorente Luis, Salazar Armando, and Gallo Angela. 1984. *Distribución de la Propiedad Rural en Colombia.* Bogotá: Editorial Presencia.

Lleras Restrepo, Carlos. 1981. *Economía Internacional y Régimén Cambiario.* Bogotá: Osprey Impresores.

Machado, Absalón. 1981. *Agricultural Policies in Colombia: 1900–1980.* Bogota, Processed.

Mejía, Millán y Perry. 1986. *Estudio sobre Políticas de Protección a los Cereales en Colombia.* Bogotá: Resumen Ejecutivo.

Montes Llamas Gabriel, et al. 1985. "La Economía del Arroz en Colombia," *Revista Nacional de Agricultura* 871.

Montes Llamas Gabriel. 1984. "Políticas Macroeconómicas y Desarollo Agropecuario." *Revista Nacional de Agricultura* (December): 125–149.

Olson, Mancur. 1982. *The Rise and Decline of Nations.* Hartford: Yale University Press.

———. 1985. "Space, Agriculture, and Organization." Washington, D.C.: International Food Policy Research Institute, Reprint No. 84.

Rueda, José O., Hortensia de Llinás, and Victor Vergara, 1982. "Dinámica Demográfica y Proyecciones de Población del Pais, los Territorios Nacionales, Bogotá, los Departamentos y las 30 Principales Ciudades: Aspectos Metodológicos y Principales Resultados." *Revista de Planeación y Desarrollo* 14 (3). SAC, *Revista Nacional de Agricultura,* several numbers 1925–1985.

Sanint Luis, et al. 1985. "Analisis de los Patrones de Consumo de Alimentos en Colombia a partir de la Encuesta de Hogares DANE/DRI 1981." *Revista de Planeación y Desarrollo* (September).

Sarmiento, Eduardo. 1981. *Objetivos del IDEMA.* Bogotá: Ministerio de Agricultura.

Scobie, Grant, and Rafael Posada. 1977. *The Impact of High Yielding Varieties in Latin America with Special Emphasis on Colombia.* Bogota: CIAT. Series JE-01 (April).

Urrutia, Miguel. 1983. *Gremios, Política Económica y Democracia.* Bogota: Fondo Cultural Cafetero-Fedesarrollo.

Vinod, Thomas. 1985. *Linking Macroeconomic and Agricultural Policies for Adjustment with Growth. The Colombian Experience.* Johns Hopkins University Press, Baltimore.

World Bank. 1984. *Colombia: Economic Development and Policy Under Changing Conditions.* Washington D.C.

World Bank. 1984. *Colombian Agriculture: Trade and Sectoral Policies for Accelerated Development.* Washington, D.C.: Report 4981-CO (March).

6 Dominican Republic

Duty D. Greene and Terry L. Roe

This analysis of agricultural pricing policies in the Dominican Republic focuses on the evolution of the prices of three agricultural commodities (sugar, coffee, and rice) relative to the price of non-agricultural goods. Sugar and coffee are the country's principal export products, and rice is the primary food staple. The analysis covers the years 1966–85 and spans the administrations of Joaquin Balaguer (1966–78), Antonio Guzman (1978–82), and Salvador Jorge (1982–86).

The years 1966–72, following the political turmoil of the revolution in 1965, were characterized by relative political stability, the initiation of an import-substitution industrialization process, fiscal and monetary restraint, and relatively high annual rates of growth in gross domestic product (GDP). The next subperiod, 1973–77, was notable for large increases in the world prices of petroleum, sugar, coffee, and grains, and their impact on the Dominican trade sector. During this subperiod, in spite of increases in the world prices of basic commodities, the Balaguer government maintained fiscal austerity and domestic food price stability. The third subperiod, 1978–81, was associated with increasing budget deficits, deficits in the economy's eternal accounts, and a rising foreign debt. The last subperiod, 1982–85, was noteworthy for a substantial decrease in the world price of sugar, increases in the country's external debt, rising fiscal and trade deficits, and efforts to liberalize trade policy, restructure the economy, devalue the peso, and adopt a floating exchange rate.

Special attention is given to the effects of agricultural pricing policy on consumer groups, primarily because the authors had access to recent studies of rural and urban household expenditures in the Dominican. One result of our analysis is the conclusion that overvaluation of the Dominican peso had a detrimental effect on agricultural producers that offset the positive effects of direct intervention. In most years, direct intervention served to subsidize producers of sugar and rice, while placing an implicit tax on coffee producers. In contrast, indirect intervention (that is, overvaluation of the peso and protection of the industrial sector) had the effect of taxing agricultural producers (except for sugarcane), while subsidizing consumers.

An Overview of the Dominican Economy

The population of the Dominican was an estimated 6.2 million in 1985 (table 6-1). The literacy rate was about 70 percent. Since about 1980, most of the country's population has resided in urban areas, with over half of the total urban population living in the country's two major cities—Santo Domingo and Santiago. As a result of an average annual population growth rate of about 2.8 percent, arable land per rural inhabitant was only 0.4 hectares in 1985. The percentage of the population active in agriculture decreased from an estimated 61 percent in 1960 to about 34 percent in 1980. During the 1966–80 period, the proportion of the population engaged in industry increased from 11 to 22 percent, in services from 18 to 28 percent, and in commerce, hotels, and restaurants, from 7 to 13 percent.

Based on the official exchange rate of one peso to one U.S. dollar, which lasted throughout the 1966–84 period, per capita real GDP grew from an annual average of about US$808 in the 1966–72 subperiod to an average annual high of about US$1,156 during the 1978–81 subperiod, and then declined to about US$1,122 during the 1982–84 subperiod (table 6-2). The primary sources of GDP growth during the 1966–72 subperiod were the industrial and service sectors of the economy. GDP grew at average annual rates of 8.4, 7.2, and 2.4 percent for the subperiods 1966–72, 1973–77, and 1978–81, respectively. The rates of growth in agricultural GDP for the same subperiods were 4.2, 3.0, and −1.3 percent, respectively (table 6-3). In the 1982–84 subperiod, average annual growth in agricultural GDP was about 2.3 percent, compared with a growth rate of about 1.4 percent for the economy as a whole.

Table 6-4 shows subperiod GDP and revenues, expenditures, and fiscal balances of the consolidated public sector, which includes public enterprises. The data in column four indicate that the Dominican government began to experience sizable deficits in 1978. These deficits averaged more than 5 percent of GDP during the 1978–81 and 1982–84 subperiods, and public saving was negative in the latter period. This steady deterioration in the solvency of the public sector appears to have been primarily the result of the fiscal policies adopted by the central government and the public enterprises (Greene and Roe 1988).

Judging by the percentage of GDP accounted for by trade, the Dominican economy seems to have been relatively open. A tendency

Table 6-1. General Demographic Data, 1960–85

(in millions)

Year	Population Total	Population Urban Total	Population Urban Concentration[b]	Population Rural[c]	Urban as percent of total[d]	Labor force total[e]	Education adult literacy[f] (percent)	Arable croplands[g] (1000 ha)	Arable land per person[h] (ha/P)	Arable land per rural person[i] (ha/P)
1960	3.04	0.92	15	2.12	30.20	0.80	65.8	1000	0.33	0.47
1970	4.00	1.62	14	2.39	40.30	1.16	66.4	1135	0.28	0.47
1980	5.43	2.77	14	2.66	51.00	1.62	68.6	1050	0.19	0.39
1985[a]	6.23	3.43	13	2.80	55.00	1.19	70.0	1100	0.18	0.39

a. 1985 estimated.

b. Computed from data provided by National Statistics Office (ONE) as number of cities in the Dominican Republic in which the most concentrated 75% of the urban population lives.

c. Column 1 divided by column 2.

d. Column 2 divided by column 1.

e. Number of people economically active.

f. Percent of total adult population (15 years old and above) that are literate.

g. Data include only land in annual and permanent crops.

h. Column 8 divided by column 1.

i. Column 8 divided by column 4.

Source: IMF Statistics, National Statistics Office (ONE), Population Census (1970, 1980), National Office of Planning (ONAPLAN) (1983), FAO Production Statistics Yearbooks (various years).

Table 6-2. National Account Statistics, Average Annual Values, 1960–84

(millions RD$)

| Year | Current GDP | Real GDP (1980 = 100) | Real GDP per capita (1980 = 100) | Percent share in GDP of | | | |
				Investment	Savings	Imports	Exports
1960–65	898.8	2345.0	702.2	12.8	13.5	19.0	20.0
1966–72	1400.1	3210.3	808.8	16.7	10.6	22.8	17.4
1973–77	3481.7	5242.9	1113.3	22.8	18.3	26.6	23.2
1978–81	5796.5	6194.0	1156.5	25.3	16.5	28.6	20.3
1982–84	8537.3	6672.5	1121.8	21.9	15.4	26.6	20.8

Note: 1984 data are preliminary estimates.

Source: IMF/IFS Statistics (1960–65), Dominican Central Bank and 1986 IBRD mission estimates.

**Table 6-3. Average Annual Growth Rates in Total GDP,
Agricultural GDP, Crop GDP, and Livestock GDP in Constant
1980 RD$, 1966–84**

Year	Total GDP	Agricultural GDP	Crop GDP	Livestock GDP
1966–72	8.36	4.22	3.98	6.83
1973–77	7.16	3.00	2.67	4.38
1978–81	2.43	−1.29	−2.60	1.38
1982–84	1.44	2.28	1.64	3.79

Source: Central Bank and 1986 International Bank for Reconstruction and Development (IBRD) mission estimates.

to incur current account deficits persisted throughout the late 1960s and the 1970s, with large trade deficits occurring in the 1980s (table 6-5). Exports as a share of GDP reached a peak of about 23 percent during the 1973–77 subperiod and then declined to an annual average of about 21 percent during the 1982–84 subperiod. During the latter subperiod the average annual value of imports exceeded the value of exports. Imports increased from a mean of about 23 percent of GDP during the 1966–72 subperiod to an average annual high of nearly 29 percent during the 1978–81 subperiod, and then declined to an average 26.6 percent during the 1982–84 subperiod. During the 1980s, foreign reserves were increasingly used to cover trade deficits (Greene and Roe 1988).

The Dominican experienced low to moderate changes in its annual rate of inflation during the 1966–84 period. The highest average annual rates in its consumer price index (CPI) occurred in the 1973–77 subperiod (12.7 percent) and in the 1982–84 subperiod (19.2 percent). The higher rate of inflation during the 1982–84 subperiod coincided with a depreciation of the country's currency relative to the U.S. dollar. The growing current account deficit in the 1960s increased the pressure to devalue the currency, and an unofficial foreign exchange market evolved. The average annual premium on purchases of U.S. dollars in the unofficial market during this period was reported by the Dominican Central Bank to have averaged about 14 percent during the 1966–77 period and about 26 percent during the 1978–81 period. It began spiraling upward in 1982 and reached 212 percent in 1985.

The average annual exchange rate for each of the four subperiods, in nominal terms, appears in column 1 of table 6-6. These rates are averages of the official and parallel market values, weighted by the respective import shares in each market. Estimates of the purchasing power parity and the real foreign exchange rate appear in columns four and six, respectively. These estimates show that the peso was depreciating in response to trade imbalances during the late 1970s

Table 6-4. Financial Accounts of the Consolidated Public Sector, Estimated Average Annual Values, 1966–85

(millions of RD$)

| Year | GDP Current | Revenues[a] | Expenditures[b] | Budget surplus deficit[c] | Budget deficit ratio to | | Current savings | Ratio of savings to GDP[f] (percent) |
					Expenditures[d] (percent)	GDP[e] (percent)		
1966–72	1713.1	458.1	445.8	12.3	2.4	0.6	125.2	7.2
1973–77	3481.7	997.7	1018.8	−21.1	−2.1	−0.6	255.7	7.4
1978–81	5796.5	1388.5	1734.0	−345.5	−19.7	−5.9	6.4	0.3
1982–84	8537.3	1928.8	2376.2	−447.4	−19.1	−5.3	−6.8	−0.3

a. Includes current revenues plus capital receipts of the Consolidated Public Sector (Central Government, decentralized agencies, municipalities, and public enterprises).

b. Includes current and capital expenditures of the Consolidated Public Sector plus expenditures of the nonconsolidated nonfinancial sector and those paid through the monetary budget.

c. Column 2 minus column 3.

d. Column 4 divided by column 3.

e. Column 4 divided by column 1.

f. Column 7 divided by 1.

Source: Central Bank estimates, 1986 IBRD mission estimates, ONAPRES.

Table 6-5. Balance on Current Account of the Balance of Payments, Average Annual Values, 1966–84

(millions of US$)

Year	Exports	Imports	Trade balance	Service exports	Service imports	Service balance	Donation transfer	Balance current account
1966–72	206.0	240.1	-34.1	42.0	108.0	-66.0	17.2	-82.9
1973–77	693.9	696.1	-2.2	118.0	323.4	-205.4	84.8	-122.8
1978–81	923.5	1242.8	-319.3	289.8	584.3	-294.5	184.1	-429.7
1982–84	808.2	1263.7	-455.5	449.8	583.7	-134.0	229.0	-360.4

Source: IMF *International Financial Statistics* yearbooks.

Table 6-6. Price Indices, Nominal and Real Foreign Exchange Rates, Average Annual Values, 1965–85

Year	Weighted nominal actual[a] (RD$/US$)	CPI DR.[b] 1965=100	WPI U.S.[c] 1965=100	Eppp DR/US[d] 1965=100 (RD$/US$)	Nominal equilibrium[d] (RD$/US$)	Real actual[f] (RD$/US$)	Real equilibrium[g] (RD$/US$)	Percentage change real and equilibrium[h] (percent)
							Real exchange rates	
1966–72	1.009	104.67	111.25	0.94	1.34	1.07	1.29	−16.820
1973–77	1.017	174.31	175.34	0.99	1.19	1.03	1.14	−9.350
1978–81	1.050	262.78	263.47	1.00	1.31	1.05	1.19	−12.020
1982–85	1.998	428.12	321.91	1.32	2.34	1.46	1.64	−11.220

Note: Values for the periods are obtained on a yearly basis and then averaged for the period.
a. Estimated weighted average nominal exchange rate.
b. D.R. Consumer Price Index. Central Bank data.
c. U.S. Producer Price Index. U.S. Dept. of Commerce.
d. Purchasing power parity (E^* (1965=1.003)*[column 2 divided by 3]).
e. Estimated nominal equilibrium exchange rate (See appendix A).
f. Real actual exchange rate (columns 1*3 divided by 2).
g. Estimated real equilibrium exchange rate (see appendix A).
h. Degree of divergence between the two given real exchange rate (columns [6 minus 7] divided by 7).
Source: Greene and Roe (1988), Table 6D.

and early 1980s. The nominal equilibrium and the real equilibrium exchange rates appear in columns 5 and 7, respectively.[1] The nominal rate is our estimate of the exchange rate that would have prevailed in the absence of distortions in the economy. This rate was used to calculate the total effects of intervention.

Contemporary industrial policy, price controls, and the legal and institutional structure needed to implement intervention in prices are a legacy from the Trujillo period (1930–61). By the end of the Trujillo era, his family and associates controlled a wide variety of manufacturing and industrial firms (Bell 1981). Most of these firms had become part of the Dominican Corporation of State-Owned Enterprises (CORDE) by 1966. The state-owned Sugar Enterprise (CEA) also evolved from the process of nationalizing private firms. Control of food prices was implemented in 1957 by the Bank of Agricultural and Industrial Credit. This bank was given the authority to market rice, to operate as a bonded warehouse, and to set rice prices for producers, wholesalers, and retailers. A reorganization of the public sector enterprises in agriculture eventually led to the creation of the National Institute of Price Stabilization (INESPRE) in 1969. Initially, INESPRE assumed the government's rice marketing and price control activities and, shortly thereafter, became the principal state-owned enterprise for implementing price policy for rice and numerous other foods. Policy implementation required INESPRE to perform many marketing activities, such as procurement, transportation, storage, and foreign trade.

After Trujillo's death in 1963, Law 13 established a Directorate General of Price Control (DGPC) within the Ministry of Commerce and Industry. This agency was given the legal authority to fix prices on agricultural and industrial goods that were designated to be of primary necessity, and to prosecute wholesalers and retailers who violated ceiling prices. In 1986, the DGPC set prices on a wide variety of food products, including sugar, rice, wheat and corn flour, soybean oil, noodles, bread, milk, chicken, eggs, chocolate, salt, soap, toothpaste, propane gas, kerosene, cement, and nails.

In 1968, with the promulgation of Law 299, the Dominican turned toward import-substitution industrialization. This law encouraged investment, through a variety of tax credits and tariff incentives, in industries specializing in either exports or import substitution.[2] Implementation of this policy tended to increase the number of firms specializing in the manufacturing of import substitutes relative to those specializing in the production of export goods. The resulting pattern of industrial growth was determined largely by the existing structure of import tariffs, quotas, domestic pricing policies on final products and, as discussed later, an overvalued currency.

The Agricultural Sector

Agriculture's share of GDP steadily declined from a mean of more than 27 percent during the years 1960–65 to a mean of about 15 percent during the 1982–84 subperiod (table 6-7). Within agriculture, the value of crop production exceeded the value of other activities by 250 percent in most years.[3] In recent years, however, the value of livestock production has increased relative to the value of crop production (table 6-7). Approximately 25 percent of the total production value of agriculture is from sugarcane. This crop constituted, on average, about 18 percent of the total cropland area (including land planted to perennial crops) between 1966 and 1985. Most of the country's rice was grown on irrigated lands, which accounted for about 11 percent of total cropland. The remaining 71 percent of the total cropland area was classified as other rainfed agricultural land. Based on the 1976 agricultural survey, land utilization was distributed as follows: food crops, 12 percent; export crops, 21.1 percent; pasture, 52.8 percent; and fallow and forest land, 14.1 percent.

Farm land ownership has been highly skewed. Data from the agricultural census for 1981 show that about 82 percent of the farms in the Dominican consisted of fewer than five hectares and occupied only 13 percent of all farmland, while 1 percent of the farms had more than 200 hectares and occupied approximately 36 percent of the land area. Approximately 40 percent of the land in farms of over 50 hectares was owned by the government. This included 173,700 hectares held by the CEA and another 392,000 hectares controlled by the Dominican Agrarian Reform Institute (IAD).

During the 1966–72 subperiod, traditional agricultural exports (that is, sugar, coffee, cocoa, and tobacco) accounted for about 76 percent of the country's total value of exports (table 6-8). By the 1982–84 subperiod, however, the value of traditional agricultural exports had declined to about 55 percent of total exports. The steady decline in the average share of agricultural exports as a proportion of total exports reflects a decrease in the value of sugar exports along with growth in the value of mining and industrial exports.[4] Although agriculture's declining share is typical of countries experiencing growth and development, our analysis in later sections will show that pricing policies that taxed agricultural exports and protected industry contributed significantly to this trend.

The share of agricultural imports (excluding manufactured agricultural goods and agricultural inputs) in the total value of all imports was small. The value of agricultural imports as a proportion of total imports increased from an annual average of about 3 percent during the 1966–72 subperiod to more than 8 percent during the 1973–77 subperiod. This change was largely the result of increases in rice and

Table 6-7. National Account Statistics for the Agricultural Sector, 1960–84
(current millions of RD$)

Year	Total current GDP	Agricultural sector value	(percent)	Crops value	(percent)	Livestock value	(percent)	Forestry & fisheries value	(percent)
1960–65	898.8	244.4	27.6	173.4	19.6	62.3	7.0	8.7	1.0
1966–72	1400.1	346.0	24.8	217.2	17.4	92.8	6.6	9.6	0.7
1973–77	3481.6	775.3	22.9	523.8	17.0	180.8	5.3	18.5	0.6
1978–81	5796.4	1039.2	18.1	711.6	12.3	281.6	4.9	31.7	0.5
1982–84	8537.3	1299.1	15.2	857.4	10.1	396.4	4.6	45.3	0.5

Source: Central Bank and IBRD data.

Table 6-8. Annual Average Values Of Traditional Agricultural Commodities, 1966–84

Exports

Year	Value total	Raw sugar value	Raw sugar (percent)	Green coffee value	Green coffee (percent)	Cocoa value	Cocoa (percent)	Tobacco value	Tobacco (percent)	Total value	Agricultural traditional exports (percent)
1966–72	206.0	103.2	50.5	22.5	11.3	14.9	7.7	14.7	6.8	155.3	76.4
1973–77	693.9	308.9	43.9	82.1	11.7	46.3	6.6	34.0	5.1	471.4	67.4
1978–81	923.5	282.6	29.3	101.3	11.7	63.6	7.5	50.3	5.6	497.8	54.0
1982–84	808.2	267.3	33.2	88.4	10.9	61.3	7.5	31.0	3.8	448.0	55.4

Imports

Year	Value total	Rice value	Rice (percent)	Wheat value	Wheat (percent)	Corn value	Corn (percent)	Soybean oil value	Soybean oil (percent)	Total value	Agricultural import (percent)
1966–72	240.1	0.7	0.3	6.0	2.6	n.a.	n.a.	n.a.	n.a.	7.5	3.1
1973–77	696.1	22.2	3.3	18.6	2.7	10.3	1.5	9.1	1.2	58.4	8.4
1978–81	1242.8	14.8	1.1	27.9	2.3	21.5	1.7	16.2	1.4	80.4	6.4
1982–84	1263.7	0.0	0.0	n.a.	n.a.	32.0	2.5	23.3	1.8	62.3	4.9

n.a. Not available.

Note: Values are in millions of US$ and percent of total exports and imports.

Source: INESPRE, Memoria Anual. Various Years and USDA/FATUS (wheat imports, various years).

wheat imports. The share of agricultural imports in total imports then declined to an annual average of about 5 percent during the 1982–84 subperiod.

Agricultural Price Policies

During the 1966–85 period there were a number of governmental policies that distorted domestic agricultural prices away from world border prices. The degree of distortion varied considerably across commodities and from year to year. The most important direct interventions during the 1966–85 period were export taxes and quotas, import tariffs and quotas, sugarcane production by CEA, and the importing and marketing of food products by INESPRE and by Dominican Wheat Mills, another state enterprise. In addition, policies that contributed to an overvalued currency and protection of the industrial sector had important indirect effects on the country's production and consumption of agricultural commodities. Obviously, overvaluing the currency in effect taxes the production of exported products and subsidizes the consumption of imported commodities. In addition, industrial protection tends to divert the domestic terms of trade from agriculture and toward the industrial sector.

The direct and indirect effects of price policy on the country's primary tradable agricultural products in each of four subperiods are evaluated in this section. Average annual rates of direct and total protection are estimated for producers and consumers of each of these products. The effects of direct intervention are derived from a comparison of average annual internal product prices with their respective border prices (after adjustment for transportation and other marketing costs) evaluated at the nominal weighted exchange rate. The effects of total intervention include the indirect effects of year-to-year overvaluation of the weighted exchange rate and distortions in the price index of nonagricultural goods. Consequently, evaluation of the effects of indirect intervention requires an estimate of the nominal equilibrium exchange rate. This rate is defined as the foreign exchange rate that would have prevailed in the absence of all policy distortions. The methodology used to derive estimates of the annual equilibrium exchange rate is given in appendix A.

The data on table 6-9 show the average annual effects of direct and total intervention on producers' prices of sugarcane, coffee, and paddy rice relative to P_{NA} in each of the four subperiods. The average producer prices relative to P_{NA} (RPP_i, i=sugar, coffee, rice) are given for each commodity and are the same for both direct and total intervention. The average world border price (evaluated at the producer level) relative to P_{NA} is first given for the direct effect (RBP_i). These relative prices were derived by multiplying the border prices of the

Table 6-9 Direct and Total Effects of Price Policy on Producer Prices of Sugar, Coffee, and Rice Relative to the Price Index of Nonagricultural Goods, Average Annual Values, 1966–85

Year	Sugar			Coffee			Rice		
	PPs/P_{NA}	BPs/P_{NA}	$RNPPRs$ (protection rate) (percent)	PPc/P_{NA}	BPc/P_{NA}	$RNPPRc$ (protection rate) (percent)	PPr/P_{NA}	BPr/P_{NA}	$RNPPRr$ (protection rate) (percent)
Direct Effects									
1966–72	6.6	3.5	580.9[a]	259.4	303.2	−13.6	159.9	144.1	11.9
1973–77	7.9	17.5	−51.0	357.2	458.4	−19.5	138.9	163.4	−4.8
1978–81	5.2	7.5	−1.4	352.7	415.5	−12.0	104.4	94.2	10.8
1982–85	4.8	2.7	182.5	121.7	240.8	−44.0	90.9	64.1	48.7
Total effects									
1966–72	6.6	6.0	143.5	259.4	389.7	−32.9	159.9	179.6	−10.3
1973–77	7.9	22.1	−62.3	357.2	531.6	−30.6	138.9	188.0	−16.3
1978–81	5.2	11.0	−38.9	352.7	521.6	−30.3	104.4	116.3	−10.3
1982–85	4.8	6.4	67.5[b]	121.7	343.9	−64.6	90.9	78.1	18.9

Note: The relative nominal protection rates are annual averages for the respective periods and, thus, they are not exactly equal to the values that would be obtained by substituting the annual averages reported in columns 1 and 2, 4 and 5, or 7 and 8 into equations 6-1 and 6-2. The notation PP.. and BP.. denote producer price and border producer price, respectively.

a. This average excludes 1967 which has an infinitely large RNPPs, because the estimated RBPs/P_{NA} for that year is negative.

b. The three year average 1982–84, RNPPRs* = −32.5. In 1985, RNPPRs* = 367.4 so that the overall average is the reported 67.5.

Source: Greene and Roe (1988).

agricultural products by the annual weighted foreign exchange rate and dividing by P_{NA}. The relative border prices for the total effects (RBP^*_i) are then given in the lower panel by multiplying the border price of the agricultural products by the annual nominal equilibrium exchange rates and dividing by the distorted price index for non-agricultural goods (P_{NA}^*).

The relative nominal producer price series (RPP_i) and the border price series (RBP_i) are used to derive the relative nominal producers' protection rate ($RNPPR_i$) arising from direct intervention according to the following equation:

(6-1) $$RNPPR_{it} = (RPP_{it}/RBP_{it}) - 1 = (PP_{it}/BP_{it}) - 1$$

where i denotes the agricultural product and t denotes the period.[5] A positive (negative) value signifies that producers of the particular commodity were subsidized (taxed) by direct intervention in prices in the *t-th* period.

The relative nominal producers' protection rate ($RNPPR^*$) arising from total intervention is given by:

(6-2) $$RNPPR^*_{it} = (RPP_{it}/RBP^*_{it}) - 1$$

where RBP^*_{it} is the ratio of the border price evaluated at the equilibrium foreign exchange rate (BP^*_{it} and $P_{NA}^*_t$).

A comparison of equations (6-1) and (6-2) indicates that an overvaluation of the foreign exchange rate will tend to make RBP^*_{it} larger than RBP_{it} and, hence, $RNPPR^*_{it}$ will be less than $RNPPR_{it}$. Consequently, any price subsidy (tax) given to producers through direct intervention will be greater (less) than the effect of total intervention. Moreover, the greater the currency overvaluation, the more $RNPPR^*_{it}$ decreases relative to $RNPPR_{it}$ and the higher the taxation rate to producers. In many cases, a subsidy resulting from direct intervention was offset by the taxation effect of an overvalued currency and the protection of nonagricultural goods, turning the total effect into an implicit tax on agricultural producers. This was the case for rice, as shown in table 6-9.

The data in columns one and two of table 6-9 indicate the evolution of the average annual relative producer price of sugarcane vis-à-vis P_{NA} and of the average sugar border price (converted to an equivalent farm price using efficient marketing and processing margins) relative to P_{NA}. The world sugar price (adjusted for transportation costs) was assumed to be the relevant border price because it represents the appropriate opportunity cost for Dominican resources allocated to sugar production. The sugar price shown in the upper panel of table 6-9 indicates that the relative producer and border prices of sugarcane increased in the second subperiod relative to the first subperiod, but then decreased significantly in the last two subperiods.

As shown in column three, direct intervention in the price of sugar-cane provided positive nominal protection to Dominican producers in the first and fourth subperiods. The negative signs in the second and third subperiods imply that producers were taxed on average during those periods. Clearly, Dominican sugarcane producers on average were taxed as a result of direct intervention when world sugar prices rose, as in the second and third subperiods, and were subsidized when sugar export prices fell, as in the first and last subperiods. Distortions in sugarcane prices were the result when producer prices were set primarily by CEA and the National Sugar Institute (INAZ-UCAR) at levels different from the respective equivalent border prices.

Columns four to six to table 6-9 show, respectively, the producer price of coffee relative to P_{NA} (*RPPc*), an the relative nominal protection rate for Dominican coffee producers (*RNPPRc*). The data in column four indicate that on average the relative producer coffee price rose significantly in the second subperiod and then declined in the third and fourth subperiods. The data in column five indicate that on average the relative border price of coffee rose in the second and third subperiods with respect to the first, but then fell dramatically in the fourth subperiod. The relative nominal protection rate for coffee producers were taxed throughout the entire 1966–85 period, and especially in the last subperiod. This was the result of export taxes assessed on coffee beans and processed coffee exports.

Columns seven to nine of table 6-9 show, respectively, the relative producer price of rice (*RPPr*), the relative import border price of rice (evaluated at the producer level after adjusting for marketing costs) (*RBPr*), an the average annual relative nominal protection rate for Dominican rice producers (*RNPPRr*). Column seven indicates that the *RPPr* declined gradually over the four subperiods. The data in column eight indicate that the *RBPr* increased significantly in the second subperiod compared with the first, but then decreased dramatically in the following two subperiods. The *RNPPRr* suggest that Dominican rice producers on average were subsidized by direct intervention in prices throughout the entire period, except in the second subperiod (1973–77). These producer price subsidies (along with taxes in the second subperiod) were implemented primarily through the marketing activities of INESPRE (the only legal importer of rice during the years 1973–86) and prohibitions on rice imports during the years 1982–84.

The total effects of intervention on the relative prices of the three agricultural products, shown in the lower panel of table 6-9, include the indirect effects of the country's foreign exchange rate policy and the distortions in P_{NA}. As explained above, domestic relative producer prices are the same ratios used for the direct effects, but the respective relative border prices are based on the estimated nominal equilibrium foreign exchange rate and $P_{NA}*$. Because the Dominican government had a policy of overvaluing its currency throughout most of the period under study, the total effect of intervention was to increase border prices and decrease relative nominal protection rates (or increase the implicit tax) for agricultural producers of tradable commodities.

As shown in the case of sugar, the RNPPRs* still suggests positive nominal rates of protection in the first and the fourth subperiods and negative rates in the second and third. As compared with the respective rates given for the RNPPRs, however, the positive protection rates (or subsidies) were less and the taxation rates were greater in the respective subperiods. In the case of coffee, the rate of taxation on Dominican coffee producers increases when the effects of indirect intervention are included. With rice, indirect intervention replaces the subsidies given to rice producers through direct intervention in the first three subperiods with implicit taxation. In the last three subperiod the subsidy provided to rice producers was reduced substantially (but not converted into a tax) because of indirect intervention.

Table 6-10 shows the relative consumer prices and nominal protection rates for Dominican consumers of the three agricultural commodities. These nominal protection rates were derived by comparing the respective domestic consumer prices with the border prices evaluated at the wholesale level (with the appropriate adjustments for marketing costs) using equations (6-1) and (6-2). In this case, a positive sign for the relative nominal protection rate indicates a consumer tax and a negative sign indicates a consumer subsidy.

The data in column one of table 6-10 show that the domestic consumer price of sugar relative to P_{NA} fell substantially throughout the entire period. The export border price of sugar relative to P_{NA} (column two) was highest in the second subperiod and lowest in the fourth subperiod. As a result of direct intervention (shown in column three), Dominican sugar consumers were taxed significantly in the first subperiod and subsidized in the last three subperiods (especially in the fourth).

With respect to coffee, the data in column four indicate that domestic consumer coffee prices relative to P_{NA} were highest in the second and third subperiods and lowest in the fourth subperiod. The same tendencies are reflected in the evolution of coffee border prices (shown in column five), except that the average relative price in the fourth subperiod is greater than in the first subperiod. The relative nominal protection rates for Dominican coffee consumers indicate that direct intervention slightly taxed consumers in the first subperiod and subsidized them in the last three subperiods. Total inter-

Table 6-10. Direct and Total Effects of Price Policy on Consumer Prices of Sugar, Coffee, and Rice Relative to the Price Index of Non-Agricultural Goods, Average Annual Values, 1966–85

	Sugar			Coffee			Rice		
Year	$CWPs/P_{NA}$ (1966 = 100)	$CBPs/P_{NA}$	RNCPRs (protection rate) (percent)	$CWPc/P_{NA}$ (1966 = 100)	$CBPc/P_{NA}$	RNCPRc (protection rate) (percent)	$CWPr/P_{NA}$ (1966 = 100)	$CBPr/P_{NA}$	RNCPRr (protection rate) (percent)
Direct effects									
1966–72	128.5	70.1	119.7	895.3	879.2	2.5	272.4	239.7	14.8
1973–77	120.7	186.3	−29.4	1025.7	1184.6	−12.6	248.1	264.0	3.3
1978–81	71.6	108.2	−19.4	1016.3	1143.7	−8.4	183.2	170.6	7.3
1982–85	39.1	61.5	−38.2	612.4	817.6	−22.6	145.1	146.6	8.7
Total effects									
1966–72	128.5	95.4	60.3	895.3	1201.1	−25.1	272.4	327.8	−16.0
1973–77	120.7	226.8	−42.8	1025.7	1452.5	−28.8	248.1	326.2	−15.2
1978–81	71.6	142.5	−39.2	1016.3	1511.7	−30.8	183.2	225.5	−18.8
1982–85	39.1	99.2	−61.6	612.4	1230.0	−50.4	145.1	183.9	−21.1

Note: The relative nominal protection rates are annual averages for the respective periods and, thus, they are not exactly equal to the values that would be obtained substituting the annual averages reported in columns 1 and 2, 4 and 5, or 7 and 8 into equations 6-1 and 6-2. The notation CW., and CB., denote consumer wholesale and consumer border price, respectively. For total effects, CBP is divided by P_{NA}^{*}.

Source: Greene and Roe (1988).

vention provided rather large consumer subsidies throughout the entire period, because overvaluation of the currency subsidizes consumers of tradable goods.

The domestic and border consumer prices of rice vis-à-vis P_{NA}, as shown in columns seven and eight, respectively, indicate that usually these prices fell continuously throughout the entire period, except in the case of rice border prices in the second subperiod. As shown in column nine, Dominican consumers were taxed as a result of direct intervention throughout the 1966–85 period on average, but only slightly in the second subperiod. The effect of total intervention was to subsidize rice consumers throughout the period. A note of caution is warranted here, however, because the use of subperiod annual averages obscures the substantial subsidies given to rice consumers in 1973 and 1974 (see Greene and Roe 1988).

The respective relative nominal rates of protection for producers and consumers of each agricultural product provide a good indication of the respective gainers and losers. Indirect intervention clearly had the effect of taxing the producers and subsidizing the consumers of tradable agricultural products throughout the period. Direct intervention, however, had very different effects, depending on the product and period in question.

In the case of sugar, for example, the results indicate that direct intervention subsidized producers and taxed consumers during the first subperiod. In the second and third subperiods, however, the results were reversed; producers were taxed, and consumers were subsidized. In the fourth subperiod, direct intervention apparently subsidized producers and consumers simultaneously, with the government covering the total costs of these subsidies. In the case of coffee, direct intervention taxed producers and subsidized consumers (except for the first subperiod) throughout the entire period.

In the case of rice, direct intervention subsidized producers and taxed consumers on average throughout the entire period. The producer subsidies resulted primarily from the rice price policies implemented by INESPRE. Dominican rice consumers paid prices slightly higher than world prices, on average, primarily because of direct intervention and the marketing inefficiency of INESPRE.

The Effects of Price Intervention

This section evaluates the primary effects (that is, the short-run direct and total effects) of direct and indirect intervention on the following variables: (a) production and consumption of rice, sugar, and coffee; (b) foreign exchange earnings from these crops; and (c) the real expenditures of different income groups on sugar, coffee, and rice. (The cumulative effects derived from the use of long-run supply elasticities for the respective agricultural products are given in Greene and Roe 1988.)

The production effects are derived from econometrically estimated supply functions for sugar, coffee, and rice. The effects on consumption are derived from an econometrically estimated two-stage complete demand system of price and expenditure elasticities for Dominican households. (The data and methodology used to derive these supply and demand results are described in detail in Greene and Roe 1988.)

Estimated Supply Functions for Sugarcane, Coffee, and Rice

The effects of intervention on sugar production were obtained using the following log-linear supply function and observed production and price data for 1966–84:

(6-3) $QPSSC = 5.892 + 0.154 RPPSC_{t-2} - 0.856 RPPRI_{t-2}$
$- 0.196 RPPBF_{t-2}$
    (3.23)   (1.15) (-1.98) (-1.05)
$-0.034D + 0.483 QPPSC_{t-2}$
    (-0.88) (2.67)
        $R^2 = 0.659$ Durbin-Watson = 1.18

where, for year t,

$QPSSC_t$ = the logarithm of sugarcane production (1,000MT)
$RPPSC_t$ = the logarithm of the producer price (RD\$/MT) of sugarcane divided by P_{NA}
$RPPRI_t$ = the logarithm of the producer price (RD4/MR) of paddy rice divided by P_{NA}
$RPPBF_t$ = the logarithm of the producer price (RD4/MT) of beef divided by P_{NA}
D = a dummy variable denoting years of bad weather (1975, 1980, 1981).

The t-statistics are given in parentheses below the coefficients. The estimated coefficients imply that the short-run supply elasticities for sugarcane are approximately 0.15, -0.86, and -0.20 with respect to the two-year lagged producer prices for sugarcane, rice, and beef, respectively. The long-run supply elasticity is approximately 0.30. The result that the cross-price elasticity of sugarcane production with respect to the price of rice is larger in absolute terms than the own price elasticity is inconsistent with the assumption of profit maximization, when the production technology is defined by a continuous quasi-concave and monotonically increasing production function with multiple outputs.[6] Given this inconsistency, the cross-price elasticities of sugarcane production with respect to rice and beef prices were omitted.

The supply function coefficients for coffee production were obtained from the following estimated linear equation, based on production and price data for 1966–84:

(6-4) $QPSCF_t = 68.13 + 7.60RPPCF_{t-3} + 3.18RPPCC_{t-3}$
$- 169.26RPPPL_{t-e}$
(5.90) (6.11)   (3.26)   (4.17)
$- 41.00D + 0.15QPSCF_{t2}$
(4.51) (1.26)
$R^2 = .91$ Durbin-Watson = 2.41

where, for year t,

$QPSCF_t$ = the annual production (1,000MT) of coffee cherries
$RPPCF_t$ = the average annual producer price ($RD\$/MT$) of coffee cherries divided by P_{NA}
$RPPCC_t$ = the average annual producer price ($RD\$/MT$) of cocoa beans divided by P_{NA}
D = a dummy variable denoting years of hurricane effects (1980–1981).

The t-statistics are given in parentheses below the coefficients. The estimated coefficients imply that the short-run supply elasticities (evaluated at the means) for coffee production are approximately 0.31, 0.22, and −0.23 with respect to three-year lagged prices for coffee, cocoa, and plantains, respectively. The long-run supply elasticity is about 0.34 (evaluated at the means).

The supply function coefficients for rice production were obtained from the following linear supply function, estimated by Roe and Senauer using annual 1966–79 production data:

(6-5) $QPSRI_t = -53.322 + 0.978RPPRI_t - 0.114RPPBF_t$
$+ 0.679QPRI_{t-1}$
(−.563) (2.051)   (2.760)   (3.606)
$= 7.918T$
(3.146)
$R^2 = 0.99$ Durbin-Watson = 2.2

where, for the year t:

$QPSRI_t$ = the annual production of rough rice (1,000 MT)
$RPPRI_t$ = the average annual producer price ($RD\$/MT$) of rough rice divided by the producer price index (PPI_t)
$RPPBF_t$ = the average annual producer price ($RD\$/MT$) of beef divided by PPI_t
PPI_t = a producer price index
T = a time trend (1=1966,. . .,14=1979).

The t-statistics are given in parentheses under the coefficients. The estimated coefficients imply that the short-run elasticities for rough rice (evaluated at the means) are approximately 0.2 and −0.2 with respect to the prices of rice and beef, respectively. The long-run own-price supply elasticity (evaluated at the means) is approximately 0.6.

Short-Term Direct and Total Effects on Production

Table 6-11 shows the effects of direct and indirect intervention on annual short-run production of sugarcane, coffee, and rice for 1966–85, based on the supply functions (1) − (3). The direct effects of price policy table 6-11 are observed by comparing the observed annual output of these crops with the estimated output that would have prevailed in the short run had producer prices been at their respective border prices evaluated at the official foreign exchange rates. The total effects of price policy are seen by comparing the observed annual output of these crops with the estimated output that would have occurred in the short run had prices been at their respective border prices evaluated at the estimated equilibrium exchange rate (and divided by $P_{NA}{}^*$).

The average annual amounts of the products that were actually produced are shown in the first, fourth, and seventh columns of table 6-11. The second column gives the estimated average annual amounts that would have been produced in the short run with border prices evaluated at the official exchange rate. The third column shows the annual averages of the change between the annual amounts produced and those estimated with border prices.

The estimated average annual changes in the amount of sugarcane production, shown in column three, are based on the difference between the annual quantity actually produced and the estimated quantity that would have been produced had border prices evaluated at the official exchange rate prevailed. These changes indicate that direct intervention in sugarcane prices had its greatest negative impact (−8.4 percent) on short-run production in the third subperiod and its most positive impact (61.9 percent) in the first subperiod.

The results in columns four to six show, respectively, the average annual quantity of coffee (cherries) actually produced, the estimated average annual quantity that would have been produced in the short run with producer prices for coffee, cocoa, and plaintains at their border prices evaluated at the official foreign exchange rate, and the average annual percentage change between these two amounts. The results in column six indicate that, on average, direct intervention in the prices of coffee, cocoa, and plaintains had their greatest negative impact on short-run production of coffee in the third subperiod (−9.2 percent). Clearly, on average, direct intervention had a negative short-run impact on Dominican coffee production in each of the four subperiods.

The data in columns seven to nine indicate, respectively, the aver-

Table 6-11. Direct and Total Effects of Price Policy on Short-Run Production of Rice, Sugarcane, and Coffee, Annual Average Values, 1966–85

Year	Sugarcane QPSC million mt[a]	QPSSC million mt[b]	QPSSC (percent)[c]	Coffee QPCF 1000 mt[d]	QPSCF 1000 mt[e]	QPSCF (percent)[f]	Rice QPRI 1000 mts[g]	QPSRI 1000 mt[h]	QPSRI (percent)[i]
Direct effects									
1966–72	8.0	6.1	61.9	84.8	92.4	−2.0	203.9	176.1	17.5
1973–77	10.3	11.0	−5.3	112.8	117.9	−4.2	278.8	289.2	−1.3
1978–81	10.3	11.4	−8.4	105.8	117.1	−9.2	379.5	362.4	4.9
1982–85	10.9	10.7	3.8	139.2	143.7	−3.1	482.3	450.6	7.5
Total effects									
1966–72	8.0	7.7	14.1	84.8	99.4	−8.8	203.9	196.7	4.4
1973–77	10.3	11.5	−9.8	112.8	126.8	−10.9	278.8	309.1	−6.8
1978–81	10.3	12.0	−13.4	105.8	129.7	−17.1	379.5	382.3	−0.5
1982–85	10.9	11.7	−6.2	139.2	158.6	−11.9	482.3	463.4	4.3

Note: The data in columns 3, 6, and 9 are averages of the annual data for each period and, hence, cannot be calculated directly from the data in the first two columns for each product.

a. Quantity of sugarcane produced.
b. Estimated short-run production of sugarcane from the removal of the direct and total price effects.
c. Estimated percentage change in sugarcane production from direct and total price effects.
d. Quantity of coffee charries produced.
e. Estimated short-run production of coffee from the removal of the direct and total price effects.
f. Estimated percentage change in coffee production from direct and total price effects.
g. Quantity of rice produced.
h. Estimated short-run production of rice from the removal of the direct and total price effects.
i. Estimated percentage change in rice production from direct and total price effects.

Source: Greene and Roe (1988).

age annual quantity of paddy rice produced, the estimated average annual quantity that would have been produced in the short run with producer prices for rice and beef at their border prices evaluated at the official foreign rate, and the average annual percentage change between these two amounts. The data in column nine indicate that, on average, combined direct intervention in the prices of rice and beef had its greatest negative impact on short-run production of rice in the second subperiod (-1.3 percent). Average annual increases in the production of rice appear to have occurred in the other three subperiods. These estimated increases indicate that direct intervention tended to subsidize the short-run production of rice, taking into account distortions in the prices of rice and beef.

The data for the total effects in table 6-11 are similar to those for direct effects. For the total effects, the estimated average annual changes in short-run production are based on total intervention in prices, which includes the effects of indirect intervention. That is, the estimated average annual outputs are derived from short-run changes in producer prices, but the respective product border prices are evaluated at the equilibrium exchange rate and divided by $P_{NA}{}^*$. Hence, the estimated changes in the short-run output of each crop result form the combined effects of direct and indirect intervention in prices.

The estimated average annual percentage changes in short-run output of sugarcane resulting form total intervention are shown in column three of table 6-11. These estimates indicate that total intervention had the effect of decreasing the change in short-run production of sugarcane compared with the effects of direct intervention alone, since estimated production with total intervention removed is greater than with only direct intervention removed. The greatest negative effect (-13.4 percent) on short-run production of sugarcane resulting from total intervention occurred in the third subperiod. An estimated increase (14.1 percent) in the average annual short-run production of sugarcane occurred in the first subperiod only as a result of total intervention.

The estimated average annual percentage changes in short-run output of coffee resulting from total intervention in the prices of coffee, cocoa, and plaintains are shown in column six under total effects in table 6-11. These estimates indicate that total intervention had the effect of decreasing short-run production of coffee compared with direct intervention alone. The greatest negative effect (-17.1 percent) on short-run production of coffee because of total intervention occurred in the third subperiod. Short-run production of coffee is estimated to have decreased in all four subperiods as a result of total intervention. These results, when compared with those for direct intervention alone, indicate the significant negative effect that the overvalued currency had on the short-run output of coffee during the 1966–85 period.

The estimated average annual percentage changes in short-run output of rice resulting from total intervention in the prices of rice and beef are shown in column nine under total effects in table 6-11. These estimates indicate that total intervention in rice and beef prices also had the effect of decreasing short-run production of rice, compared with direct intervention alone. The greatest negative effect (−6.8 percent) on short-run production of rice because of total intervention occurred in the second subperiod. In addition, the average annual change in production was negative (−0.5 percent) in the third subperiod. Estimated increases in the average annual short-run production of rice occurred in the first (4.4 percent) and third (4.3 percent) subperiods as a result of total intervention.

The Estimated Demand Functions for Sugar, Coffee, and Rice

The effects of direct and total intervention in prices on consumption of sugar, coffee, and rice were derived from a matrix of a complete and internally consistent system of demand elasticities (Greene and Roe 1988). This demand matrix was derived from the elasticities of a larger econometrically estimated complete two-stage demand system of Dominican households (Yen 1986). The demand equations for rice, sugar, and coffee are assumed to be approximated by a constant exponential function (that is, a double logarithmic-linear form), with the respective estimated elasticities given as the exponents.

Calculation of the effects of intervention on consumption includes the effect of total intervention on the prices of rice, sugar, coffee, other foods, and nonfood goods. Total per capita income per year is held constant. However, changes in total income over time are captured in the calculation of the constant term (A_{it}) for consumption of the ith good in each year ($t=1966,\ldots,1985$). The price index of non-agricultural goods (P_{NA}) is used as the numeraire to calculate the relative prices for each agricultural product.

The estimated consumption of sugar in the year t was based on the following demand equations:

$$(6\text{-}6)\ QCSG_t = a^{lt} - .136PRI_t - .931CPSG_t - .008CPCF_t - .121CPFD_t \\ + .073P_{NAT} + 1.124EXP_t$$

where

$QCSG_t$ = annual per capita consumption of sugar [pounds(lbs)/person(N)]

a_{lt} = the constant term

$CPRI_t$ = the consumer price of rice

$CPSG_t$ = the consumer price of sugar
$CPCF_t$ = the consumer price of coffee
$CPFD_t$ = the consumer price of all other food
P_{NAT} = price index of nonagricultural (nonfood) goods
EXP_t = total expenditure on all goods and services consumed.

Analysis of the effects of price policy on the consumption of coffee was based on the following demand equation:

$$(6\text{-}7) \quad QCCF_t = a_{2t} - .170CPRI_t - .012CPSG_t - 1.038CPCF_t$$
$$- .169CPFD_t + .069P_{NAT} + 1.21EXP_t$$

where, for year t,

$QCCF_t$ = annual per capita consumption of coffee and the dependent variables are the same as those defined in the sugar equation.

Analysis of the effects of price policy on consumption of rice was based on the following demand equation:

$$(6\text{-}8) \quad QCRI_t = a_{3t} - .566CPRI_t - .018CPSG_t - .032CPCE_t$$
$$- .339CPFD_t + .065P_{NAT} + .89EXP_t$$

where,

$QCRI_t$ = annual per capita consumption of polished rice and the dependent variables are defined in the sugar equation.

The methodology and data used to calculate the estimated changes in per capita annual consumption caused by direct and total intervention in the prices of the respective commodities are presented in (Greene and Roe 1988).

The Effects of Price Policies on Consumption

Table 6-12 shows the effects of direct and total intervention on average annual short-run consumption of sugar, coffee, and rice for the four subperiods. These effects were calculated from the estimated per capita consumption derived from the demand equations presented above. The data for the direct effects of price policy in table 6-12 compare the observed annual per capita consumption of these commodities with the estimated consumption that would have prevailed had consumer prices been at their equivalent border prices evaluated at the official foreign exchange rate. The data for the total effects in table 6-12 compare the observed average annual per capita consumption with the estimated consumption that would have prevailed had consumer prices been at their equivalent border prices and evaluated at the estimated equilibrium exchange rate.

The data in columns one to three for the direct effects show the average annual per capita quantities of sugar consumed during each

Table 6-12. Direct and Total Effects of Price Policy on the Per Capita Consumption of Rice, Sugar, and Coffee, Average Annual Values, 1966–85

	Sugarcane			Coffee			Rice		
Year	QCSG/N[a] (LBS/N)	QCBSG/N[b] (LBS/N)	QCSG/N[c] (percent)	QCCF/N[d] (LBS/N)	QCBCF/N[e] (LBS/N)	QCCF/N[f] (percent)	QCRI/N[g] (LBS/N)	QCBRI/N[h] (LBS/N)	QCRI/N[i] (percent)
Direct effects									
1966–72	71.1	144.3	–42.5	2.2	2.3	–3.2	77.8	84.4	–7.4
1973–77	77.2	51.7	58.2	2.3	1.8	27.6	109.0	91.2	25.2
1978–81	82.2	65.9	55.6	2.2	2.0	13.7	111.6	107.8	3.6
1982–85	90.0	55.5	93.4	2.5	1.8	46.0	115.6	104.2	22.1
Total effects									
1966–72	71.1	99.0	–16.8	2.2	1.5	49.1	77.8	62.8	24.9
1973–77	77.2	40.3	100.5	2.3	1.3	69.4	109.0	75.4	52.9
1978–81	82.2	47.0	116.5	2.2	1.4	67.6	111.6	82.5	35.3
1982–85	90.0	32.7	197.7	2.5	1.0	152.1	115.6	76.2	54.8

Note: The data in columns 3, 6, and 9 are averages of the annual data for each period and, hence, cannot be calculated directly from the data in the first two columns for each product.

a. Apparent per capita consumption of raw sugar.
b. Estimated consumption of raw sugar resulting from the removal of the direct and total price interventions.
c. Percentage change in the consumption of raw sugar from direct and total price interventions.
d. Apparent per capita consumption of green coffee.
e. Estimated consumption of green coffee resulting from the removal of the direct and total price interventions.
f. Percentage change in the consumption of green coffee from direct and total price interventions.
g. Apparent per capita consumption of rice.
h. Estimated consumption of rice resulting from the removal of the direct and total price interventions.
i. Percentage change in the consumption of rice from direct and total price interventions.
Source: Greene and Roe (1988).

period, and are presented in the same format as those in the previous table. The estimated percentage change in per capita consumption of sugar, shown in column three indicates the effect of direct intervention in consumer prices. The average annual effects of direct intervention on sugar consumption were negative in the first subperiod and positive in the remaining three subperiods. The greatest implicit tax (93.4 percent) because of direct intervention occurred in the fourth subperiod. The average annual change in per capita consumption of sugar for all four subperiods as a result of intervention in prices was an estimated increase of 29.5 percent.[7]

The results in columns four to six for the direct effects show the estimated levels of per capita consumption of milled coffee induced by direct intervention. The effects of direct intervention on average annual coffee consumption are shown to have been positive for the first subperiod and negative for the following three subperiods. The greatest positive change (46.0 percent) in coffee consumption as a result of direct intervention is estimated to have occurred in the fourth subperiod. The average annual change in per capita coffee consumption resulting from direct intervention is estimated to have been an increase of approximately 17.7 percent per year over all four subperiods.

The data in columns seven to nine of table 6-12 show, respectively, the average annual apparent per capita consumption of polished rice, the estimated average annual per capita consumption of polished rice that would have been consumed with consumer prices at their equivalent border prices evaluated at the official exchange rate, and the average annual percentage change between these amounts. According to these calculations, direct intervention had the effect of significantly increasing per capita rice consumption during the second (25.2 percent) and fourth subperiods (22.1 percent). The average annual percentage increase in per capita rice consumption over all four subperiods is estimated to have been 8.9 percent, despite a negative change in the first subperiod (−7.4 percent).

According to the data, which shows effects of total intervention on per capita consumption of rice, sugar, and coffee, total intervention had the effect of substantially increasing per capita sugar consumption in every subperiod except the first. The average annual percentage increase in per capita consumption for all subperiods was estimated to have been about 82.1 percent. These results, when compared with the effects of direct intervention, reflect the significant implicit subsidy given to consumers of sugar by the overvalued currency.

The average annual percentage change in per capita consumption of coffee resulting from total intervention is shown in column six of the table 6-12. Total intervention is shown to have had a positive effect on coffee consumption for every subperiod of the analysis. The greatest positive change (152.1 percent) in consumption as a result of total intervention is estimated to have occurred in the fourth subperiod. The average annual change in per capita consumption of coffee as a result of total intervention is estimated to have been an increase of approximately 78.5 percent a year.

The estimated percentage change in per capita consumption of rice, shown in column nine, indicates the effect of changing the actual consumer prices of all the given price variables to their equivalent border prices evaluated at the estimated equilibrium exchange rate. Total intervention is estimated to have had positive effects on rice consumption in all four subperiods. The greatest positive effects of total intervention on rice consumption are estimated to have been in the fourth (54.8 percent) and second subperiods (52.9 percent). The average annual change in per capita consumption of rice for the entire period as a result of total intervention is estimated to have been an increase of 42.1 percent.

Expenditure Distribution Effects of Price Policy on Consumers

This section focuses on the effects of intervention on the standard of living. These effects, summarized in table 6-13, were analyzed by estimating the average annual change in the per capita consumption of three income groups in both rural and urban areas. These partial equilibrium estimates (which follow the same methodology used above with the demand system for the total population) are based on a complete and consistent system of demand elasticities for each of the six population groups. As in the aggregate consumption analysis presented above, annual incomes were not adjusted for the within-year effects of intervention. Nevertheless, factors not accounted for in the estimated demand equation, which caused the demand function to shift from year to year, were accounted for by recalculating the constant term of the demand equation for each year.

The estimates reported in table 6-13 are the sum of the annual average changes in value of per capita consumption of sugar, coffee, and rice that would have resulted from the removal of intervention. These changes for each period are measured relative to consumption in a base period (1976–77) evaluated at 1984 prices. The 1976–77 base was chosen because data on this period were available from an extensive Dominican household expenditure survey. Had undistorted prices [$p^*(i,t)$] been used in the formula reported in the note to table 6-13, the value of the numerator would have increased when $p^*(i,t)$ was greater than $p(i,t)$. Of key importance is the relative magnitude in these estimates among consumer income groups. A negative value in table 6-13 implies that price distortions caused a decrease in consumer

Table 6-13. Direct and Total Annual Average Effects of Price Policy on Consumer Welfare, by Income Group, 1966–85
(percent)

	Low		Medium		High	
Year	Direct	Total	Direct	Total	Direct	Total
Rural income groups						
1966–72	−14.34	0.87	−17.87	0.50	−12.67	1.22
1973–77	8.12	17.08	3.69	14.46	6.11	14.03
1978–81	0.96	13.30	0.07	14.37	1.76	12.69
1982–85	1.82	15.34	0.10	16.47	2.82	15.13
Urban income groups						
1966–72	−26.93	−3.10	−14.19	2.59	−11.64	−1.70
1973–77	10.71	22.20	7.02	17.59	3.31	9.25
1978–81	3.26	18.94	1.94	16.16	0.46	8.39
1982–85	5.48	22.43	3.26	19.16	1.28	10.12

Note: The change in the standard of living (welfare), based on the consumption of these three commodities, is computed as a percent of total expenditure on these commodities in 1976–77, evaluated at 1984 prices. That is, for the *j-th* income group in the *t-th* year: Percentage changes = $[TE(rj,t) + TE(sj,t) + TE(cj,t)]/[EX(rj) + EX(sj) + EX(cj)]*100$. The indices r,s,c denote rice, sugar, and coffee, respectively. $TE(ij,t) = p(i,t)[q(ij,t) - q^*(ij,t)]$, $i = r,s,c$ and $p(i,t)$ denote the price of the *i-th* good; $q(ij,t)$ denotes quantity of the *i-th* good purchased by the *j-th* income group at distorted prices $p(i,t)$; $q^*(ij,t)$ denotes the estimated quantities of the good purchased at direct prices (top panel) and at undistorted prices (bottom panel). $EX(ij)$ denotes income spent on good i in 1976–77 by the *j-th* income group evaluated at the 1984 prices.

Consider the case of a single good. If distorted prices caused: $q(ij,t) > q^*(ij,t)$, then the numerator above is positive. The value of this difference is evaluated at distorted prices $p(i,t)$, converted to percentage of base period expenditures.

Per capita income categories are:
rural consumers; low < RD$100, RD$100 < medium < RD$160, high > RD$160.
urban consumers; low < RD$165, RD$165 < medium < RD$300, high > RD$300.
Source: Greene and Roe (1988).

welfare. A large positive value suggests that price distortions caused a larger increase in consumer welfare than occurred in the case of a smaller value. The differences in magnitude are the result of differences in the price and expenditure demand elasticities for each income group.

The results shown in table 6-13 suggest that direct intervention in prices decreased the standard of living of all income groups during the 1966–72 subperiod. Direct intervention during this period, on average, appears to have had the greatest adverse impact (−26.9 percent) on low-income urban consumers. High-income urban consumers appear to have been the least affected (−11.6 percent) by direct intervention during this period.

During the first subperiod, total intervention appears to have resulted in small welfare changes for all income groups. As shown in table 6-13, for example, total intervention caused only a 1.2 percent increase in the consumer welfare of the high-income rural group. The greatest welfare effects from total intervention generally occurred during the second subperiod (when the effects of direct intervention were large relative to other subperiods) and during the fourth subperiod, when the effects of total intervention on consumption were large relative to other periods.

These results also suggest that the largest positive values resulting from total intervention, in most cases were associated with low-income rural and urban consumers, while the smallest positive values were associated with high-income rural and urban consumers. Consequently, the removal of price subsidies, on average, would have had the greatest negative effect on the welfare of low-income urban and rural consumers. That is, low-income consumer groups appear to have received the greatest benefits from total intervention, at least in this short-run partial equilibrium context.

The Effect of Agricultural Price Intervention on Foreign Exchange Earnings

This section focuses on the short-run effects of price policy intervention on foreign exchange earnings from exports of sugar, coffee, and rice. The estimated changes in foreign exchange earnings from these crops are based on the production and consumption changes estimated above. Therefore annual changes in the foreign exchange earnings for each crop as a result of direct and total intervention are estimated separately, based on short-run supply and demand changes obtained in the previous section. Income changes and second-round shifts in the supply and demand functions for the commodities and for foreign exchange earnings, which would undoubtedly change in response to changes in relative prices and first-round shifts, are not included in this analysis.

Changes in the annual foreign exchange earnings from the respective commodities are based on the assumptions that the Dominican always filled its quota in the U.S. sugar market first, and any excess was then exported to the world market; the f.o.b. export price of coffee was the average annual price received by Dominican exporters, and any estimated additional excess would have been exported at these prices; and the c.i.f. import price of polished rice was equal to the f.o.b. export price.

The results of analyses are summarized in table 6-14. The estimated annual changes in foreign exchange earnings (in millions of U.S. dollars) and as a percentage of the value of total exports are shown for sugar, coffee, and rice in the first six columns of this table. The respective sums of these values are given in the last two columns. Positive

Table 6-14. Direct and Total Effects of Price Interventions on Foreign Exchange Earnings with Short-Run Supply Changes, Average Annual Values, 1966–85

(millions of current US$)

Year	Effect on sugar exports	Effect on sugar exports to value of total exports (percent)	Effect on coffee exports	Effect on coffee exports to value of total exports (percent)	Effect on rice exports	Effect on rice exports to value of total exports (percent)	Total effect on foreign exchange earnings[a]	Total effect on foreign exchg. earnings to value of total exports (percent)
Direct effects								
1966–72	42.7	22.2	–1.3	–0.3	7.9	3.6	36.8	19.3
1973–77	–57.9	–7.6	–6.5	–0.9	–24.1	–4.6	–88.4	–13.1
1978–81	–28.3	–4.0	–13.7	–1.5	0.2	0.1	–41.9	–5.4
1982–85	–13.7	–3.7	–7.8	–1.0	–1.9	1.0	–24.4	–3.7
Total effects								
1966–72	9.8	5.4	–4.7	–1.9	–5.4	–2.8	–1.0	–0.2
1973–77	–83.8	–11.3	–15.6	–2.3	–44.8	–7.9	–144.2	–21.5
1978–81	–61.3	–7.4	–30.9	–3.3	–35.2	–3.7	–127.5	–14.5
1982–85	–46.5	–8.5	–25.7	–3.3	–34.8	–4.4	–106.9	–16.2

Note: Negative values denote a decrease in foreign exchange earnings from direct and total price effects relative to the observed level of foreign exchange earnings on these commodities.

Column 7 = 1 plus 3 plus 5.

a. Gain (+) or loss (−).

Source: Greene and Roe (1988).

values indicate that the observed distorted prices had the effect of increasing foreign exchange earnings (that is, exports increased, or imports decreased) relative to the estimated undistorted situations that would have resulted from the removal of direct and total intervention. Negative values denote a decrease in foreign exchange earnings (that is, decreased exports or increased imports).

The effects of direct intervention on average annual foreign exchange earnings are reported in table 6-14. Direct intervention with short-run supply and demand changes had the following average annual effects:

- Foreign exchange earnings from greater exports of sugar increased by 22.2 percent in the first subperiod above the estimated value that would have prevailed if direct intervention had been removed. Foreign exchange earnings from sugar exports decreased by 7.6, 4.0, and 3.7 percent, respectively, in the following three subperiods.

- Foreign exchange earnings from decreased coffee exports decreased in all four subperiods by 0.3, 0.9, 1.5, and 1.0 percent, respectively.

- Because of increased rice imports, foreign exchange earnings decreased in the second subperiod by 4.6 percent; decreased rice imports in the first and last two subperiods resulted in increases in foreign exchange earnings of 3.6, 0.1, and 1.0 percent, respectively.

- Total foreign exchange earnings from international trade in the three crops increased in the first subperiod by 19.3 percent but decreased in the last three subperiods by 13.1, 5.4, and 3.7 percent, respectively.

The results of the effects of total intervention on foreign exchange earnings are as follows:

- Foreign exchange earnings from increased sugar exports increased in the first subperiod by 5.4 percent but decreased because of decreased exports in the last three subperiods by 11.3, 7.4, and 8.5 percent, respectively.

- Foreign exchange earnings from reductions in coffee exports decreased in all four subperiods by 1.9, 2.3, 3.3, and 3.3 percent, respectively.

- Because of increased rice imports, foreign exchange earnings decreased in all four subperiods by 2.8, 7.9, 3.7, and 4.4 percent, respectively.

- Total foreign exchange earnings from international trade in these crops decreased by 0.2 percent in the first subperiod, 21.6 percent in the second, 14.5 percent in the third, and 16.2 percent in the fourth.

The contrast between the effects of direct and total intervention shows the large negative impact of an overvalued exchange rate on foreign exchange earnings.

Resource Transfers In and Out of Agriculture

Estimates of the annual average sum of transfers from producers of sugar, coffee, and rice appear in table 6-15. These estimates approximate the average annual values of the quasi rents resulting from direct and total effects of intervention in prices on short-run supply. The largest transfers resulting from direct and total intervention occurred during the second subperiod, when the producers of all three crops were taxed and resources thus were transferred from the agricultural sector. Average annual agricultural expenditures, both current and capital, include expenditures by the government on agriculture, fishing, irrigation, rural roads, agricultural bank expenditures (BAGRICOLA), and expenditures on the government's agrarian reform program, IAD. A summation of average annual expenditures and the transfers resulting from direct and total price intervention suggests that there was a net transfer of resources from these three crops only during the second subperiod. This interpretation, however, could be misleading. The reported capital expenditures are lump sum annual amounts that should be amortized, depending on the type of investment. Then, these expenditures include some that are associated with marketing agricultural products, government salaries, and others that are associated with the administration of agricultural development and food policy. Finally, these public sector transfers to the agricultural sector may not have generated returns to resources that, at the margin, were equal to or greater than the opportunity costs of the direct and total intervention that served to transfer resources out of the sector. If the resources transferred to agriculture were less productive than those extracted, a zero net transfer would still amount to an implicit tax on the sector. Nevertheless, the results shown in table 6-15 suggest that there were sizable net resource transfers from the public sector to the food sector throughout the 1966–85 period, except for the years 1973–77.

The Political Determinants of Agricultural Pricing Policies

The object of this section is to provide insight into the political determinants of pricing policies and their evolution. This section attempts to explain why intervention took the forms that it did in each subperiod and why the degree of intervention was not greater or less than it was.

A basic premise underlying our analysis is that the Dominican government was pursuing policies in response to political pressure from

Table 6-15. Average Annual Transfers into (+)/ out of (−) Agriculture as a Result of Government Expenditures and Price Interventions, 1966–85

(millions of constant 1984 RD$)

Year	Agricultural expenditure		Sum of transfers		Total agricultural expenditures plus price transfers		Total transfers as a share of GDP[a]	
	Total current[a]	Total capital[b]	Direct[c]	Total[d]	Direct[e]	Total[f]	Direct[g]	Total[h]
1966–72	95.0	78.1	98.8	−56.1	222.5	67.6	15.9	5.2
1973–77	115.6	271.9	−501.7	−783.4	−114.2	−395.9	−5.6	−20.0
1978–81	177.0	239.9	−30.4	−391.9	386.5	25.0	17.8	1.1
1982–85	163.0	152.1	99.6	−211.1	336.0	25.3	22.1	1.7

a. Sum of current expenditures of central government and autonomous government institutions on agricultural infrastructure.

b. Sum of capital expenditures of central government and autonomous government institutions on agricultural infrastructure.

c. Sum of transfers to agriculture resulting from direct price intervention on short-run output of rice, sugar, and coffee; transfers are estimated as quasi rents from direct price interventions.

d. Sum of transfers to agriculture resulting from total price intervention on short-run output of rice, sugar, and coffee; transfers are estimated as quasi rents from total price interventions.

e. Sum of columns 1, 2, and 3.

f. Sum of columns 1, 2, and 4.

g. Sum of government transfers and direct price interventions as a percent of agricultural GDP.

h. Sum of government transfers and total price interventions as a percent of agricultural GDP.

Source: Greene and Roe (1988).

various interest groups. Hence, the government's policy choices were probably influenced by the relative political power of these groups. If our hypothesis is true, the magnitude of direct nominal rates of protection for various interest groups should reflect the levels of political influence that these groups were able to exercise. A related premise is that the amount of political pressure that the interest groups exerted to influence policy was proportional to their expected gains or losses from policy intervention. If these hypotheses are true, the next question that must be answered is whether the relative political power of the various interest groups changed over time.

A primary concern of this analysis is to relate changes in the economic welfare of producers and consumers of agricultural products and of nonagricultural goods to shifts in the relative political power of these interest groups in the presence of exogenous shocks to the Dominican economy. The changes are assumed to be determined primarily by the magnitude of taxation or subsidy given to each interest group in each subperiod by direct and indirect intervention in prices. Hence, this section begins with a comparative analysis of the structures of the Dominican sugar, coffee, and rice industries.

The Political Determinants of Direct Intervention in Sugar Prices

As mentioned earlier, direct intervention in prices served to subsidize sugarcane producers in the first and fourth subperiods and to tax them in the second and third subperiods. In contrast, direct intervention implicitly taxed sugar consumers in the first subperiod and subsidized them in the last three subperiods despite the direct consumer tax put in place in 1974. CEA, as the dominant enterprise in the sugar industry, implemented the government's pricing policies. Retail sugar prices were implemented primarily through wholesale marketings by sugar processors to INESPRE, which then distributed sugar to retailers. The general policy decisions were to subsidize sugar producers when world sugar prices fell below their trend line and to tax them when the price exceeded the trend line, and to subsidize sugar consumers, except during the first subperiod, when world sugar prices were substantially above their trend line.

Direct intervention by the government in the sugar industry began in the 1950s, when the government began to nationalize the sugar industry. By 1960, all but two of the private firms in the country had been acquired by the Trujillo government. By 1980, CEA owned approximately 101,100 hectares (36.7 percent) of the land planted in sugarcane, and its private contract growers, *colonos,* managed an additional 77,800 hectares (28.3 percent). That is to say, CEA controlled about two-thirds of the land used to raise sugarcane. The remaining 96,000 hectares were owned by Central Romana (a subsidiary of Gulf-

Western Corporation from 1960 to 1984) and Casa Vicini. Central Romana had around 43,900 hectares of sugarcane land and purchased sugar from its *colonos*, who managed some 27,400 hectares of sugarcane. Casa Vicini had 24,700 hectares planted in sugarcane and did not purchase any sugarcane from *colonos*. Throughout the 1966–85 period, CEA owned approximately 69 percent of the country's sugarcane processing capacity of 67,350 metric tons a day.

Prices, obviously, were strongly influenced by the price at which CEA bought sugarcane. The average annual price appears to have been based on a value-weighted average expected price for CEA raw sugar exports sold in the U.S. quota market and in the world market at the prevailing nominal official exchange rate. Assuming that the sugar price in the world market represented the appropriate opportunity cost for domestic resource utilization, the analysis above indicated that sugarcane producers were subsidized when world prices fell and taxed when they rose.

The policy of taxing sugarcane producers during the mid-1970s created significant net public revenues, which were transferred through INESPRE to the state-owned Electricity Corporation (CDE) to subsidize electricity generation. Private sugarcane producers did not complain vigorously about this tax, because their nominal price rose when world price rose, but not as much. Subsidies for sugarcane producers and for CEA's operating costs were financed by direct transfers from the government and loans from foreign sources. Obviously, the primary beneficiaries of these subsidies were the sugarcane producers and employees of CEA, but the losers were the country's present and future taxpayers.

The extent of the direct effects of intervention on sugar prices was largely determined by the relative political power of the key interest groups affected by sugar price policy and by the inability of the government, CEA, and others involved in determining sugar price policy to forecast world sugar prices accurately when sugar price policy decisions were made. The key interest groups include sugar producers, CEA and its employees, the consumers and processors of sugar products, and producers of other crops that compete for resources allocated to sugar production.

Another broad-based group includes those who stand to benefit (lose) from any inflow (outflow) of revenue to the government treasury that might result from sugar price policy. These interests are important because the inflow of revenue can be used to subsidize or otherwise transfer income to other sectors of the economy. For example, in the second subperiod, when the world sugar prices and energy prices were rising, the government appears to have responded to this latter group by transferring the windfall gains from rising sugar prices to consumers of electricity. This transfer prevented the total effect of rising world energy prices from being reflected in the domestic economy.

In the fourth subperiod, when world sugar prices fell relative to petroleum prices, the government responded by subsidizing sugar consumers and processors of sugar products, and also by subsidizing sugar producers. During this period, CEA experienced large deficits that were eventually financed by the central government and from foreign borrowing. Our interpretation of the policy followed during this subperiod is that the government underestimated the decrease in world sugar prices. As world sugar prices fell, the pressure from the growers and their employees was sufficient, along with rigidities in the Dominican planning-policy formation process, to prevent any readjustments in sugar price policy.

As the value of the subsidies accumulated toward the end of the fourth subperiod, there was greater political pressure to reduce them from the adversely affected broad-based groups mentioned above. The policy reform of 1986 resulted in the reorganization of CEA and the removal of INESPRE from sugar marketing. This reform amounted to a compromise between the government, the above-mentioned interest groups, and the policy adjustments supported by the International Monetary Fund (IMF) and by external financial institutions, primarily Western banks. The reform reduced the subsidies to sugar producers, CEA, and the two private firms; it also prevented losses to the rest of the economy that would otherwise have been taxed to support the subsidy to the sugar sector. Gulf and Western Corporation sold its holdings in Dominican sugar production in 1984, possibly because it foresaw the reduction in subsidies.

Political Determinants of Direct Intervention in Coffee Prices

Earlier, it was reported that direct intervention in coffee prices took the form of a tax on Dominican coffee producers throughout 1966–85, and particularly in the fourth subperiod. Direct intervention was also shown to have slightly taxed consumers in the first subperiod and subsidized them in the last three subperiods. The policy instruments that affected producers were progressive tax surcharges and specific fees assessed on coffee exports. The policy instrument that affected consumers was price controls administered by the DGPC. Consumer prices, however, were below world prices probably not so much because of price controls but because the coffee quota likely gave rise to excess supplies of coffee in the domestic market.

Most Dominican coffee is grown on small farms located in mountainous areas. According to the 1981 agricultural census, coffee was produced on some 71,200 farms and 152,700 hectares of land, for an average farm size of 2.1 hectares. There were only 123 large coffee producers—those whose holdings totaled more than 37.7 hectares.

The ability of coffee producers to lobby successfully for their interests was probably impaired by their geographical dispersion and their lack of political power relative to sugar and rice producers.

In 1968 the Dominican signed the International Coffee Agreement (ICA), which subjected its exports to quotas determined annually by the International Coffee Organization (ICO) and a "voluntary" tax on coffee exports to establish a national fund to support diversification. In August 1968 a Dominican Coffee Commission was established in the Secretariat of Agriculture (SEA) to determine the share of coffee to be provided by each region of the country in fulfilling the quota. The Commission consists of twelve members (equally divided between coffee producers and exporters) and the Secretary of Agriculture, who directs meetings and casts the deciding vote in the event of a tie.

The Dominican coffee-processing sector has become increasingly concentrated. By 1982, the private firm Industrias Banilejas (INDUBAN) owned about two-thirds of the country's coffee-processing capacity and employed approximately 81 percent of the processing industry's labor force (Del Villar 1985).

In the early 1970s Dominican coffee exports were controlled largely by twelve private export houses, although there were some forty export firms. The government did not intervene directly in the marketing of coffee during the 1966–85 period, except for the export quota arrangement. There were, however, some unsuccessful attempts in the early 1970s to form a semipublic coffee-marketing institute, and several interest groups urged INESPRE to buy coffee from small farms.

The primary losers from taxation of coffee exports were the coffee producers. Although the taxes were levied on exporters of coffee beans and processed coffee, they simply passed the tax on to the producers by paying lower prices for coffee cherries. The primary gainers appear to have been coffee consumers and the numerous sectors of the economy that received government subsidies and transfers financed in part by coffee tax revenues. The disincentive effects of the tax tended, in the long run, to reduce production capacity as well as the quality of raw coffee, which, in turn, caused a decline in coffee tax revenues. The reasons that help to explain the relatively large amounts of these taxes and subsidies are probably similar to those given for sugar.

Political Determinants of Direct Intervention in Rice Prices

Direct intervention in rice prices caused rice producers to be subsidized throughout the 1966–85 period. Producer subsidies were lowest (2 percent) during the second subperiod and highest (60 percent) during the fourth subperiod. Direct intervention also had the effect of taxing rice consumers throughout the entire period. As shown in table 6-10, the smallest consumer tax (3 percent) occurred during the second subperiod, while the largest (15 percent) occurred during the first.

INESPRE was granted exclusive control over the importation of basic foods in 1969; in 1973 it was given the authority to regulate wholesale marketing of polished rice. INESPRE announced prices at the farm and wholesale market levels and then engaged in transactions until the markets cleared or its budget was exhausted. Dominican rice consumers, on average, paid more for rice than it cost on the world market, except during the years 1973–74. The government's stated objective, especially in the fourth subperiod, was to become self-sufficient in rice. As a result, INESPRE paid prices that protected domestic rice producers in most years during 1973–85.

In the mid-1980s, about 20 percent of total rice production came from some 5,000 farms of five hectares or less, which were generally located in highly accessible areas. Production of paddy rice in the Dominican accelerated greatly during the 1960s and 1970s with the completion of a number of irrigation projects, primarily in the Cibao Valley. Approximately 50 percent of the total area planted to rice was found on the agrarian reform farms administered by the Dominican Agrarian Institute (Consejo Nacional de Agricultura, UEA, 1986); these farms produced about 38 percent of total annual production. This structure tended to support a relatively effective lobbying organization.

The objective of direct intervention appears to have been the maintenance of stable producer and consumer prices while subsidizing producers and taxing consumers. INESPRE achieved these objectives through control of rice imports, storage facilities, and marketing subsidies. These subsidies were limited, obviously, by INESPRE's budget constraints, which became more severe after 1981 because of declining government revenues. The direct taxes assessed on rice consumers were substantial, probably because the government wanted to dampen excess demand to minimize rice imports. The decrease in imports of rice also saved on foreign exchange, which indirectly benefited the importers of other goods and services.

The Relative Levels of Political Influence

The estimated nominal rates of protection arising from direct intervention appear to reflect the different degrees of influence of the agricultural groups. Rice producers were found to have been the most subsidized (or the least taxed) by direct intervention, and it appears that they were relatively well-organized into regional and national grower associations throughout the period of analysis. The rice producer associations, geographically concentrated in the Cibao Valley, were politically influential within the SEA, INESPRE, the Congress, and the presidential office (all three presidents in the 1966–85 period were from the Cibao region). The completion of a number of irrigation projects and implementation of agrarian reform laws in the early 1970s caused the number of agrarian reform farms producing rice to expand rapidly. These farms added their weight to the political efforts of the private producer associations in obtaining stable prices and positive nominal rates of protection. The agrarian reform farms lobbied for higher farm support prices, greater volumes of rice purchases by INESPRE, and subsidized inputs (especially land, credit, and irrigation water).

In contrast to the many small farms where rice is grown, the large firms of Central Romana and Casa Vicini and the *colonos*, who sold their production to Central Romana and CEA, were responsible for sugarcane production. Throughout most of the period, sugar exporters were forced to pay explicit and progressive export taxes—in 1985, for example, a 36 percent exchange rate surcharge. These export taxes were largely passed back to private sugarcane farmers and workers, as shown by negative nominal rates of protection in most years. Windfall gains from changes in the U.S. sugar quota were captured by the Dominican government and the exporters. From 1981 to 1986, CEA produced about 60 percent of the Dominican share of the U.S. quota market. As indicated by the pattern of taxes and subsidies, and changes in world sugar prices, sugarcane producers were not as successful as rice producers in obtaining border prices, especially in periods of high prices in the world market. Nevertheless, sugarcane producers were able to maintain stable farm prices in the face of substantial decreases in world sugar prices in the fourth subperiod.

Among producers of the three commodities, producers of coffee paid the highest average annual levels of taxation because of direct intervention. This group was also the least organized politically. As discussed above, a majority of the coffee farms are small and isolated, and numerous producers sell their coffee to a small group of processors and exporters. Given the structure of the industry, coffee producer groups (especially those representing small farms) had limited political influence.[8]

Decisions regarding taxes on export products were made by presidential order on the recommendation of the Monetary Board and the Secretary of Agriculture. The imposition of export taxes on coffee suggests that the political influence of the producers and exporters was not sufficient to allow them to capture all the windfall gains resulting from increases in world prices. Taxation of exports was probably implemented because this policy instrument is easily managed and is a highly cost-effective way (at least in the short run) to raise government revenue.

As a result of direct intervention, Dominican food consumers were generally subsidized in most years during the 1966–85 period. Rice consumers, however, were explicitly taxed. These results suggest that, despite the efforts of the DGPC and INESPRE to reduce food prices, Dominican consumer groups did not have enough influence to bring about a reduction in the rice price to its equivalent border price. The obvious exceptions were in 1973 and 1974 (when world rice prices increased dramatically) and in 1984 to 1985 (when the Dominican peso price of rice imports rose dramatically with the transfer of these imports to the parallel foreign exchange market). The subsidy to rice consumers in 1984 increased INESPRE's annual deficits until the institution was virtually insolvent by 1986.

The Political Economy of Indirect Intervention

As discussed earlier, our estimates of the peso's overvaluation range from an annual average of about 16 percent during the 1966–72 period to 9 percent during the mid-1970s, followed by a rise to an annual average of about 11 percent during the 1982–85 period. In 1985, as part of a standby agreement with the IMF, all imported merchandise (except petroleum and petroleum products) and foreign exchange earnings from exports (except for traditional Dominican exports) were transferred into the parallel foreign exchange market. Thus, starting in 1985, only a small divergence is found between our estimate of nominal equilibrium and the official exchange rate.

Our estimate of the undistorted price index for nonagricultural goods (Pna^*) was lower than the observed distorted index (Pna) by only 2 to 3 percent in most years. This reflects two adjustments: first, a downward adjustment to account for the removal of trade distortions, and second, an upward adjustment to account for overvaluation of the peso for the trade component of this index. Because of the relatively small divergence, the difference between the effects of direct and total intervention is largely explained by the overvaluation of the currency.

The effect of indirect intervention was to increase the tax (or lower the subsidy) to producers and increase the subsidy (or lower the tax) to consumers. Moreover, the effects of indirect intervention tended to exceed the effects of direct intervention in many years (especially vis-à-vis rice), except during the mid-1970s and in 1985, when the equilibrium exchange rate was estimated to depart only slightly from the observed rate. The government's intervention contributed to increases in the fiscal deficits of the consolidated public sector and deterioration in the country's external accounts. The policy choices discussed below are those that most contributed to the country's fiscal and trade deficits and, consequently, led to overvaluation of the peso.

THE 1966–72 SUBPERIOD. During 1966–72, the Dominican was in its initial phase of import-substitution industrialization. Direct intervention in agricultural prices was limited to rice and the traditional export crops. Revenues from import duties averaged about 45 percent of total government revenues during this period, while revenues from income and sales taxes accounted for about 40 percent (Greene and Roe 1988). Government revenues averaged about 14 percent of GDP per year, while revenues from public enterprises averaged about 10 percent. Total public sector expenditures were slightly less than total revenues, so that a modest surplus averaging about 0.6 percent of GDP per year was realized. The four major public enterprises (CDE, CORDE, CEA, and INESPRE) incurred small deficits which, added together, averaged about 0.1 percent of GDP.

Certain policies that were implemented during this period, however, would have consequences that would become increasingly costly to the government in later periods. These policies include tax and tariff incentives granted under the Industrial Incentive Law of 1968. Although these incentives were initially effective in promoting private investment, they eventually caused a decrease in the government's revenue while expenditures continued to increase. The trade and service components of the current account were negative during this period, averaging about 2.0 and 3.8 percent of GDP, respectively, which accounts for our estimate of the overvaluation averages in real terms about 16.8 percent per year of the estimated real equilibrium exchange rate (see table 6-6).

THE 1972–77 SUBPERIOD. The effects of indirect intervention in agricultural prices were lowest (averaging about 9.4 percent per year) during the 1972–77 period. The reason was that overvaluation of the currency was at its lowest. The rise in the world price of sugar during the years 1974–76 and the rise in the world coffee price in 1977 increased the government's revenues from export taxes despite increased expenditures on oil imports.

Government revenues averaged about 14 percent of GDP per year, with over 16 percent of those revenues attributable to export taxes. This was in contrast to the previous period, when government revenues from export duties averaged only about 5.6 percent of government revenues per year. Government revenues from import duties, and income, property, and sales taxes, tended to decline as a percentage of GDP during this period.

Total expenditures of the consolidated public sector increased from an annual average of about 26 percent of GDP in the 1966–72 sub-period to an average of nearly 30 percent per year during the 1972–77 subperiod. The net result was a modest deficit of about 0.6 percent per year. More important, the government's decision to prevent the increase in the oil import price from being fully reflected in domestic prices required substantial subsidies, which eventually led to large fiscal deficits. CDE alone had deficits averaging almost 0.4 percent of GDP per year, primarily from subsidizing the cost of electricity generation.

The importation of rice in 1974 and 1977 at costs that exceeded INESPRE's domestic prices gave rise to deficits in INESPRE's accounts that amounted to 1.1 and 0.4 percent of GDP in those respective years. Revenue surpluses generated by CEA (except in 1976) and INESPRE (except in 1974 and 1977) were substantially less than the total deficits of public sector enterprises. Hence, the modest consolidated public sector deficit (0.6 percent of GDP per year) was partly a consequence of direct intervention in agricultural prices during this period. Meanwhile, the Dominican pursued its import-substitution policy by increasing the number of import prohibitions and restrictions and by raising tariff rates on selected commodities that competed with locally produced goods. Although the tariff system became more complex, the aggregate tariff rate declined from an annual average rate of about 39 percent during the 1966–71 period to about 25 percent a year during this period.

The deterioration in the country's current account (see table 6-5) is largely explained by the increasing debit for investment income in the services account. The real interest rate on commercial bank time deposits averaged about −6.6 percent (Greene and Roe 1988). Net direct foreign investment remained constant (averaging about US$45 million a year), while medium- and long-term loans (averaging about US$50 million a year at the beginning of the period) doubled to over US$100 million during the last two years of the 1972–77 period.

In summary, as a result of an increase in government revenues associated with the rise in world market prices of sugar and coffee, the government was able to subsidize the rising costs of petroleum and food imports. This policy prevented the total transmission of higher import prices into the domestic economy and kept inflation rates relatively low. At the same time, the government expanded its policies of import-substitution industrialization without any official devaluation of the peso.

THE 1978–81 SUBPERIOD. The indirect effects of overvaluing the currency increased substantially during the 1978–81 period, with the estimated overvaluation averaging about 12 percent per year (table 6-6). During this period, under the Guzman administration, policy was generally a continuation of policies pursued in the previous two subperiods, notwithstanding the sharp rise in the world price of petroleum in 1979, the decline in world prices for sugar and coffee, and the devastating effects of the 1979 hurricanes. An increase in the world price of sugar in 1981 then alleviated some of the shortfalls in export earnings of previous years. Hence, adverse changes in the country's financial situation during this period were largely the result of the continuation of previous policies despite falling revenues.

Import quotas were increasingly used in an effort to curtail the outflow of foreign monetary reserves, and by August of 1982 about 200 products were prohibited from importation. Export Incentive Law No. 69 of 1979 increased the number of producers of nontraditional exports who received tariff and income tax exemptions and exchange rate premiums. The overall tariff rate declined from an annual average of about 27 percent to an annual average of about 18 percent during this period (although tariff rates remained high for selected imports, and import licensing became more common). At the same time, the aggregate tax rate on exports declined from an average of about 10.8 percent to 6.8 percent a year.

Government revenues declined to an annual average of 11 percent of GDP, with export taxes accounting for an average of only about 10 percent of these revenues, compared with 16 percent in the previous period. Government revenues from virtually all other sources also declined. Consolidated government expenditures remained unchanged from the previous period, averaging about 30 percent of GDP per year, while revenues declined to an annual average of only 24 percent of GDP.

The direct effects of price policies and the increasing inefficiency of the expanding public enterprises induced a public enterprise deficit averaging about 2.7 percent of GDP per year. Of this deficit, the deficits of CDE, CEA, and INESPRE averaged 0.9, 0.9, and 0.1 percent of GDP per year, respectively (Greene and Roe 1988). These deficits produced a total consolidated government deficit averaging 5.9 percent of GDP annually during the period (table 6-4). The country's trade deficit grew from an average of only US$2.2 million a year in the second subperiod to an annual average deficit of US$319.3 million during this third subperiod.

The government's deficits were largely financed by medium- and long-term loans, which increased from an annual average of US$70 million during the 1973–77 subperiod to about US$188 million a year during the third subperiod. Meanwhile, foreign monetary reserves were decreasing by an annual average amount of US$23.6 million. Real interest rates on commercial bank time deposits and loans of the BAGRICOLA remained negative. Errors and omissions in the balance of payments (an indication of capital flight) were the highest of any period, averaging about US$126.5 million a year (Greene and Roe 1988).

The annual trade deficits put strong pressure on the government's foreign monetary reserves. To alleviate this pressure, individuals holding U.S. dollars were permitted to buy pesos from the parallel foreign exchange market. Meanwhile, the 1979 Export Incentive Law permitted receipts from certain nontraditional exports to be wholly or partially exempted from the requirement that all foreign exchange had to be remitted at the official rate. Exports of the four traditional agricultural commodities, however, remained subject to earlier exchange rules. INESPRE was permitted to import rice and other food commodities with a limited amount of foreign exchange evaluated at the official parity exchange rate.

In sum, the expansion of policies initiated in the previous two subperiods increased both the indirect tax on producers and the subsidies to consumers of tradable crops. The indirect effects probably served to make the urban industrial sector appear more profitable than the rural sector. The perceived change in relative profitability, in turn, may have increased rural-to-urban migration during this period.

THE 1982–85 SUBPERIOD. The policies of this period were a continuation of the policies pursued in previous periods despite a decline in world sugar prices after 1982 and an increase in the real interest rate on the country's external debt. Our estimates suggest that overvaluation was about 11.2 percent per year during the 1982–84 subperiod, then dropping to only 0.9 percent in 1985 after the IMF standby agreement was signed and the exchange rate was unified.

The trade legislation of this period had some very restrictive effects. The number of prohibited import items jumped from about 200 in August 1982 to over 350 by the end of 1983. Law 145, enacted in June 1983, was an attempt to address the complexities and inequities of trade legislation enacted in previous years by extending the highest tariff exemption on identically imported inputs to all firms. By the end of 1984 the industrial incentive law had reduced the number of final products that could be imported at the official parity exchange rate. Law 21, enacted in 1984, created a minimum tariff for the purpose of increasing nominal tariff rates to at least 30 percent on previously nonexempt goods, and from 5 to 15 percent on previously exempt goods. Nevertheless, many inputs remained exempt from these rates, including petroleum and raw materials imported by the state-owned oil refinery. Although the average annual tariff rate (around 14 percent) remained unchanged from the previous subperiod through 1983, it rose to 22 percent during 1984.

During the 1982–84 subperiod, government revenue declined slightly to an annual average of about 10 percent of GDP; export duties accounted each year for about one-tenth of these revenues. Revenues from other sources declined only slightly relative to the previous subperiod. Consolidated government revenues and expenditures also declined slightly from the previous subperiod to an annual average of about 22.6 percent and 27.8 percent of GDP, respectively (Green and Roe 1988). The account of public enterprises as a group remained in deficit, averaging about 1.8 percent per year of GDP. The annual deficits of CDE, CEA, and INESPRE averaged about 0.6, 0.9 and 0.2 percent of GDP, respectively. In 1985, INESPRE's deficit increased to 0.4 percent of GDP as a result of the direct consumer price subsidy following the riots in April 1984 and the government's rule that INESPRE's imports could no longer be imported at the official parity rate of exchange.

The 1982–84 fiscal situation led to a slightly smaller consolidated government deficit averaging about 5.3 percent of GDP per year during this subperiod. The country's trade deficit increased, however, reaching US$455.5 million (or nearly 5.5 percent of GDP, as shown in table 6-5). At the same time, the deficit in the country's service balance declined from an average of about US$294 million in the previous subperiod to an average of US$134.0 million during this subperiod. As in the previous subperiod, these deficits were financed by medium- and long-term loans (averaging about $210.4 million a year), a large drop in foreign monetary reserves (an average decline of US$82.8 million a year, compared with an average of about US$23.6 million a year during the previous subperiod), and increased IMF transfers (growing from an average of about US$47 million a year during the 1977–81 subperiod to US$91 million a year during the 1982–84 subperiod). The IMF transfer in late 1983, as part of the standby agreement, was about US$235.2 million.

The IMF agreement required a unification of the official and unofficial foreign exchange rate markets. This policy change raised the official nominal foreign exchange rate from parity to DR$2.37 and DR$3.12 per dollar in 1984 and 1985, respectively. Largely to address the government's financial situation, a temporary exchange rate surcharge of 36 percent was levied on all traditional exports. This tax was lowered to 18 percent in February of 1986 and eliminated in June 1986. The realignment of the exchange rate contributed to inflation rates of about 24.5 and 37.5 percent during 1984 and 1985, respectively. As a result of capital market restrictions and increased inflation, real interest rates on commercial bank time deposits dropped to a negative 16 percent in late 1984.

The Jorge administration attempted to pursue the economic policies of the previous administrations, but with some adjustments to account for the country's worsening economic situation. The Jorge and the previous administrations appear to have pursued policies largely based on the relative political influence of various interest groups. Changes in economic policy appear to have been largely forced on the Jorge administration by the possibility of illiquidity and, hence, a withdrawal from foreign trade, followed by recession. The myopia and self-interest of the various interest groups probably explain the failure of those groups to foresee this impending economic crisis, to negotiate alternative economic policies, and then to pressure the government to carry them out.

Conclusion

This study has focused on the political economy of agricultural pricing policies in the Dominican Republic, with special attention given to sugar and coffee (the country's major earners of foreign exchange) and rice (the major food crop). The country's policy regime during 1966–85 was characterized by moderate levels of intervention with a number of quantitative trade and capital market restrictions. One conclusion of this analysis is that overvaluation of the Dominican peso generally tended to have a detrimental effect on agricultural producers that offset the subsidies resulting from intervention. More precisely, direct intervention generally served to subsidize producers of sugar and rice and to tax coffee producers. The effects of indirect intervention were often sufficiently large to reverse the effects of direct intervention, so that sugar and rice producers were taxed while consumption of these commodities was subsidized. The analysis also suggests that, in the short run, intervention provided low-income rural and urban consumers with the largest welfare gains as a percentage of household income.

One premise underlying our analysis was that the Dominican government, in a general sense and in light of the conditions that evolved from the Trujillo period, pursued policies in response to political pressure from various interest groups. Direct intervention was implemented by state-owned enterprises and the Director of Price Control, and by export taxes, tariffs, and quotas. Decisions regarding the structure of taxes and tariffs on traded commodities were made by the presidential office and the ministries of Industry and Commerce, and Agriculture.

With respect to direct intervention in the prices of sugar, coffee, and rice, the relative political power of these industries appears to have influenced the respective levels of producer protection. In the case of sugar, CEA was a focal point at which lobbying efforts for direct intervention were concentrated. These efforts appear to have been only partially successful, because sugar producers were taxed in years when border prices for sugar exports were used to partially offset the deficits incurred by the state-owned electrical company (CDE). These deficits occurred because the government prevented the costs of rising petroleum imports from being transmitted in full to the domestic economy.

In the case of rice, the government appears to have followed a policy of direct intervention while maintaining stable producer and consumer prices. In most years, direct intervention served to subsidize rice producers. The rice producers were relatively well organized through producer associations and were highly concentrated geographically. They were also politically influential within SEA, INESPRE, in the Congress, and in the presidential office. Support for rice price policy was also provided by the IAD. In contrast, coffee was produced on relatively numerous small farms in remote regions of the country. Direct intervention taxed coffee producers relative to the other two crops. The imposition of the tax on coffee seems consistent with the relatively weak political influence of these producers.

Policies contributing to the overvaluation of the Dominican peso include direct intervention in agricultural prices and other interventions in the economy. These interventions contributed to the country's fiscal deficits and deterioration in its external accounts, both of which helped to produce overvaluation.

The administrations of the period 1966–85 essentially pursued a policy of import-substitution industrialization until late 1984. At that time, the IMF standby agreement gave rise to a devaluation of the currency, a partial revision of the country's foreign trade tax structure, and later, some changes in the structure of state-owned enterprises. The import-substitution industrialization policy was characterized by declining government revenues relative to expenditures, increasing restrictions on import-competing goods, and greater licensing requirements and firm-specific legislation that provided protection from foreign competition while allowing the importation of inputs at relatively low tariff rates (that is, at the official rather than the higher parallel market exchange rate).

These policies accompanied the practice of not permitting increases in world market price for petroleum, rice, and other commodities to be fully transmitted to the domestic economy. The country was able to do this largely because of the rises in sugar and coffee prices that followed the 1973–74 increase in the prices of primary commodities. In addition, the 1979–80 shock to world oil prices was absorbed without an official devaluation of the currency because of a rise in the prices of traditional Dominican exports and an increase in the government's external debt.

Overvaluation of the domestic currency is a subtle but effective way to subsidize consumers of imported goods. Consumer groups probably did not lobby directly for overvaluation because of its subtlety. Nevertheless, the urban riots of 1984, protesting the IMF agreement and the devaluation of the Dominican currency, reflect this group's awareness of the relationship of overvaluation to its welfare. More-over, interest groups may support overvaluation when institutional structures exist that increase the probability that lobbying efforts will permit the capturing of economic rents that invariably exist in a dis-torted economy. Policy instruments that permit the capturing of rents include licensing, quotas, other import restrictions, and import exemptions.

The interest groups most likely to lobby for an overvalued currency consist of producers who do not produce for export or who do not use a high percentage of imported inputs in their production process, merchants who sell imported goods, and debt-holders who hold a high percentage of their debt in foreign currency. These interest groups, aided by urban consumer groups, appear to have been suc-cessful in their efforts to maintain an overvalued currency throughout the 1966–84 period.

The decisions of various interest groups to seek direct intervention were probably related to their support for a policy that overvalued the currency. For instance, consumers might have been willing to pay a direct tax on rice if they had received a subsidy from the overvalued currency. In addition, rice producers might have been willing to ac-cept indirect taxation (as they did in some years) if direct intervention took the form of a subsidy. The various taxes and subsidies may have reflected the reality that each interest group was not fully aware of the reaction of other groups to the benefits received by them, because the benefits to a narrow-based interest group invariably came at a cost to some other group. From the government's perspective, direct inter-vention would have been undone if the peso had been permitted to float. To reward (or penalize) particular interest groups through total intervention, the government had to control exchange rates.

Appendix A. Estimation of a Shadow Equilibrium Exchange Rate

The estimates of the shadow equilibrium exchange rate used in this study were based on the elasticity estimates of imports and exports of goods and services. This approach, developed graphically and alge-braically in Roe and Greene (1988), derives the exchange rate formula directly from the conditions for equilibrium in the foreign exchange market; equilibrium in the foreign exchange market is determined solely by trade in goods and services (that is, flows in the capital account and short-run speculative trade in foreign exchange are not considered explicitly). The uniqueness of this approach is that the determination of the demand and supply for foreign exchange is directly related to the trade in goods and services in a manner that facilitates the estimation of a shadow exchange rate under alternative situations. A base and an extended version of the model is specified below.

The Base Model

The demand for foreign exchange in the t-th period is derived from the importation of goods and services (M) which is expressed as a function of the domestic price of imports P_m, and, for our purposes here, other exogenous variables (Z), such as the prices of substitutes, complements, income, and so forth. The domestic price P_m equals the product of the exchange rate (E), the world (border) price (P_{mw}) of imported goods, and the import tariff rate (t_m). Thus, the demand for imports in t can be expressed as:

(1a) $$M_t = B^*(Z_t)[P_{mt}]^\eta = B^*(Z_t)[E_t P_{mwt}(1+t_{mt})]^\eta$$

where, for the t-th period, $B^*(Z_t)$ is a real valued function of the variables Z, (these variables are unobservable in the empirical analysis so that $B^*(Z_t)$ is computed as constant value in each period) and η is the constant elasticity of demand for imported goods and services. If the level of imports does not affect the border price, the demand for foreign exchange (Q_d) is derived by multiplying both sides of equation (1a) by the border price P_{mw}:

(1b) $$Q_{dt} = B^*(Z_t)(P_{mwt})^{1+\eta}[E_t(1+t_{mt})]^\eta.$$

The supply of foreign exchange is derived from the excess supply of goods and services, which is a function of the domestic price (P_x) of exports of goods and services (X). This price is a product of the exchange rate, the tax rate (t_x), and the relevant border price for exportable goods and services P_{xw}. The exports of goods and services may be expressed as:

(2a) $$X_t = A^*(W_t)[P_{xt}]^\epsilon = A^*(W_t)[E_t P_{xwt}(1-t_{xt})]^\epsilon$$

where, for any t-th period, $A^*(W_t)$ is a real valued function of exogenous variables W_t (assumed to be unobservable in the empirical analysis), and ϵ is a parameter. If the level of exports has no effect on the border price, multiplying both sides of equation (2a) by the border price P_{xw} yields the supply function for foreign exchange:

(2b) $$Q_{st} = A^*(W_t)(P_{xwt})^{1+\epsilon}[E_t(1-t_{xt})]^\epsilon.$$

The elasticity of E in the foreign exchange equations is identical to the elasticities in their "parent" excess demand and supply equations. Moreover, in this model, it is not necessary that demand equal the supply of foreign exchange.

The simplicity and tractability of this framework for computing exchange rates that might have prevailed if the current account or taxes, or both on exports and tariffs were changed from historical levels can now be shown. The first step is to derive values for $B^*(Z_t)$ and $A^*(W_t)$ in each period. From equation (1b), the constant term for imports can be expressed as:

(1c) $$B_t = B^*(Z_t)(P_{mwt})^{1+\eta} = Q_{dt}/[E_t(1+t_{mt})]^\eta$$

and, from equation (2a), for exports:

(2c) $$A_t = A^*(W_t)(P_{xwt})^{1+\epsilon} = Q_{st}/[E_t(1-t_{xt})]^\epsilon.$$

Thus, if data are available on the annual value of imports (Q_{dt}), the nominal exchange rate (E_t), the tariff rate (t_{mt}), and the demand elasticity η, then the constant term in (1c) can be computed for each period. Likewise, knowledge of Q_{st}, t_{xt}, and ϵ permits the calculation of the constant term in (2c) for each period.

Substituting these estimates into equations (1b) and (2b) gives the following foreign exchange demand and supply equations:

(1d) $$Q_{dt} = B_t[E_t(1+t_{mt})]^\eta$$

(2d) $$Q_{st} = A_t[E_t(1-t_{xt})]^\epsilon.$$

Now, equating (1d) and (2d) and solving for E_t permits an estimate of the exchange rate that might have prevailed under alternative assumptions of the level of t_{mt}, t_{xt} and the current account balance. This estimate can be obtained by substituting equations (1d) and (2d) into

(3a) $$Q_{dt} = kQ_{st},$$

and solved for E_t, where k is a parameter. Values of $k > 1$ would imply a current account deficit, $k < 1$ a surplus, and $k = 1$ implies a balanced current account. For the latter case ($k = 1$), the equilibrium exchange rate is derived from the following equation:

(3b) $$E_t^* \equiv E_t = (B_t/A_t)^{1/(\epsilon-\eta)}[(1+t_{mt})^\eta/(1-t_{xt})^\epsilon]^{1/(\epsilon-\eta)}.$$

Setting $t_{mt} = t_{xt} = 0$, provides an estimate of E_t that might have prevailed for the case where the current account was in balance and tariffs and taxes were removed. The variables Z_t and W_t are exogenous in this model; the effects of these variables on E_t are implicitly included through the observed levels of the variables M_t and X_t. Nevertheless, because these variables are held constant within any particular period, the above framework is clearly a partial equilibrium model.

The Extended Model

The above framework is easily extended to allow for a home good and for substitution among traded goods. The demand for imports in the $t-th$ period is stated as:

(1-1a) $\qquad M_t = B^*(Z_t)[P_{mt}]^{\eta 1}[P_{xt}]^{\eta 2}$
$\qquad\qquad = B^*(Z_t)[e_t P_{mwt}(1+t_{mt})]^{\eta 1}[e_t P_{xwt}(1-t_{xt})]^{\eta 2}$

where P_{mt}, P_{xt} are the domestic prices of import and export goods relative to the price of home goods and e_t is the real exchange rate (the nominal rate divided by the price of home goods). The demand for foreign exchange is derived by multiplying both sides of equation (1-1a) by the border price P_{mw}:

(1-1b) $\quad Q_{dt} = B^*(Z_t)(P_{mwt})^{1+\eta 1}[P_{xwt}]^{\eta 2}[e_t]^{\eta 1+\eta 2}[(1+t_{mt})]^{\eta 1}[(1-t_{xt})]^{\eta 2}.$

The export of goods and services may be expressed as:

(2-1a) $\qquad X_t = A^*(W_t)[P_{xt}]^{\epsilon 1}[P_{mt}]^{\epsilon 2}$
$\qquad\qquad = A^*(W_t)[e_t P_{xwt}(1-t_{xt})]^{\epsilon 1}[e_t P_{mwt}(1+t_{mt})]^{\epsilon 2}$

and the supply of foreign exchange can be expressed as:

(2-1b) $\quad Q_{st} = A^*(W_t)(P_{xwt})^{1+\epsilon 1}[P_{mwt}]^{\epsilon 2}[e_t]^{\epsilon 1+\epsilon 2}[(1-t_{xt})]^{\epsilon 1}[(1+t_{mt})]^{\epsilon 2}.$

Following the procedure used in the base model, the constant terms can be expressed as follows:

(1-1c) $\qquad B_t = B^*(Z_t)(P_{mwt})^{1+\eta 1}[P_{xwt}]^{\eta 2}$
$\qquad\qquad = Q_{dt}/[e_t]^{\eta 1+\eta 2}[(1+t_{mt})]^{\eta 1}[(1-t_{xt})]^{\eta 2}$

and, from equation (2.1'), for exports:

(2-1c) $\qquad A_t = A^*(W_t)(P_{xwt})^{1+\epsilon 1}[P_{mwt}]^{\epsilon 2}$
$\qquad\qquad = Q_{st}/[e_t]^{\epsilon 1+\epsilon 2}[(1-t_{xt})]^{\epsilon 1}[(1+t_{mt})]^{\epsilon 2}.$

Substituting these values into the above equations yields:

(1-1d) $\qquad\qquad Q_{dt} = B[e_t]^{\eta 1+\eta 2}[(1+t_{mt})]^{\eta 1}[(1-t_{xt})]^{\eta 2}$

(2-2d) $\qquad\qquad Q_{st} = A[e_t]^{\epsilon 1+\epsilon 2}[(1-t_{xt})]^{\epsilon 1}[(1+t_{mt})]^{\epsilon 2}.$

Now equating (1-1d) and (2-1d) and solving for e_t, as in the base model, permits an estimate of the real exchange rate that might have prevailed under alternative assumptions of the level of t_{mt}, t_{xt} and the current account balance:

(3-1a) $\qquad\qquad\qquad Q_{dt} = k Q_{st}.$

The real equilibrium exchange rate for the case where $k = 1$ is derived from the following equation:

(3-1b) $\qquad e_t^* \equiv e_t = (B_t/A_t)^{1/\gamma}[(1+t_m)^{(\eta 1-\epsilon 2)}/(1-t_{xt})^{(\epsilon 1-\eta 2)}]^{1/\gamma}$

where $\gamma = \epsilon_1 + \epsilon_2 - (\eta_1 + \eta_2)$. Notice that the empirical tractability is owing to the functional form we have chosen. Otherwise, numerical methods would likely have been needed to solve either the nominal or the real rate.

Appendix B. Additional Empirical Evidence of Government Behavior

In this appendix we briefly summarize the results from regressing the producer and consumer prices of sugar, coffee, and rice on the expected value of a two-period autoregressive lag of the exogenous variables: the border prices of these three crops, medium- and long-term loans, and our estimate of the real equilibrium exchange rate that would have prevailed in the absence of economic distortions. Dummy variables were also included to account for policy differences that may have arisen among each of the four subperiods.

The framework underlying this approach is sketched in Greene and Roe (1988). A more fully developed framework appears in Roe and Yeldan. This approach assumes that the government forms preferences among interest groups in the economy. In turn, these preferences are influenced by the rent-seeking behavior of these interest groups. In addition, the government is assumed to choose the level of its policy instruments (that is, the dependent variables in the regression equations) in period t based on its expectation of the state of the economy in period $t + 1$, as though it sought to optimize its welfare over these interest groups. In principle, the result is a set of policy decision rules (our regression equations) that are functions of the expectations (in period t) of the level of the variables exogenous to the government that might prevail in period $t + 1$. The results from fitting these equations to the Dominican data appear in table 6-B1.

We interpret the key implications of these results as providing support to the government behavior inferred in the preceding discussion; that is, (1) the various government administrations pursued essentially the same policies over the four subperiods, (2) there is some evidence that price policies for rice, sugar, and coffee are not independent of each other, and (3) in the formulation of direct price policy, the government gave some consideration to the indirect effects of intervention. Evidence in support of (1) is provided by the insignificance of the coefficients associated with the dummy variables (Di, representing different periods) in each of the six equations. This result was robust. In the various specifications of the regressions, no significant differences were found that would differentiate the policies pursued during one period from those of another. This result is consistent with the view that the relative political power of the various pressure groups to influence government policy remained fairly constant over the entire period. Consequently, despite changes in administrations, the government's price policy decision rules were relatively stable throughout the study period.

Evidence supporting the interdependencies of pricing policies is given by the significance of the cross-price coefficients of sugar and

Table 6-1B. Estimates of Policy Instrument Equations for Rice, Sugar, and Coffee, 1966–85

| | Dependent variables: Domestic Price of | | | | | |
| | Rice | | Sugar | | Coffee | |
Independent variables	Producer	Consumer	Producer	Consumer	Producer	Consumer
Constant	4.6933+	8.6104+3	2.4897+3	−2.7144+3	−4.3546+4	6.0643+4
	(2.9114−8)	(3.9537−8)	(2.3415−8)	(3.2983−8)	(4.2961−8)	(3.7747−8)
Expected border price of:						
Rice	4.0139−1	7.3217−1	4.2013−1	4.1418−1	−6.5495−1	−5.7388−1
	(2.0690+0)	(2.7936+0)	(3.2832+0)	(4.1819+0)	(5.3691−1)	(2.9682−1)
Sugar	8.7738−1	9.1485−1	5.8603−2	3.3519−1	4.7260+0	8.4306+0
	(3.8533+0)	(2.9741+0)	(3.9019−1)	(2.8835+0)	(3.3008+0)	(3.7151+0)
Coffee	1.0053−1	1.0147−1	−2.3919−2	2.9109−2	9.9366−1	1.2781+0
	(4.0619+0)	(3.0347+0)	(1.4651−2)	(2.3037+0)	(6.3849+0)	(5.1816+0)
Expected equilibrium ex-change rate	−3.8184−1	5.6102−1	2.5004−2	−2.8799−1	−5.9125+0	−1.0468+1
	(8.4381−1)	(−9.1768−1)	(8.3766−2)	(1.2466+0)	(2.0779+0)	(2.3212+0)
Expected medium-long-term loan	6.4903+2	4.9336+2	5.3234+1	−3.0503+1	2.1785+2	4.0790+3
	(5.1293+0)	(2.8860+0)	(6.3781−1)	(4.7218−1)	(2.7381−1)	(3.2346+0)
Dummy variables						
D1	−5.6796+3	−9.3860+3	−2.6275+3	2.7477+3	4.2592+4	−6.7374+4
	(3.5234−8)	(−4.3099−8)	(2.4711−8)	(3.3387−8)	(4.2019−8)	(4.1937−8)
D2	−5.6589+3	−9.2342+3	−2.5921+3	2.7572+3	4.2622+4	−6.7049+4
	(3.5105−8)	(−4.2815−8)	(2.4378−8)	(3.3502−8)	(4.2049−8)	(4.1734−8)
D3	−5.5040+3	−9.0880+3	−2.5280+3	2.8800+3	4.2880+4	−6.6560+4
	(3.3411−8)	(−4.1730−8)	(2.3775−8)	(3.4995−8)	(4.2303−8)	(−4.1420−8)
R²	0.97	0.97	0.92	0.96	0.97	0.94
D.W.	1.96	2.053	2.15	2.405	2.91	2.534

Note: t-values in parentheses, note that, for example, the t-value for the expected exchange rate coefficient in the rice producer price equation (8.4381−1) equals (.84381).

coffee in the respective producer and consumer rice price equations, the cross-price coefficients of rice and coffee in the consumer sugar price equation, and from the significance of the price coefficient of sugar in the producer and consumer coffee price equations. These interdependencies are to be expected, if price policy is the outcome of the lobbying efforts of political interest groups (Olson 1987, pp. 203–205).

The insignificance of the coefficient associated with the border price of sugar in the producer's sugar price equation is not unexpected, because producer sugar prices were strongly influenced by a weighted average price of the exports to the U.S. quota market and to the world market. This result lends support to the earlier discussion that the actual producer price of sugar was not based on its opportunity cost.

Some evidence supporting the earlier observation that direct price policy gave some consideration to the indirect effects of intervention is provided by the significant coefficients associated with medium- and long-term loans in the coffee price equations. Additional evidence is given by the significance of the coefficients associated with our estimates of the real equilibrium exchange rate variable in the respective producer and consumer coffee price equations. These variables were chosen as proxies to account for the extent to which the economy was distorted.

Notes

1. These estimates were obtained by finding the exchange rate for each year (1966–85) that equated the excess supply and demand for foreign exchange in the absence of price and trade distortions. This methodology is explained in appendix A.

2. See Bell (349–357) and IBRD, *Dominican Republic: Its Main Economic Development Problems,* World Bank Country Study, 1978 (53–57).

3. For purposes of later analysis, it should be noted that a drop in the GDP from crops in 1980 was the result of hurricanes David and Frederick, which occurred in the fall of 1979.

4. World sugar price increases during the mid-1970s and early 1980s, and high world coffee prices in the late 1970s mitigated, but obviously did not reverse, the decline in agriculture's share in total exports.

5. The averages presented in the third column cannot be calculated directly from those in the first two columns for each product because these results are the annual averages of each period. That is, the data in the third column are averages of the yearly data in each period that indicate the average amount of change in each of the four periods. This note of caution in interpreting these annual averages applies throughout this analysis.

6. Because CEA may not have allocated resources in a least-cost manner, the value of the estimated cross-price supply coefficients is not consistent

with profit maximization. Because the counterfactual analysis presupposes a distortion-free economy and because cane production is a multiyear crop, the cross-price supply elasticities should be smaller than 0.15. In this analysis, they are assumed to be zero.

7. Although the percentage changes in the consumption of sugar, coffee, and rice may appear large in table 6-12, the estimated quantities consumed (using the undistorted prices) are within the range of actual observations from the 1976–77 survey of Dominican households. Yen (tables 5.4 and 5.5) shows that the standard deviations of household consumption expenditures in 1976–77 for individual food items were typically 50 percent (and higher) of the reported mean expenditures. Also, recall that the estimated percentage changes include both the own-price and the cross-price effects of price policy distortions.

8. Following the line of reasoning advanced by Mancur Olson (1987, 203–205), the costs to coffee producers of mounting a lobbying effort would likely exceed the costs of lobbying by rice and sugar producers. Relative to the other groups, coffee producers are likely to face higher lobbying costs because they are spatially dispersed and because of the free rider problem that, as Olson suggests, is common when a sector contains a relatively large number of producers that are also engaged in other activities. Under these circumstances, producers are likely to be less willing to pay for lobbying activities relative to producers of rice and sugar and, hence, have less influence or political power relative to these groups.

References

Bell, Ian. 1981. *The Dominican Republic*. Boulder, Colorado: Westview Press.

Conde, Luis E. 1977. "Imported vs. Policy Induced Prices and Payments in the Dominican Republic," Ph.D. diss., Boston College. Processed.

Consejo Nacional de Agricultura, Unidad de Estudios Agropecuarios. 1986. "Racionalidid de la Autosuficiencia Arrocera con Referencia a los Subsidios en los Medios de Producción y Alternativas de Precios, Vols. I and II." Santo Domingo.

Del Villar, Juan Danilo. 1985. "El Cafe Molido para Consumo Interno de la Republica Dominicana: Periodo 1950–80." *Análisis Cafetalero*, Edicciones nos. 5 y 6, Departamento de Dare, Santo Domingo, SEA.

Greene, Duty, D., Jerome Hammond, Terry Roe, Benjamin Senauer, and Loraine West. 1981. "An Overview of the Food System in the Dominican Republic: Planning Policies and Constraints." Minnesota: University of Minnesota.

Greene, Duty D. and Terry L. Roe. 1988. *Trade, Exchange Rate, and Agricultural Pricing Policies in the Dominican Republic*. The World Bank, Washington D.C.

Mann, Arthur J. 1977. "Agricultural Price Stabilization Policy in a Developing Economy: The Case of the Dominican Republic," *Social and Economic Studies* (26):190–91.

Musgrove, Philip. 1984. "Household Income Distribution in the Dominican Republic: A First Look at New Survey Data" in *The Collection and Analysis of*

Economic and Consumer Behavior Data: In Memory of Robert Ferber, eds. S. Sudman and M.A. Spaeth. Urbana: University of Illinois Press.

―――. 1985. "Household Food Consumption in the Dominican Republic: Effects of Income, Price, and Family Size." *Economic Development and Cultural Change* 34 (October): 83–101.

Olson, Mancur. 1987. *The Rise and Decline of Nations.* Hartford, Conn: Yale University Press.

Quezada, Norberto A. 1981. "Endogenous Agricultural Price and Trade Policy in the Dominican Republic." Ph.D. diss., Purdue University. Processed.

Roe, Terry and Duty D. Greene. 1987. "The Estimation of a Shadow Equilibrium Exchange Rate." *Revista Brasileira de Economia,* 41, no. 4.

Roe, Terry and Erinc Yeldan. 1988. "An Open Economy Model of Political Influence and Competition Among Rent Seeking Groups," *Economic Development Center Bulletin.* University of Minnesota.

Senauer, Benjamin. 1983. "Foodgrain Price and Trade Policy in the Dominican Republic," *Food Policy.* (November): 313–25.

Sharpe, Kenneth E. 1977. *Peasant Politics: Struggle in a Dominican Village.* Baltimore, MD: The Johns Hopkins University Press.

World Bank. 1978. "Dominican Republic: Its Main Economic Development Problems." A World Bank Country Study, Washington, D.C.

―――. 1980. "Major Social Concerns and Policy Recommendations." Washington, D.C.

―――. 1984. "Dominican Republic: Economic Prospects and Policies to Renew Growth." Washington, D.C.

Yen, Tze-yi and Terry L. Roe. 1986. "Determinants of Rural and Urban Household Demand: An Analysis of Dominican Household Consumption." Economic Development Center, University of Minnesota.

Yen, Tze-yi. 1986. "Stagewise Estimation of Complete Demand Systems with Limited Dependent Variables: An Analysis of Dominican Household Consumption." Ph.D. diss., University of Minnesota. Processed.

Appendix

Anne O. Krueger
Maurice Schiff
Alberto Valdés

We provide here a summary of the principal concepts and measures used in the eighteen country studies. For the country chapters of this volume, authors selected the most relevant material from their country studies, so all chapters do not necessarily cover in the same detail all the items presented here.

The first part of the appendix discusses concepts used in measuring the impact of sector-specific and economywide policies on incentives. The second part describes concepts used for measuring the effects of these policies on output, consumption, foreign exchange, the budget, transfers between agriculture and the rest of the economy, and rural and urban income distribution. The relationship between price policy and government investment is then addressed, and in the final section price variability is discussed.

The Impact of Policies on Incentives

The agricultural sector consists of hundreds of products in most countries. To make the research manageable, authors were asked to identify key agricultural products for their studies. Authors generally covered crops that were important to trade and to domestic consumption, although they also considered the degree to which the crops chosen for analysis were representative of agriculture as a whole.

Sector-Specific Pricing Policies

Most agricultural crops are tradable, and most countries have so small a share in world trade that the prices at which they can buy or sell these commodities are given. In such cases, the border prices of the commodities examined can be used as reference prices to measure the impact of sector-specific or direct price interventions on agricultural prices. To be sure, border prices must be adjusted for transport costs and other factors to make them comparable to producer prices. Nonetheless, it is a reasonable assumption that in most unregulated markets, producer prices would be closely related to border prices, plus or minus the margins for transport, storage, differences in quality, and handling costs.

The following analysis deals with nominal protection measures, but effective rates of protection were also computed in those countries where the required data were available.

The domestic producer price, P_i, of an exportable product i is given by:

$$(A\text{-}1) \qquad P_i = P_i^W E_0 (1 - t_i) - C_i$$

where P_i = domestic producer price, P_i^W = foreign-currency border (f.o.b) price, E_0 = nominal official exchange rate, t_i = export tax ($t_i > 0$) or subsidy ($t_i < 0$), and C_i = adjustment for differences in quality, location (transport), time (storage), and other margins.

If a different exchange rate E' is applied to the exports of product i, then the official exchange rate E_0 should be replaced by E' in equation A-1.

The export tax t_i may be explicit (as in the case of Argentina), or it may be implicit, as when there is an export quota or prohibition, or when output is procured by a government agency at a price below what would have prevailed in the absence of direct interventions.

The producer price in the absence of direct intervention is given by

$$(A\text{-}2) \qquad P_i' = P_i^W E_0 - C_i'$$

where C_i' = adjustment for quality, transport, storage, and other margins, all measured under competitive conditions.

Similarly, for importables the corresponding expressions are:

$$(A\text{-}3) \qquad P_j = P_j^W E_0 (1 + t_j) - C_j$$

and

$$(A\text{-}4) \qquad P_j' = P_j^W E_0 - C_j'$$

where P_j^W = foreign-currency border (c.i.f.) price, and t_j = import tariff ($t_j > 0$) or subsidy ($t_j < 0$).

We are interested in determining t_i and t_j. These are not always explicit. Data may be available on P_i and P_j, as well as on P_i^W and P_j^W, but not on the hypothetical prices P_i' and P_j'. Border prices P_i^W and P_j^W must first be adjusted for C_i' and C_j' to obtain P_i' and P_j', which are comparable to the actual producer prices P_i and P_j, in order to determine the direct protection rate.

Uncontroversial as they may appear, these adjustments between domestic prices and the relevant border prices have often not been considered in much of the literature that reports nominal rates of protection to agricultural tradables. Taxes or subsidies on agriculture are often calculated by simply comparing border prices and producer prices. Some exceptions are Beenhakker (1987), Ahmed and Rustagi (1985), and Westlake (1987). However, not all differences between P_i (P_j) and $P_i^W E_0$ ($P_j^W E_0$) result from intervention; the differences may partly reflect actual "competitive" costs or compensating differentials.

For example, producing areas may be located far from the ports or consumption centers, so adjustments must be made for transportation costs. Also, the time of import may differ from harvest time, so storage costs must be included. Moreover, the border price of tradable products (such as powdered milk) influence the domestic price of the nontradable related products (fluid milk) and the relation between these two prices through processing margins must be considered in the calculations. Finally, in taking these factors into account, the actual marketing and distribution costs often need adjustment for products whose transportation is subsidized or whose marketing is done primarily by parastatals with costs that differ significantly from competitive margins.

The nominal protection rate NPR_D for direct price policies affecting product A is given by

(A-5)
$$NPR_D = \frac{P_A/P_{NA} - P_A'/P_{NA}}{P_A'/P_{NA}} = \frac{P_A - P_A'}{P_A'}$$

where P_{NA} is a price index of the nonagricultural sector.

As can be seen from equation A-5, the impact is calculated relative to the price that would have prevailed in the absence of intervention. This is done throughout the study.

P_{NA} is not affected by direct (sector-specific) price interventions, so the direct measures of intervention related to P_A or P_A/P_{NA} are identical.

For a nontradable product, calculating the impact of price policies on its price is more difficult because we need to know the impact on both demand and supply, and for that we need to know the elasticity of those functions with respect to all their arguments. This task is much simpler when the product is a close substitute for a tradable product in production or consumption.

Economywide Policies

Relative agricultural prices P_A/P_{NA} are also affected by trade policies affecting nonagricultural products (mostly industrial goods) and by policies affecting the real exchange rate. Agriculture tends to be more tradable than the nonagricultural sector, which includes such nontradables as public and private services (retail, transportation, banking), housing, construction, and so forth. Consequently, P_A/P_{NA} will vary with the level of the real exchange rate.

The price index in the nonagricultural section (P_{NA}) consists of P_{NAT} (price index of the tradable component of the nonagricultural sector) and P_{NAH} (price index of the nontradable component of nonagriculture), with

(A-6) $$P_{NA} = \alpha P_{NAT} + (1-\alpha)P_{NAH}$$

where α = share of tradables in nonagriculture.

Exchange-rate policies will affect both P_A and P_{NAT} relative to P_{NAH}. Also, trade policies on nonagriculture will affect P_{NAT}.

To capture the exchange-rate effect, a simple three-sector model (exportables, importables, and nontradables) was constructed to estimate the equilibrium real exchange rate e^* in the absence of interventions, which for a given price of the nontradable sector P_{NAH} corresponds to the equilibrium nominal exchange rate E^*. E^* is defined as the exchange rate that equilibrates the current account (or leads to a current account deficit that is sustainable in the long run)[1] in the absence of tariffs and quotas on imports (t_M) and in the absence of export taxes and other export restrictions (t_x) for a given price of nontradables P_{NAH}. E^* is given by

(A-7) $$E^* = \left(\frac{\Delta Q_0 + \Delta Q_1}{\epsilon_s Q_s + \eta_D Q_D} + 1\right)E_0$$

where ΔQ_0 = nonsustainable part of the current account deficit, ΔQ_1 = current account deficit that would result from removing trade taxes t_M and t_x at exchange rate E_0, $Q_s(Q_D)$ = quantity supplied (demanded) of foreign exchange, $\epsilon_s(\eta_D)$ = elasticity of supply (demand) of foreign exchange with respect to the real exchange rate e (η_D is defined as being positive), $E^*(E_0)$ = equilibrium (actual) nominal exchange rate, which corresponds to $e^*(e)$ for a given P_{NAH}, and ΔQ_1 is given by

(A-8) $$\Delta Q_1 = \frac{t_M}{1+t_M} Q_D \eta_D - \frac{t_x}{1-t_x} Q_s \epsilon_s$$

where t_M = average equivalent tariff (including effect of quotas) and t_x = average equivalent export taxes.[2]

Changes in monetary or fiscal policies will tend to be reflected in ΔQ_0, in ΔQ_1, or in E_0 and will therefore be captured by E^* in equation A-7. The same is true of change in terms of trade, world interest rates, and other exogenous shocks. For example, an increase in government expenditures financed through money creation will lead to an increase in ΔQ_0 if trade taxes and E_0 are unchanged. If the rate of protection, t_M, is increased, it will lead to an increase in ΔQ_1. Alternatively, the government may decide to raise E_0. Possibly, a combination of these three adjustments will occur. In any case, the change in policy will be reflected in E^*.

Similarly, an increase in the world price of importables (for example, oil) will lead to an increase in ΔQ_0, or in ΔQ_1 if tariffs and quotas are used to reduce imports, or possibly in E_0, or in combination of the three, and it will lead to an increase in E^*.

The nonagricultural price, P_{NA}, in the absence of trade taxes, t_{NA}, on nonagricultural tradables and at the equilibrium exchange rate E^* is given by

$$(A-9) \qquad P_{NA}^* = \alpha \frac{E^*}{E_0} \frac{P_{NAT}}{1+t_{NA}} + (1-\alpha)\, P_{NAH}$$

where t_{NA} = effect of trade policies on the price of nonagricultural tradables.

t_{NA} differs from t_M because t_M applies to all importables, while t_{NA} applies to nonagricultural tradables (importables and exportables).

Elimination of trade taxes as well as a change from E_0 to E^* will affect P_{NAH} over time because of substitutions in production and consumption leading to a reallocation of factors of production between the tradable and nontradable sectors. However, we are interested in the effect of these policies on P_A/P_{NA} before the reallocation of resources occurs, and we therefore abstract from the effect on P_{NAH}.[3]

Indirect or economywide policies will change P_A/P_{NA} to $\frac{E^*}{E_0} P_A/P_{NA}^*$, so that the indirect effect is given by

$$(A-10) \qquad NPR_I = \frac{P_A/P_{NA} - \frac{E^*}{E_0}P_A/P_{NA}^*}{\frac{E^*}{E_0}\, P_A/P_{NA}^*} = \frac{1/P_{NA} - \frac{E^*}{E_0}/P_{NA}^*}{\frac{E^*}{E_0}\, /P_{NA}^*}$$

$$= \frac{P_{NA}^*}{P_{NA}} \frac{E_0}{E^*} - 1.$$

The indirect effect measured by NPR_I is due to 1) the official exchange rate (E_0) not being at its equilibrium value, E^*, (in the absence of trade policies), which affects both P_A and P_{NAT}, and 2) t_{NA}, which affects P_{NAT}. As can be seen from equation (A-10), the indirect effect is independent of the specific tradable product analyzed; that is, it is the same for all tradable agricultural products and depends only on E^*/E_0, on t_{NA}, and on α. If the product is not tradable, then the indirect effect is due exclusively to the effect on P_{NA}.

The sum of the direct and the indirect effects, or the total effect, on P_A/P_{NA} is given by

(A-11)
$$\text{NPR}_T = \frac{P_A/P_{NA} - \dfrac{E^*}{E_0} P'_A/P^*_{NA}}{\dfrac{E^*}{E_0} \; P'_A/P^*_{NA}} .$$

NPR_D had to be adjusted to npr_D so that $\text{npr}_D + \text{NPR}_I = \text{NPR}_T$. npr_D is defined as $\text{npr}_D = \text{NPR}_D(1 + \text{NPR}_I)$. This is equivalent to replacing the denominator P'_A/P_{NA} in equation A-5 by the denominator $(E^*/E_0)P'_A/P^*_{NA}$ in equation A-11. Since NPR_I in equation A-10 can also be written as

(A-12)
$$\frac{P'_A/P_{NA} - \dfrac{E^*}{E_0} P'_A/P^*_{NA}}{\dfrac{E^*}{E_0} \; P'_A/P^*_{NA}}$$

it follows that npr_D, NPR_I, and NPR_T have the same denominator, and $\text{npr}_D + \text{NPR}_I = \text{NPR}_T$. The measure of direct intervention reported in this volume is npr_D.

The total effect of price policies on P_A/P_{NA} is due to sector-specific or direct price interventions (resulting in P_A instead of P'_A), to the exchange-rate effect, and to the trade policies t_{NA} affecting the non-agricultural sector (mostly industrial protection).

Wherever the data were available, the same was done for effective rates of protection (ERP), measuring the impact of those policies on value added for the agricultural products and, in the case of Chile, also for the nonagricultural sector.

The Effect of Policies on Economic Variables

Throughout the studies, both the direct (sector-specific) and the total (direct plus indirect or economywide) effects on output (short- and long-run), consumption, foreign exchange, budget, intersectoral transfers, and income distribution are reported. We start with the effects on output.

Output

The matrix of own- and cross-elasticities of output with respect to the prices of the products analyzed and of variable inputs was derived from the estimation of a system of supply functions or was borrowed from other studies.

Assuming all variables are in logs, we have for any product i (using a Nerlovian approach):

(A-13) $Q_i = a_i + \sum_j a_{ij} P_{j,-1} + \sum_k a_{ik} P_{k,-1} + b_i Q_{i,-1}$

where $Q_i(Q_{i,-1})$ = output of product i in period t (period $t - 1$); $P_{j,-1}(P_{k,-1})$ = price of product j, including product i (input k) relative to P_{NA} (at $t - 1$); $a_{ij}(a_{ik})$ = elasticity of Q_i with respect to $P_{i,-1}(P_{k,-1})$; and b_i = coefficient of adjustment.

Assume $\hat{X}$ = dlog X. For small changes:

(A-14) $$\hat{Q}_i = \sum_j a_{ij} \hat{P}_{j,-1} + \sum_k a_{ik}\hat{P}_{k,-1} + b_i\hat{Q}_{i,-1}.$$

For large changes, the new values for $P_{j,-1}$, $P_{k,-1}$ and $Q_{i,-1}$ must be inserted in equation (A-13) to obtain the new value for Q_i ($Q'_{1,SR}$ for the short-run direct effect, $Q^*_{i,SR}$ for the short-term total effect, and Q'_{iC} or $Q^*_{i,C}$ for the corresponding long-run, cumulative effects).

In the short run (where prices change at $t - 1$ but are assumed to be unchanged before that), $Q_{i,-1}$ is assumed to be given (that is, $\hat{Q}'_{i,-1} = 0$ in equation A-14) so that for direct intervention the short-run output effect, $\hat{Q}'_{i,SR}$, is

(A-15) $$\hat{Q}'_{i,SR} = \sum_j a_{ij}NPR_{D(j,-1)} + \sum_k a_{ik}NPR_{D(k,-1)}$$

and for total intervention it is

(A-16) $$\hat{Q}^*_{i,SR} = \sum_j a_{ij}NPR_{T(j,-1)} + \sum_k a_{ik}NPR_{T(k,-1)}.$$

The Nerlovian long-run effect on Q_i is obtained by dividing all elasticities a_{ij} and a_{ik} by $1 - b_i$. This measures the effect on Q_i of the price intervention NPR at $t - 1$ being constant indefinitely, and provides little insight on the long-term effect of price intervention.

An alternative measure is the cumulative effect, which measures the effect on $Q_{i,t}$ of the prices being at their nonintervention value since $t = 1$, the first year of the sample period. In this case, we are measuring the alternative, dynamic path that Q_i would have followed if the interventions had been removed at $t = 1$ and prices had followed a nonintervention path.

We assume that interventions were removed at $t = 1$ but were not announced at $t = 0$, so that the impact on Q_i at $t = 1$ is zero. At $t = 2$, the short-run and cumulative output effects are the same, since $\hat{Q}_{i,t=1} = 0$. At $t = 3$, $\hat{Q}_i$ will depend both on $\hat{P}_j$ and $\hat{P}_k$ at $t = 2$ and on $\hat{Q}_i$ at $t = 2$. At $t = 4$, $\hat{Q}_i$ will depend on $\hat{P}_j$ and $\hat{P}_k$ at $t = 3$ and on $\hat{Q}_i$ (cumulative) at $t = 3$, which depends on $\hat{P}_j$ and $\hat{P}_k$ at $t = 2$ and on $\hat{Q}_i$ at $t = 2$. It can be shown that the cumulative effect on Q_i is given by Equation A-14 if $\hat{Q}_{i-1}$ is reinterpreted as the cumulative effect at $t = 1$.[4] The direct cumulative effect, $\hat{Q}'_{i,c}$, is obtained by replacing $\hat{P}_{m,-1}$ by $NPR_{D(m,-1)}$, where $m = j,k$. For the total cumulative effect, $\hat{P}_{m,-1}$ is replaced by $NPR_{T(m,-1)}$.

If the elasticities a_{ik} are not available, and data on value added for products j are available, then a measure of $\hat{Q}_i$ can be obtained from equation A-17:

(A-17) $\hat{Q}_i = \sum_j c_{ij} \, \hat{\text{VA}}_{j, \, -1} + d_i \hat{Q}_{i, \, -1}$

where VA = value added; $c_{ij} = a_{ij} \, (\text{VA}_{j, \, -1}/P_{j-1})$, or the elasticity with respect to VA$_j$; and d_i may or may not be equal to b_i in equation A-14.

In some studies, the long-term process of investment and labor migration underlying the long-run supply response was explicitly incorporated, including the allocation of investment between agriculture and nonagriculture. An application of such an approach is presented in the study on Chile.

Consumption

We assumed that short-term effects are equal to cumulative effects; that is, that the effect of $\hat{P}_j$ (consumer price of any j) at t on consumption of $i(Q_i^c)$ occurs entirely at t, and there are no lagged effects as in output. This assumption is not entirely valid for consumer durables, nor in the case of endogenous tastes depending on past consumption, but we believe it provides a good approximation in the case of food products. The consumption effect is

(A-18) $\hat{Q}_i^c = \sum_j f_{ij} \, \hat{P}_j$

where f_{ij} = elasticity of $Q_{i,t}$ with respect to $P_{j,t}$.

The direct and total effects on Q_i^c are obtained by replacing $\hat{P}_j$ by NPR$_{D,j}$ and NPR$_{T,j}$, respectively.

The income effect on Q_i^c has been ignored except then the income change relative to GDP of eliminating the interventions is large enough to affect Q_i^c, or when income elasticities are available by income group, and changes in income or the elasticities vary by income group.

Foreign Exchange

Four effects on foreign exchange were calculated, related to the four effects on output (direct, total, short-run, and cumulative). The foreign exchange effects include the change in excess supply for each product multiplied by the border price and summed over all products analyzed, as well as the change in value of imported inputs accompanying the changes in output.

Two comments are in order. First, some products may have switched categories after the removal of interventions. For instance, in the case of an imported product, it may remain as an imported good and the foreign exchange effect is calculated at the c.i.f. border price; it may become a nontraded good because of excess-supply at the c.i.f. price and excess demand at the f.o.b. border price; or it may become an exported product because of excess supply at the f.o.b. border price. These considerations were taken into account for the effects on foreign exchange. Second, in the case of total intervention, only the effect on agricultural foreign exchange was taken into account. For instance, the effect of the removal of restrictions on industrial imports was not included.

Budget

In this section, an estimate was made of the effect on the budget of direct price policies on agricultural products and inputs. These include taxes or subsidies on output, exports, imports, inputs, consumption, marketing, and processing, including the profits and losses of parastatals involved in these activities. Wherever possible, data on actual expenditures or revenues, rather than the announced tax or subsidy rates, were used.

Intersectoral Real Income Transfers

The purpose was to estimate whether the agricultural sector gained or lost from the set of direct and total price interventions as well as from nonprice transfers. Nonprice transfers include the subsidy element of government expenditures specific to agriculture (for example, on irrigation, research and extension, and rural transportation), as well as transfers out of agriculture, such as tax revenues specific to agriculture but not included in the price transfers (for example, land taxes).

The price-related transfers measure the effect of the price policies on agricultural GDP. These differ from the effects on the budget for several reasons. First, some of the gains (or losses) to producers are often captured by the consumers, with only a part going to the government. An extreme case would be a control on the price of a food product, which would tax producers and subsidize consumers but have no effect on the budget. Similarly, some input subsidies may be captured by the industries producing those inputs rather than by the agricultural sector. Second, the measure of real income transfers includes the effect of intervention not only on nominal income but also on the cost of the consumption basket of rural households. For that purpose, authors of the individual studies estimated the impact on the consumer price index (CPI) of the removal of direct interventions (CPI′) and of total interventions (CPI*).

CPI, CPI′, and CPI* are defined as

(A-19) $$\text{CPI} = \Sigma\beta_i P_i + (1 - \Sigma\beta_i)P_{\text{NA}}$$

where β_i = share of agricultural product i in the rural CPI, and $1 - \Sigma\beta_i$ = share of nonagricultural goods and services in the rural CPI.

(A-20) $$\text{CPI}' = \Sigma \beta_i P_i' + (1 - \Sigma \beta_i) P_{NA}$$

where CPI' reflects the cost of the consumer basket in the absence of direct interventions.

(A-21) $$\text{CPI}^* = \Sigma \beta_i (E^*/E_0) P'_i + (1 - \Sigma \beta_i) P^*_{NA}$$

where CPI* reflects the cost of the consumer basket in the absence of total interventions.

Income Distribution

STATIC EFFECTS. Urban consumers were classified by income groups. Their real income is affected because direct and total intervention influence the cost of their consumption basket. The effect varies by income group because of differences in the weights of the various products in each group's consumption basket. When data permitted, other classifications were used, such as the effect on the urban functional distribution of income.

Rural household classification in each country depended on the structure of production, on the political influence of various rural groups, and on the availability of data. In some countries households were classified according to whether members were large-scale farmers, small-scale farmers, farm laborers, or rural nonagricultural laborers. In other countries, where farmers tend to grow one product and where farm size is associated with the product grown (for example, estates producing an export crop and small-scale farmers producing a food crop), the classification was by product. In other cases, the effect on the functional distribution of income was estimated.

The real income effect of direct and total intervention for each group was obtained by calculating the effect on nominal income (value added) and on the cost of the consumer basket. Some small-scale farmers may have been net buyers of the food product grown and may have used off-farm income to acquire the additional food. Where data on off-farm income were available, an effort was also made to estimate the effect of intervention on that source of income.

For hired labor, the static income effect was estimated based on the assumption that nominal income remained unchanged. This assumption was relaxed for the dynamic effects.

DYNAMIC EFFECTS. Over time, income of farm labor may change because of changes in the demand for and supply of labor. The supply of labor may vary because of changes in hours worked and because of migration, which depends in part on the relative returns to labor in urban and rural areas.

From a model of migration and of demand for and supply of labor in rural and urban areas, a reduced-form equation for real income for rural labor was derived as a function of current and lagged values of agriculture's domestic terms of trade and real urban labor income, and of the unemployment rate. Equations of that type were estimated in those countries for which data were available. Using the empirical results, it was then possible to assess the dynamic effect of intervention on the real income of rural labor.

Government Investment and Expenditure Index

It has been claimed that taxation of agriculture was compensated by increased public expenditures on agriculture. To verify this, authors calculated indexes of government investment and total expenditures for agriculture.

The index of government investment bias (GIB) is defined as the share of agriculture in government investment relative to the share of agriculture in GDP:

$$\text{(A-22)} \qquad \text{GIB} = \frac{\text{AGI}/\text{GI}}{\text{AGDP}/\text{GDP}}$$

where AGI = agricultural public investment expenditures, GI = total public investment expenditition and AGDP = agricultural GDP (evaluated at prices in the absence of direct interventions).

Two questions of interest arise. First, what is the relation over time between GIB and agricultural price policy and incentives? Second, is government investment biased in favor of or against the agricultural sector, or is it neutral?

The answer to the second question depends on the criterion used. If a neutral policy is defined as one under which the share of agriculture in public investment expenditures equals the share of agriculture in GDP, then a value of GIB larger (smaller) than 1 indicates a bias in favor of (against) agriculture. If efficiency is used as a criterion, then a neutral policy is one under which the marginal social returns to public investment in agriculture and in nonagriculture are equalized, and a higher (lower) return in agriculture indicates a bias against (in favor of) agriculture.

An index of government expenditure bias was also calculated as

$$\text{(A-23)} \qquad \text{GEB} = \frac{\text{AGE}/\text{GE}}{\text{AGDP}/\text{GDP}}$$

where AGE = agricultural government expenditures, and GE = total government expenditures.

Price Variability

Three indexes of price variability were calculated: the standard deviation, the coefficient of variation (equal to the standard deviation of the price relative to the average price), and the Z-statistic.

The Z-statistic is defined as

(A-24)
$$Z = \left(\frac{\sum\limits_{t=2}^{n} (P_t - P_{t-1})^2}{n - 1} \right)^{1/2}$$

where P is the price of any product relative to P_{NA}.

The standard deviation (SD) of the price series is the square root of the average squared deviation of the price from the sample mean. The Z-statistic is the square root of the average squared deviation of the price from its value lagged one period (or of the first difference in the price). The two statistics SD and Z are thus directly comparable.

Producers may be more concerned with annual changes in their prices than with the deviation from the sample mean. Moreover, two very different price series may have the same SD value even though one would be considered more stable than the other, and this would be reflected in the Z value. For example, assume $P_1 = 100$ for ten periods and then rises to 200 for ten additional periods, whereas P_2 varies annually from 100 to 200. That is,

(A-24)
$$P_{1t} = \begin{cases} 100, & 0 \le t \le 9 \\ 200, & 10 \le t \le 19 \end{cases}$$

and

$$P_{2t} = \begin{cases} 100, & t = 2n, 0 \le n \le 9 \\ 200, & t = 1 + 2n, 0 \le n \le 9. \end{cases}$$

Both series have the same mean of 150 and have the same standard deviation, $SD = 50$, but P_{1t} has a much smaller Z value. $Z = 100$ for P_{2t} and $Z = 23$ for P_{1t} (approximately). Thus the Z-statistic seems to better reflect the relative stability of the two series, in the sense that P_{1t} experiences only one change over the period whereas P_{2t} changes every year.

The calcuations of the various measures of intervention and of their effects were then used as a quantitative basis for the analysis of the political economy of agricultural pricing policies in each country.

Notes

1. The sustainable current account deficit may be positive because of long-run commitments on foreign aid, worker remittances, foreign investment, and so forth.

2. In some cases (for example, Chile) a real exchange rate equation was also estimated as a function of the terms of trade, trade policies, and other variables reflecting absorption and wage policy.

Equations A-7 and A-8 are correct for small changes and are good approximations for larger changes. The exact solution for large changes with constant elasticities is shown in the study of the Dominican Republic, and the difference between the two solutions is small even for large t_M, t_x, and ΔQ_0. Derivation of equations A-7 and A-8 and methodologies for estimating the equivalent tariff, t_M, are available from the editors of this volume.

3. In a few studies (for example, Chile) the effect on P_{NAH} is taken into account.

4. The solution is found in the methodological memoranda, which are available from the editors of this volume.

References

Ahmed, R., and N. Rustagi. 1985. "Agricultural Marketing and Price Incentives: A Comparative Study of African and Asian Countries." International Food Policy Research Institute, Washington, D.C.

Beenhakker, Henri L. 1987. "Issues in Agricultural Marketing and Transport Due to Government Intervention." Discussion Paper, Transportation Issues Series, Report TRP7 (May), World Bank, Washington, D.C.

Westlake, M.J. 1987. "The Measurement of Agricultural Price Distortion in Developing Countries." *Journal of Development Studies*, Volume 23 (April), pp. 367–81.